INGREDIENT MEASUREM

All-purpose flour, unsifted and spooned in

Volume	Ounces	
¼ cup	1.1 oz	31 g
⅓ cup	1.5 oz	42 g
½ cup	2.2 oz	63 g
1 cup	4.4 oz	125 g

Granulated sugar

Volume	Ounces	Grams
1 teaspoon	.1 oz	4 g
1 tablespoon	.4 oz	12 g
¼ cup	1.8 oz	50 g
⅓ cup	2.4 oz	67 g
½ cup	3.5 oz	100 g
1 cup	7.1 oz	200 g

Firmly packed brown sugar

Volume	Ounces	Grams
1 tablespoon	.5 oz	14 g
¼ cup	1.9 oz	55 g
⅓ cup	2.6 oz	73 g
½ cup	3.9 oz	110 g
1 cup	7.8 oz	220 g

Confectioners sugar

Volume	Ounces	Grams
¼ cup	.1 oz	35 g

Abbreviations

Cup	c.		Large	lge.
Tablespoon . . .	tbsp.		Small	sm.
Teaspoon	tsp.		Package	pkg
Pound	lb.		Dozen	doz.
Ounce	oz.		Pint	pt.

To Meg
Cook with love!

Carole J. Kantel

NY 2002

SAILco Press
P.O. Box 2099
Key Largo, FL 33037
(305) 743-0626 Tel. & Fax
e-mail: kisscook@aol.com

For additional copies of this book, order forms are included in the back of this book. Single copy $24.95 plus $3.75 shipping and handling (Florida residents add $1.62 tax). See order form for other books offered by **SAILco Press**.

Library of Congress Catalog Card Number: 96-68625
Kanter, Corinne C.
The Cruising **K.I.S.S.** COOKBOOK
ISBN: 0-9618406-3-3

$24.95

Cover Creation by:
Teall's Guides/Global Cartographics Inc.
111 Saguro Lane
Marathon, FL 33050
305-743-3942

Edited: Denis Blaise

Manufactured by
Favorite Recipes® Press
P.O. Box 305142
Nashville, Tennessee 37230

Manufactured in the United States of America
First Printing, October, 1996

Dedication

To some of the unsung heroines with whom I have the pleasure of sailing and camaraderie:

Fran Beckley, Linda Blaise, Ruth Bowman, Betty Brock, Helen Caesar, Nancy Harris, Kathy Johnson, Josie Kalpen, Joan Morse, Sara Marsh, Sheila Nickles, Betty Pollard, Eileen Rugg, Sarah Tompson, Barbara Towner, Priscella Wormell, Judy Snow, Angela Wellman.

My husband *Charles*, who gave me support and patiently waited for me to complete this book. He was my constant critic, editor and business manager. Most important, he was my primary taste-tester.

To our children *Noah, Seth*, and *Jill*, their spouses and our eight grand-children who also were test kitchen families.

Most important to the cruising folks who have contributed to this book, to those who have used my first book, *The Galley K.I.S.S. Cookbook*. Enjoy this new companion in your galley.

To The Newcomers Cruising:

Start your adventure now. A guiding light in my own cruising experience is that marvelous quote by *Betsy Hitz Holman:*

"We went cruising not to escape from life but to keep life from escaping us."

Author's Note:

The Cruising *K.I.S.S.* COOKBOOK is the culmination of twenty years of research and experimentation. Hundreds of recipes and scores of cooking hints have crossed my path during those years and any that fit the KISS principle (*Keep It Simple System*) were tried and tested. In this book are 563 recipes that passed the scrutiny of a group of tough food testers.

Nutrition is always a primary factor in my published recipes and cooking hints. My theme, "Delicious, Nutritious, Economical and Convenient" is the heart-beat of my *Corinne's Culinary Corner* and *Living Aboard* columns and of my first book: *The Galley K.I.S.S. Cookbook.*

Within this book, you will find charts on food, weights and measures, ingredients, oven temperature conversions, a capacity chart for pots and pans and an all-important chart of substitutions. Complete lists of unique and useful items not found in any other single cookbook are listed in the table of contents and the inside covers.

Packed into 448 pages are 563 *new* recipes, each complete on the page, printed in easy-to-read large type and hard bound with an innovative binding that will lay flat during use.

Cruisers in their wanderings come across all sorts of uncommon vegetables. In my helpful-hints section I discuss how to identify, purchase and prepare these vegetables. I have simple short-cuts for stowage and handling of foods; long term cruising helpful hints; descriptions of pots and pans, kitchen tools, galley gear and gadgets. Cooking methods that conserve fuel and produce less unwanted heat and fumes are outlined. There are tips on microwaves and the advantages of the pressure-cooker. There are easy-to-use charts, guidelines and an easy to use Lite Section.

The Cruising **K.I.S.S.** COOKBOOK, will help you prepare your own biscuit mix, pudding, granola mix, mayonnaise, yogurt, sourdough starters, soup stocks, all from scratch. There are details on how to grow your own sprouts, make and wax your own cheese, new and uncommon grains and vegetables, lite meals, fish, vegetarian meals and seafood meals. All in this one book!

There are descriptions of those esoteric little bottles of international sauces, detailing what is in them and how to use them. There is mail order information on canned cheeses, meats, spices, long shelf-life milk and dried eggs; where to purchase an easy to use pressure cooker; details about a smoke-less top-stove grill which requires no charcoal or fuel, a hand operated food beater-chopper, and even where to purchase a hand grinder for grains.

The philosophy of the Cruising **K.I.S.S.** COOKBOOK is the premise that basic cookery uses wholesome fresh foods, cooked in the most healthful manner. It encourages experimentation with local and seasonal fresh fruits and vegetables. Imaginative cooks experiment with herbs, spices, vinegars, extracts, and tomato products. The Cruising **K.I.S.S.** COOKBOOK will bring you an unbeatable combination of tasty ingredients, time-saving hints, exciting recipes, and it will become your constant galley companion.

The Cruising *K.I.S.S.* COOKBOOK

Table of Contents.

The Cruising

K.I.S.S.

Keep It Simple System

COOKBOOK

by Corinne C. Kanter

TERMS USED IN COOKERY & COOKING METHODS

Acidulated Water: The addition of lemon juice or vinegar to cold water, which prevents discoloration of some fruits and vegetables. To 1 cup of water, add 1 tsp. of lemon juice or vinegar.

A La King: Food prepared in a creamy white sauce containing mushrooms and red or green peppers.

A La Mode: Food served with ice cream.

Al Dente: Cooked, but firm to the bite; refers to pasta.

Antipasto: Assorted appetizers of fish, cold cuts, vegetables.

Appetizer: Small portion of food or beverage served before or as the first course of a meal.

Au Gratin: With a crust, usually applied to scalloped dishes topped with browned covering or crust of fine bread crumbs, often mixed with butter or shredded cheese.

Bake: A method of cooking by dry heat in an oven or over hot coals.

Barbecue: Roast meat slowly over coals on a spit or in an oven, basting intermittently with a special sauce.

Baste: To spoon pan liquid over meats while they are roasting to prevent surface from drying.

Batter: A smooth mixture of flour, fat and other ingredients which can be poured or dropped from a spoon.

Beat: Mix with a brisk motion with fork, egg beater or electric mixer.

Béchamel: White sauce made of butter, flour, cream.

Béarnaise: Sauce of egg yolk and butter, flavored with tarragon.

Bisque: A thick, creamy soup usually of shellfish. Using tomato or vegetable base.

Blanche: To immerse, usually vegetables or fruit, briefly into boiling water to inactivate enzymes, loosen skin or remove excess salt.

Blend: To combine ingredients, of which at least one is liquid or soft, to uniform consistency.

Blintz: A cooked crepe stuffed with cheese or other fillings.

Boil: To heat liquid until rapidly bubbling.

Bordelaise: Brown sauce flavored with red wine.

Borscht: A soup containing beets, usually with a meat stock base.

Bouillabaisse: Fish soup, highly seasoned, has two or more kinds of fish.

Bouillon: A clear soup made by cooking meat, beef, with vegetables and seasonings, then straining the stock. It also can be prepared from bouillon cubes in various flavors.

Bouquet Garni: Herbs tied in cheesecloth which are cooked in a mixture and removed before serving. (see page 178)

Braising: Browning in hot fat, less-tender cuts of meat, slowly in a small amount of liquid in a tightly covered pan.

Bread: Coat with crumbs before cooking, usually in combination with egg or other binder.

Broil: Cook by direct heat under a flame or electric unit.

Broth: A thin soup, or a liquid in which meat, fish, or vegetables have been boiled.

Brush: To spread thinly on surface of food, using a pastry brush.

Butterfly: To split almost in half, leaving enough flesh intact to keep the food whole.

Caramelize: Cook white sugar in a skillet over medium heat, stirring constantly, until sugar forms a golden-brown syrup.

Casserole: An ovenproof baking dish, usually with a cover.

Chill: To cool in the refrigerator or in cracked ice before serving.

Chop: Cut into pieces about the size of peas.

Clarify: Make liquids clear by filtering, such as stock or broth.

Coat: Evenly cover food with crumbs, flour, or a batter.

Cobbler: A deep-dish fruit pie made with pastry or biscuit dough on top.

Coddle: Cook food in water just below the boiling point.

Compote: Usually mixed fruit cooked slowly in syrup.

Condiments: Seasonings that enhance the flavor of foods with which they are served.

Cool: Remove from heat and let stand at room temperature until not warm to the touch.

Consommé: A light colored, highly seasoned clear soup made from one or a combination of meats and vegetables.

Cream: Blend a mixture until it becomes soft and smooth. When applied to combining shortening, sugar, the mixture is beaten till light and fluffy.

Cream Whipped: Cream that has been whipped until it is stiff.

Crêpe: A small thin pancake filled with fruit, cheese, fish, meat or potato filling, rolled or folded around its contents.

Croquette: Minced food, shaped like a ball, patty, bound with a heavy sauce breaded and fried.

Croutons: Cubes of bread, toasted or fried, served with soups, salads, or other foods. (see page 393)

Crush: The process of using a spoon or fork to break a whole piece into a smaller piece without actually cutting it.

Cube: Cut into pieces that are the same size on each side.

Custard: A pudding, a mixture of eggs, milk and sugar, baked until set.

Cut In: To disperse solid shortening into dry ingredients with two knives, pastry cutter. Mixture texture should resemble coarse cracker meal.

Deglaze: To heat stock, wine or other liquid in the pan in which meat has been cooked, mixing with pan juices to form a gravy or sauce base.

Degrease: To remove accumulated fat from the surface of hot liquids.

Dice: Cut food into small cubes of uniform size and shape.

Dissolve: To thoroughly mix a solid or granular substance with a liquid until no sediment remains.

Dollop: A small spoonful of a semi-liquid food to garnish another food.

Dot: Distribute small bits of food over another food.

Dough: A mixture of flour and liquid of such consistency that it can be handled or kneaded.

Dredge: To cover thoroughly with a fine, dry ingredient such as flour, fine cracker crumbs, sugar or corn meal

Drippings: The fat and juice which cook out of poultry or meat and drip into the roasting pan.

Dust: Sprinkle foods lightly with sugar, flour.

Entrée: The main dish of an informal meal or a light savory course served between the soup and main course of a formal dinner.

Fillet: To remove bones from meat or fish. Pieces of meat, fish or poultry from which bones have been removed are called fillets.

Flake: Break food lightly into small pieces.

Flambé: Process of adding liquor to food and igniting it to produce a flaming effect.

Flour: To coat with flour.

Flute: A decorative scalloped crust around the edge of a pie or tart .

Fold: To blend a delicate, frothy mixture into a heavier one preferably with a rubber spatula so that none of the lightness or volume is lost. The motion used is one of turning under and bringing up and over, rotating the bowl ¼ turn as you go.

Fondant: Sugar mixed with other ingredients to form a paste. It may be cooked or uncooked, but it is always beaten or kneaded to its proper consistency.

French: To cut into thin slivers, as green beans.

Fricassée: A stew, usually of poultry.

Fritter: Vegetable or fruit dipped into batter and fried.

Frost: To cover a cake with icing of confectioners' sugar.

Fry: To pan fry, cook food in a small amount of fat. To deep fat fry, cook the food immersed in a large amount of fat.

Garnish: To decorate with a sprig of parsley or one food with another.

Glaze: Brush pastry, biscuits, or buns with a liquid such as a beaten egg, milk, or water and sugar. This will add firmness, and a hard glaze finish.

Grate: To rub food against a rough, perforated utensil to produce slivers, chunks, curls, etc.

Grill: Cook food over direct heat.

Grind: To crush or force through a chopper to produce small bits.

Hollandaise: A sauce made of butter, egg, and lemon juice or vinegar.

Infusing: Steeping herbs, tea leaves, or coffee in water or other liquid to extract the flavor.

Julienne: Cut vegetables, fruits, or meats into match-like strips.

Jus: Juices from roasting meat; used as gravy.

Knead: To work a dough with the heels of your hands in a pressing and folding motion. Kneading makes the dough smooth and elastic, which helps the dough trap gas bubbles, enabling it to rise.

Maître D'Hôtel Butter: Butter mixed with finely chopped parsley and flavored with lemon juice, salt and pepper.

Marinade: A spicy, herbed liquid, usually containing vinegar or wine, in which food is allowed to stand to become tenderized and gain flavor.

Marinate: Let stand in a marinade, sour cream, lemon juice or vinegar until well seasoned.

Mask: Cover with a thick sauce very smoothly.

Matelote: In the sailor's style; e.g., fish stew made with wine or cider.

Melt: To liquefy solid foods by heating.

Meringue: An egg white-sugar combination for pie topping.

Microwave: To cook, heat or defrost foods with microwave energy.

Mince: To chop foods into very small pieces. Minced food pieces are finer than chopped foods.

Mix: To combine ingredients by stirring or beating to distribute them uniformly.

Mold: To shape into a particular form.

Mousse: A sweetened chilled or frozen dessert made with flavored whipped cream or egg whites.

Pan-broil: Cook over direct heat in an uncovered skillet containing little or no oil, butter or shortening.

Pan-fry: Cook in an uncovered skillet in a small amount of oil or shortening over low heat.

Parboil: Partially cook in boiling water before final cooking.

Parch: To brown with dry heat.

Pare: To cut off the outside covering.

Partially set: When the consistency of a gelatin mixture resembles unbeaten egg whites after chilling.

Paste: A thick, smooth mixture of a dry ingredient and a liquid, usually flour and water, used to thicken other foods.

Pâté: A paste made of liver or meat.

Patty: Small, flat, round or oval cake of food, such as potato cake or fish cake, that is served hot.

Pickle: To preserve meat, fish, fruit, or vegetables in brine or vinegar solution.

Pipe: To force meringue, icing, savory butter, potato purée, or the like, through a pastry bag fitted with a tube, to decorate various dishes.

Pit: To remove the inedible seed from fruit, etc.

Plump: To soak fruits, usually dried, in liquid until puffy and softened. Can also refer to chicken.

Peel: Remove the outer layer or skin from a fruit or vegetable.

Poach: Cook in liquid held below the boiling point.

Preheat: To turn on oven so that desired temperature will be reached before food is placed inside for baking.

Pressure cooking: Cooks foods faster, saves time, retains the vitamins and minerals in food. Tenderizes tough meats in very little time.

Pulp: Soft, fleshy tissue of fruit or vegetables. To reduce food to a soft mass by crushing or boiling.

Purée: A thick sauce made by forcing cooked food through a sieve.

Quiche: Open-face pastry shell filled with a savory custard mixture.

Ramekin: An individual portion, baking-serving dish or casserole.

Reduce: Boil stock, gravy or other liquid until volume is lessened and liquid thickened.

Render: Reducing solid animal fat to a liquid to separate it from skin or other parts by heating.

Rind: Outer shell or peel of melon or fruit.

Roast: Cook by dry heat either in an oven or over hot coals.

Roux: Flour and oil cooked together slowly, used as a thickening agent in soups and sauces.

Sauté: To cook, stirring frequently, in a small amount of oil or non-stick cooking spray.

Scald: To heat milk or cream to just below boiling point. To plunge fruit or vegetables briefly into boiling water to loosen the skins for removal.

Score: Cut shallow gashes on surface of food, with knife as in scoring fat on ham before glazing.

Sear: Brown surface of meat over high temperature quickly on both sides to seal in juices.

Set: A term used to describe the consistency of gelatin when it has jelled enough to unmold.

Shred: To cut or shave food into slivers.

Sieve: To press a mixture through a meshed utensil to make it uniform.

Sift: Putting flour or other dry ingredients through a sieve or sifter to obtain a finer, lighter consistency.

Simmer: To cook slowly in liquid that is just below the boiling point.

Singe: To touch lightly with flame.

Soak: Immerse in water for a period of time.

Steam: Cook food in a closed pot on a rack above the boiling water.

Steep: Allowing food to stand in not quite boiling water until the flavor is extracted. Usually refers to tea.

Stew: To simmer, usually meats; for a long period of time to tenderize.

Stir: Mix ingredients with a spoon in a circular motion till combined.

Stir-fry: Cook food quickly in a small amount of hot fat, stirring constantly. Often associated with using a wok.

Strain: To pass through a strainer, sieve or cheesecloth to remove solids.

Stock: Broth in which meat, poultry, fish, or vegetables have been cooked.

Toast: Brown by direct heat, as in a toaster or under broiler.

Toss: Mix ingredients lightly by lifting and dropping them with two forks, spoons, or a pair of chopsticks.

Truss: To bind poultry legs and wings close to the body before cooking.

Velouté: Basic white sauce made with chicken, veal, or fish stock. Soup with a creamy consistency.

Vinaigrette: A mixture of oil and vinegar, flavored with parsley, finely chopped onions and other seasonings.

Whey: Liquid that separates from the curd when milk curdles; used in making cheese.

Whipping: Beating air into a substance, such as egg whites and cream, with a fork, whisk, rotary beater, or electric mixer to lighten it into a froth and increase its volume.

Zest: The fine grating of the colored outermost coatings of citrus fruits.

BASIC EQUIPMENT and then some!

• All my gadgets, knives, flatware and chopsticks are stored in a three tier carousel holder. This gadget stands on my counter top and holds everything in place even in the roughest seas. I never have to rummage through drawers or lockers with sticky hands to find anything.

• Good quality cooking utensils, good knives, last a lifetime. If you are starting from scratch, your initial investment will be high, but it's worth it. Hold each knife and see which feels most comfortable for you. One doesn't have to purchase a complete set, you may want to buy individual pieces. Consider looking at commercial quality pots. Put good thought to this. Don't hesitate to lift the utensil, how does it feel in one hand, or both. Aluminum heats well, but food sticks. Copper heats best; stainless steel cleans easily. There are combinations of stainless steel and copper core. Nonstick means an egg slides right off. Stick-resistant surfaces need pampering. Enamel surfaces chip easily. Weight increases durability.

• If your refrigeration area is a deep compartment, make a graph of the inside and opening hole to see what various size open stackable container crates you could use in this space. This way you can place items in each container crate enabling you to pick up 3 or 4 container crates instead of rummaging around for loose items piled or balanced on one another. This can be quite annoying, and allows cold air to escape at the same time. It always seems the item you want is on the bottom and by eliminating rummaging, you now are able to select from three or four crates easily.

• I have a hand operated "*quick chopper*" Salsa Maker. It comes with the sharp triple blade, an egg beater attachment, an easy to grip handle, a pouring spout, and a opening to add liquid from the top hole. It's a durable plastic and very easy to clean. Send for information to; L.A. Casseday, P.O. Box 821 South St., St. Paul, Minnesota 55075. OR . Show-Me Products, 2705 61st. Street, #B448, Galveston, TX.77551 (409-986-5154)

• The tea kettle is a very important piece of equipment. I am mentioning the brand name, because of its durability, and good design of handle, spout and *SAFETY*. Why? You fill the kettle and pour the hot boiling water out of the

same spout. Some tea kettles are cute looking, but often dangerous.
Accidents happen from the handle pivoting or the top falling off.
I have a 6-quart Revere Ware tea kettle, its single-opening trigger operated spout and fixed handle are a basic design that hasn't changed in
years. I'm glad, because it's functional and *SAFE*. This utensil will be
used daily. It even is a whistler.

• *A portable mixer* can beat, mix, cream, and whip; some even come with
a dough blade for bread recipes. If you do not have sufficient electric
power for this, use a hand operated quick chopper (see above how to
order), whisk , or just plain hand power.

• *Pressure Cooker:* Very valuable utensil see pressure cooker (see page
329) how to order, use, recipes.

• *Peelers:* Vegetable, buy two for paring
vegetables, potatoes and fruits.
 (for peeling thin strips of rind)

• *Loaf Pans:* Choose at least four. Two
standard size 8½ x 3½; several mini-loaf
pans so you can divide that banana bread,
or quick loaf recipe with a friend.

• *Custard Cups:* Select four of the 5 ounce size, used for baking custards,
flan and small molds for dessert.

• *Grinder:* Baking on board requires either carrying your own flour or
finding it ashore. Send for information; K-Tec Inc.,420 N. Geneva Rd.,
Lindon, UT. 84042,801/785-3600, has a small, lightweight, electric grain
grinder . It has a 1¾ peak horsepower 120 vac motor, a permanently
lubricated stainless steel milling chamber that never needs maintenance
and the entire unit measures 10x8x6 and weighs 8lbs. It will mill 15-20
cups of grain. The advantages to grinding your own grain: one cup of
grain produces 1½ cups of flour, so you save
space. Grain is less expensive per pound than
flour, so you save money. Grinding only the
flour you need for a week insures freshness.
There are no preservatives in the grain itself,
therefore none in your flour.
You can carry various grains such as rye and
whole wheat to vary your baking. By taking
proper storage precautions you can store grain much longer than flour.

• *Knives:* Sharpening your knowledge of knives. If I had to live with only five knives, they would be a 10-inch chef's knife, a 3-inch paring knife, a 10-inch serrated bread knife, a utility knife and a fillet knife, and knife sharpener.

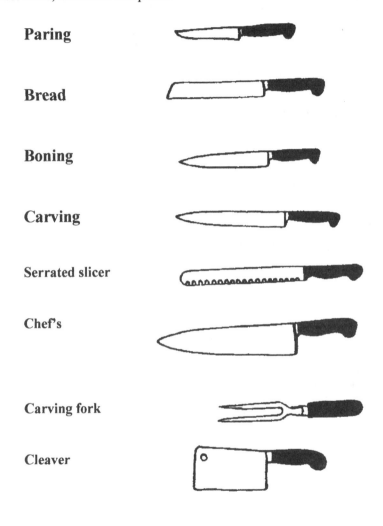

Paring	
Bread	
Boning	
Carving	
Serrated slicer	
Chef's	
Carving fork	
Cleaver	

• My first choice is a set of *Wusthof-Trident*, forged high carbon steel stored in a knife block. *Kershaw* makes a complete set which consists of detachable handle for all blades, cook's blade, carving blade, bread slicing serrated blade, fish fillet blade, paring/utility blade. The set rolls up and stores in its own carry case.

• *Knife sharpener:* The FOLD-A-Vee Sharpener works on knives, fish hooks, scissors or any edge. Total cost $19.95 includes shipping and handling; Tri-Seven Sales, 1614 SW Seagull Way, Palm City, FL. 34990.

• *Smokeless grill:* What a great gadget! The reason grills smoke is because the fat from the food drips into the fire. The smokeless grill channels the fat down into a "moat" filled with water cooling it, thus the fat never gets to burn. The grill consists of two interlocking pieces. The bottom, (looks a little like a hub-cap) houses the water; the top piece, (looks a little like the astrodome) fits into it and has the groves that channel the fat. They are inexpensive and you can find them in the housewares department or kitchen shops. Some people even put their veggies in the water section to cook while the meat or fish is grilling. Fits on one burner of your top stove. Easy to clean, no need for charcoal or fluid. *(K.I.S.S. principle)*

• *Stovetop smoker:* In addition to having a smokeless grill consider the Smoking Box, the Burton Stovetop Smoker, which can be bought through Nature's Own, 11 Roddy Ave., Attleboro, MA 02703. It is a stainless steel rectangular pan with a lid that is designed to be able to cook and smoke fish, chicken, or meat on top of your stove with very little preparation and in a short amount of time. Purchase the commercial grade. The regular unit is too lightweight to give long term service.

• *Rolykit:* Compact 8½"wide 9½"high 11" long, unrolls to 6ft. long, with many adjustable compartments for storage of small items. Ideal for first-aid kit, radio and electronic parts, nuts, bolts, sewing supplies or any other small hard to find or store items. Made of durable plastic and nylon with no metal parts.

GALLEY EQUIPMENT:

1 food processor (hand operated); unless you have electric power
1 10 or 12-inch iron skillet use on top of stove and in oven
1 1-quart saucepan, with cover
1 tea kettle, Revere 6 quart copper bottom
1 10 or 12-inch nonstick deep skillet with cover
1 6-quart stainless steel "FAGOR" pressure cooker with rack; it doubles
as a pasta pot; don't put the pressure valve on and it's an oven. (see
pressure cooker section page 329)
1 wok with cover; use to stir-fry or as a steamer by placing a rack inside.
1 plunger type coffee maker.
1 stainless steel pasta pot (optional)
1 set of 3 nesting mixing bowls
1 large colander
1 roasting pan (big enough for a small turkey)
1 smokeless grill (see above)

TOOLS:

corkscrew	egg slicer (also used for mushrooms)
2 can openers	bottle combination opener
cheese slicer	pancake turner
chopsticks	long slotted kitchen spoon
kitchen tongs	solid kitchen spoon
rubber scraper	vegetable steamer
potato masher	2 chopping boards, large and small
set of strainers	2 ladles, large and small
large spatula	large two-pronged fork
whisk	basting syringe (*optional)
wooden spoon	2 large serving spoons
rolling pin	tenderizer hammer (wood)
ice pick	2 vacuum thermos bottles (see page 23)
vegetable brush	assorted size serving trays
poultry shears	set of inexpensive paint brushes
pepper mill	2 vegetable peelers
kitchen timer	four-sided box grater
garlic press	pastry blender

BAKING EQUIPMENT:

2 heavy -duty cookie sheets
plastic pastry sheet
loaf baking pans (2 small, 2 medium)
muffin tins (12)
9-inch pie plate, 9-inch square cake pan, 9-inch quiche pan
ovenproof baking casserole dish with cover
4 custard cups
wire rack; to cool cookies, breads, and pies
sifter (flour) or use a large mesh strainer

MEASURE AND MIX:

large liquid measuring cup
set of dry measuring cups
each plastic slide rule measure teaspoon and tablespoon

CLEAN UP SUPPLIES:

Bleach, Soft-Scrub, scouring powder, fabric softener
Joy detergent works great in sea-water
fly swatter and old fashioned pull down sticky traps
stain remover
steel wool pads and soap pads (stainless steel or bronze)
laundry detergent (concentrate powder)
buckets, plastic and canvas
rubber gloves, disposable gloves
furniture polish

PAPER, PLASTIC AND KITCHEN PRODUCTS:

aluminum foil	matches
plastic wrap	sturdy garbage bags
wax paper	mop
clothespins	cheesecloth
dustpan and brush	coffee filters
toothpicks	dish towels (cotton)
long nose butane lighter	flashlights (regular/disposable)
office supply kit	

2 regular pot holders, glove pot holder

first aid kit and supplies (Rolykit, see page 16)

candles, large pair, birthday, and citronella

paper products; tissue, toilet paper, paper towels, white paper plates, paper muffin holders

assorted air vent and regular zip-lock bags, roll of inexpensive plastic bags (the kind in the produce department of the supermarket, see page 19) hand terry towels (6); use as everyday napkins

1 apron, select a long apron that goes around your neck, with a loop in front to hold a towel.

DINNERWARE, FLATWARE, GLASSES

• *Service for 4 or 6;* my first choice is Corelle, lightweight, easy to clean, stacks very well, chip resistant, comes in a variety of patterns. These sets also include a serving platter, microwave and oven proof. Inexpensive, durable a good investment.

• *Stainless-steel flatware;* a complete service for 4 or 6.

2-4 large mugs, (use for hot drinks, soups)

assorted drinking glasses, wine glasses, shot glasses

2 large insulated mugs with tops easy to sip from when underway.

HELPFUL HINTS FOR LONG TERM CRUISING

• *Mark* all bilge-stored canned goods on one end with an indelible marker, write the contents and date of purchase. To read easily and identify, but to determine how long it has been there. Paper labels may fall off, especially if you get water in the bilge.

• *Remove* all paper or cardboard boxes, store the contents in plastic containers or additional Zip-lock plastic bags. Cardboard is notorious for carrying a variety of insects. Cardboard draws and holds moisture as well.

• *Plants aboard:* an Aloe plant and perhaps a few fresh herbs. My aloe plant lives aboard, grows very easily in a small pot, needs limited amounts of sunlight and water. You can feed it coffee grinds; water it with your sprout water. Besides its beauty, it helps heal cuts, burns, bruises, some people even use it as a tonic. It is world renowned for its curative powers on skin. Take one along, as it multiplies give a baby arm to a friend to start their own. A few fresh herbs such as basil, parsley and chives will also take the same treatment and prosper aboard as well.

• *Backpacks-fanny packs-insulated soft coolers:* tote them bags! Have on board one back pack for each crew member. The modern light-weight back pack makes toting the groceries easy. The miniature fanny packs leave your hands free and they stay safely attached to you. Insulated soft coolers come in various sizes. Take a medium one to the store, let it cool in the AC, then pack it in the store to help food it keep cool until you return to the boat. I use the same one to make my yogurt in. I also use these coolers as sea-going emergency packs because they float. My large softpack holds a block of ice for 3-4 days. It is about the size of one of those hard chest coolers. When not in use soft coolers stow easily unlike bulky hard coolers. For a good nautical version with no metal fittings, Write to: Horizons Ltd., 858 C Dauls Dr.,Conyers, GA 30207, phone 800-969-4583, ask for Paul Niemi.

• *35 MM- film canisters:* are great for storing small amounts of seasonings, especially things like Old Bay or oregano which will get damp and stale in the original cartons. These canisters are also great for making little baking-soda filled odor-fighters. Instead of using the entire cardboard box of baking soda, which gets soft and sticky, fill the canisters with baking soda, punch a few holes in the lids, place them in drawers, cabinets and wastebaskets and in the refrigerator.

• *Cheesecloth:* carry one large package of this cloth. *Use:* Wrap a piece of cheesecloth moistened with vinegar around the hard cheese to keep it fresh. Run out of filters for your morning brewed coffee? Cut a piece of cheesecloth into eight inch square. If your coffee is finely ground use a double amount. Fill with 3 scoops of coffee, tie with a piece of string. Place in your coffee pot or filter holder and brew that coffee, yields 4 cups of coffee. Make your beef stock by placing bones wrapped in cheesecloth. Make your yogurt cheese. (See how to, page 421)

• *Cutting boards:* wood? plastic? or glass? I use wood, one side to cut bread, the other for vegetables. Plastic I find doesn't hold up to well and I worry about the minute scraps of plastic in my food, so I opted for the corning glass for poultry, meat, veal or pork. This cleans easily with soap and water. I do have a wooden fish holder with a strong steel tail-clamp to clean the fresh catch of the day.

• *Fresh water spray rinse:* to help conserve your fresh water supply, wash dishes in salt water whenever it's clean enough and just rinse with your precious fresh water. In my galley I use an ordinary small plastic spray bottle.

• *Folding bikes;* a pair of 20" folding bikes are our main means of shore side transportation and we wouldn't be without them. On a carrier over the rear fender we carry our saddle bags. They are designed to carry a full case of adult beverage each side and to slip off easily with a central carry handle to take right into the store. Or you can make saddle bags from two back packs joined together at the top. Our bikes have a generator driven light set , a bell attached to the handlebars, reflectors on the pedals and rear fender and a small rear-view mirror. Biking is a great way to get around town, do your shopping or laundry, and explore new areas. The local people love having all the yachties biking through town. We have zippered canvas covers for them when they are stowed away.

• *Garlic crock jar:* I use a small one with the vented holes in my galley. I keep my main stock in a large netted bag below in a cool, dark area and place a small supply in the crock jar for easy use.

• *Ginger:* see below *seasickness.*

• *Ice cubes;* E-Z Ice maker bags, come in packages of 10 bags. Each bag makes 18 cubes. Fill through built-in funnel, double tie and freeze. A nice feature of this bag is that it takes up little room and can be folded in half. It is great to store your homemade clear cooled soup stock, pop out one cube of stock at a time. EZ POR Corporation, Wheeling, IL 60090.

• *Ice stretcher:* two nights before going away for the weekend cruise, place your favorite fruit drink in plastic re-useable milk containers and freeze. Pack them instead of ice in your insulated bag or ice-chest. Your frozen drink will keep other items cold as it defrosts and you get truly cold drinks as a bonus, instead of dealing with that wasted melted ice water.

• *Meat tenderizer:* can be purchased in the grocery store and aside from its tenderizing qualities, it's great on sea nettle stings and insect bites. Just sprinkle on and away goes that itch or sting.

• *MICROWAVE:* see *Microwave* section (page 314).

• *Mixing Bowls:* purchase a set of three nest mixing bowls. Many uses, mixing, serving and letting the dough rise in them.

• *Non-skid matt:* comes in rolls, use it to make crockery slip resistant. *Use* it under your carousel, binoculars or whatever you place on a smooth surface. Perfect for under your doggie dish.

• *Paint brushes:* purchase the assorted small size package of paint brushes, turn them into your pastry and BBQ brushes. They clean easily in soap and water, when you are through using them in the galley, send them to the workshop. *Use* the small narrow paint brush to clean coffee grinders. The brush can get around the metal blade in a blade grinder and also get into the corners of a mill grinder. A soft paintbrush is an excellent tool for dusting areas that are hard to get into with a dust rag.

• *Paper products:* paper products in the USA are very inexpensive, so before you sail away from it all, stock up on toilet paper, paper towels, and tissues. To make ordinary paper towels last twice as long, I cut them in half before putting them on the paper towel holder. Be sure the factory edges face one another. Buy a cheap serrated knife at the next flea market or garage sale to cut the paper towels.
There are so many times when half a sheet will do. I learned a new trick instead of cutting, try this. Hold your one hand on the top edge where the paper is perforated, tear half way across then tear straight down quickly half a sheet. It's that easy and economical.

• *Plastic bags:* have zip-lock bags in various sizes. *Uses* range from little goody-bags for the night watch, thru keeping your sandpaper from disintegrating. You can stretch the use of the large, expensive ones by double-bagging using the inexpensive vegetable store bags as liners. New on the market are vented vegetable zip-locks. De-box cardboard boxed items. If they are in sealed inner-liners, put the entire inner liner along with an identification label and instructions into the large zip-lock.

• *Salsa Master:* hand controlled food chopper. It chops onions, garlic, coarse, or fine without tears or odors. Chop or mince fresh herbs, all types of chili peppers, bell peppers, raw cabbage, carrots, celery and zucchini. Make a complete tuna, egg or seafood salad. Whirl cooked applesinto instant applesauce, make creamy mashed potatoes. Prepare ingredients for all types of Mexican and Hispanic specialties. Make fillings, topping for tortillas, tacos and enchiladas. Made of heavy duty plastic, easy to clean and store.

• *Seasickness:* mal-de-mer oops, try Ginger! It does not work as well for everyone, but it sure is worth a try and a delicious, nutritious try at that! Ginger is a well documented aid in the fight against mal-de-mer. Try a gingersnap cookie, chunks of ginger in syrup, ginger beer, ginger tea, crystallized ginger candy (found in Oriental food markets). There are claims of soothing effects from ginger that help calm an upset stomach. Sailors Ginger Delight is a sparkling beverage with papaya and pineapple juices. Others recommend Karo Syrup; 1 tablespoon at first sign of queasiness and repeat as necessary. Karo is a dextrose: a type of sugar that is absorbed directly into the system with little change needed in digestive track.

• *Sprouts and sprouting;* (see page 399)
• *Smokeless grill;* (see page 16)
• *Stovetop Smoker;* (see page 16)
• *Tableware;* (see page 19)

• *Trash, the disposal dilemma:* I'm quoting a dear friend, cruiser *"Liza Copeland*: " When provisioning for a cruise, the amount of trash that will accrue can be greatly reduced by removing unnecessary packaging prior to departure." Items such as flour, rice, cake mixes, breakfast cereals, herbs, and cookies can be stowed in robust air-tight and reusable containers. Follow U.S. and international pollution guidelines. *Liza Copeland and her family recently circumnavigated aboard Bagheera. order her books, Cruising, Still Cruising, and a video Just Cruising, by writing to Romany Enterprises, 3943 W. Broadway, Vancouver, B.C., Canada V6R 2C2.*

• *Vacuum-Thermos Bottles:* Take two on board, one for coffee, the other for hot water *ONLY*. Don't waste the hot water from the kettle you just boiled up, store it. Now you have instant hot water for tea, coffee, instant cereal or cup of soup during the day. Saves on cooking fuel as well.

• *Weevil:* one of "the pets from Hell!" Store flour, rice, grains, pastas, beans in air-tight containers, place a couple of bay leaves inside. The bay leaves keep those critters away.

• *Wok:* stir-fry or steamer. Read the instructions carefully and season this utensil properly. They are inexpensive and easy to clean up. Wash with hot water, rinse and dry. Fill a small amount of water up to a wooden rack or steamer basket, cover the wok and you have an efficient instant steamer. To season the wok; place over low flame with about 4 tablespoons of oil, wiping it around with a paper towel. Heat about 15 minutes. Remove from heat, cool down and store. If you do not have a wooden rack, make one by taking two pairs of chopsticks and place them across the wok tic-tac-toe fashion, or make a weave out of ice-cream sticks and you have an instant rack.

• *Wraps:* Paper Products (see page 19,20,22)

HELPFUL HINTS ON FOOD

A compilation of valuable information including tips on purchasing, storing, and cooking. An introduction to some fascinating uncommon fruits, vegetables, rices and grains.

• *Apples:* Fall or winter apples keep best, they are generally the crisper varieties and will keep about up to 3 months. Fall is the best time for farm fresh apples.

Apples store well in a cool dark area. Wash before storing to get rid of any potential pests and insecticides. Dry well and wrap individual fruit in tissue paper or newspaper.

Apple juice: use it to poach the fish catch of the day. Use a small amount in a non-stick skillet. Cooking time for fish is 10 minutes per inch. After cooking, place fish on a serving platter and top with thinly sliced lemon pieces. Bring the remaining apple juice in the skillet to a boil until syrupy. Pour onto the cooked fish.

Apple juice: substitute apple juice for ¼ of your water when cooking rice.

Keep apple peel from splitting during baking: use the peeling edge of an apple corer or a vegetable peeler, remove a strip of peel around the center of the apple.

Apple substitute: 1 cup firm pears, chopped, plus 1 tablespoon lemon juice = 1 cup chopped apple.

• *Arrowroot:* (a thickener): substitute equal amount of cornstarch.

• *Asparagus:* Choose spears with firm green stalks and hard-closed tips. *Use* quickly after purchasing, wash and store in air-vent plastic zip-locks. *Steam* in wok or microwave. Rinse thoroughly, cut away lower bottom just up to the more tender part.

Leftovers go nicely into an omelet for breakfast.

Jury rig if you have no asparagus pot or steamer rack. Cut off the bottom two to three inches of the asparagus stems. Lay them at the bottom of a deep skillet (making them the steaming rack) place remaining spears on top. They get steamed and stems are cooking in the water.

Very thin asparagus can be eaten raw.

Top with hot melted butter, cream sauce, or a cold vinaigrette dressing.

• *Artichokes:* (Globe); select artichokes with compact heads that feel heavy for their size. The leaves should cling together, not gap open. Brown spots on the leaves were caused by frost. In fact some folks believe a frost enhances the flavor. Simple to cook in your microwave or pressure cooker and easy to eat. You may eat them hot, warm, or cold.

Trimming: trim the stem even with the base, then trim 1-inch from the top of the artichoke or snip the points of the leaves. If you're working with a lot of artichokes, either rub the cut edges with lemon to prevent discoloring or plunk the trimmed chokes into a bowl of cold water spiked with lemon juice.

Steaming: steam artichokes, stem side down, on a steaming rack over at least 1-inch of boiling water. Cover and steam until base is tender or a petal near the center pulls out easily.

Pressure cooking: put water up to rack, place artichoke on rack, secure cover and cook 7 minutes. Let pressure come down on its own accord.

Microwave: place in deep bowl, cover with plastic wrap, and make a few slits in wrap. Cook 5 minutes, check if more time is needed.

Eating: pull off leaves individually, use the fleshy end to scoop dip, and draw the leaf between your teeth to scrape off the flesh. Scoop out the fuzzy core and discard, cut the remaining heart into bite-size dipping pieces or store in a glass jar with a small amount of olive oil and garlic, refrigerate for your next tossed salad.

Jerusalem: can be pressure cooked with skin on and then peel. Serve with hot melted butter, cheese or white cream sauce, cold with a vinaigrette sauce or mayonnaise.

• *Avocados:* a ripe avocado will be firm but soft to the touch. They are peeled, cut up in salads, sandwiches or omelets. Select a ripe avocado with skin uniformly dark, not just in spots.

Making your guacamole early in the day, place the pit in the center of the dip to prevents discoloration. Discard pit just before serving.

To keep a leftover piece of avocado, sprinkle a few drops of lemon juice, cover tightly with plastic wrap.

Ripen at room temperature, preferably in a dark place; ripening takes 3 to 5 days. Refrigeration will slow the process.

• *Bananas:* Can be bought from green to bright yellow. Buy small hands at different stages of ripeness. If you are in the islands and buy a huge stalk, hang it in the shade to ripen after dipping it in seawater for a few seconds to stop spiders and bugs from getting on board.

Bananas will ripen quite quickly at room temperature.

One medium-sized banana equals ½ cup sliced, ⅓ cup mashed.

• *Bacon:* Canned bacon and whole ham can be found at variety stores. They need no refrigeration, are delicious and inexpensive.

2 ounces of raw bacon will yield about ⅓ cup diced.

• *Beans:* (canned) Stock up on green, yellow wax, lima, chick peas, pinto, black and red kidney beans. Not only do you have the makings of a bean salad, but you have vegetables that can be added to cooked stew, or clear broth soup just 2 minutes before serving.

Add: mashed kidney beans to ground beef before shaping meatloaf or meatballs as a filler.

Dried: keep a variety of beans on hand. Make your own mixture of dried beans for a great bean soup. Store them in an air-tight container.

• *Bean Sprouts:* sprouting, *(see page* 399)

• *Beef-Chicken-Turkey:* (Canned) beef, chicken, turkey, pork, smoked pork sausage, Amish noodles. Order; Beech Bound Farm, Rt.2 Box 251, Shiloh, Ohio 44878 or Brinkman Turkey Farms inc. 16314 S.R. 68, Findlay, Ohio 45840. They are a small farm cannery & turkey farm. Canned Beef Company, Montana Ranch Beef, Gilt Edge Route, Lewiston, MT 59457.

• *Beets:* (fresh) Come with red-leaf or green-leaf tops. Available all year long. If they arrive at the grocer with their leaves removed, these are called clip tops and more than likely have come out of storage. If you purchase fresh beets with tops, cut them off and use in salads or as a cooked vegetable. Store unwashed in a cool dry place. Select fresh beets that are smooth skinned, hard, and dark red. Do not peel until after beets are cooked with the skin on.

Use your pressure cooker, see how to: (see page 329).

Cold beets can be served as a side dish, or diced in salads.

Peel uncooked fresh beets, cut in match stick strips for crunch in salad. *Canned beets,* add to salads, make into pickled beets, or serve as a cold or hot beet soup.

• **Berries:** Don't wash berries until you need them. Wet berries don't keep as long in the refrigerator as dry ones.

• **Black Beans:** (fermented) Found in Oriental markets, they come in half to one pound cans, or in plastic bags. They are moist, soft, tender, taste beany, salty, and tangy. *Uses* are: condiment, flavoring agent, darkens sauces.

Black beans, (dried) (canned) with thin skins, are also used in Hispanic cuisines.

Purchase, dried (see cooking index) or ready to eat canned for quick soups, salads.

• **Bok choy:** Available all year. Select large-leaved types for soup making, narrower and longer stems for stir-frying. Store unwashed in a perforated plastic bag in the refrigerator. Trim off the heavy base, discard blemished or tough leaves. Separate stalks from the base as you would celery. Slice stalks and leaves, rinse well. Use for stir-frying and in soups. *No bok choy?* use Napa , Savoy, or green cabbage.

• **Bones:** After you have finished that baked ham, roasted turkey or the chicken pieces after deboning whole chickens, don't discard the bones. These parts make great stock, or a homemade soup. (page 428-430)

• **Boniato:** Treat it just like a North American sweet potato. Bake, boil, roast, fry, steam, sauté, mash or purée. *Used* in puddings, pies and muffins. It is available year round but is prone to bruising and rapid spoilage, but will keep at room temperature in a ventilated area for a few days.

• **Bread:** Save stale bread; if one or two days old make french toast; if a bit older, make croutons, bread pudding or stuffing for a roast chicken.

Canned date-nut bread needs no refrigeration. Keep it on board for your emergency and heavy weather meals. Serve as a dessert with jam.

Rusks, make your own. Take a fresh loaf of Italian, French or sourdough bread, cut into thick slices, place on a rack in a warm oven. Lightly brown, remove and store in a airtight container. Will last for two months.

Pita pockets makes a great stuffed sandwiches.

Make pizzas on party breads, English muffins, split pita rounds or bagels.

• *Breadfruit:* The green scaly fruit should feel dense and heavy for its size, not spongy.

Use like the white and sweet potatoes, boiled, baked, roasted, fried, steamed, mashed, creamed or in puddings, cakes, and pies.

Cored, stuffed and baked with a rich filling of meat or cheese. *Stores poorly,* keep at room temperature until ripe. Can be refrigerated after that for a day or two.

Peel a hard breadfruit, quarter it lengthwise, cut out the darker core. Pare off the skin, rinse, place pieces in water as you continue to pare. For softer fruit, score the peel, pull it off gently.

• *Broccoli:* Look for green heads, leaves and stems. Tender firm stalks, compact dark green or purplish green buds. Avoid yellow or purple flowers visible inside buds.

Wash immediately, store in air-vent plastic zip-lock bag in the refrigerator.

Broccoli raab; thin, leafy, sparsely budded broccoli stalks.

Serve as you would string-beans, spinach.

Choose firm, small stems and relatively few buds and open flowers. Keep in a perforated vegetable bag, in refrigerator for a few days.

Clean by rinsing it quickly, shake off water, cut off heavier base stems. Leave whole or cut into bite-size pieces.

Cook as you would broccoli. Top it with garlic and hot peppers, or a white cream sauce.

• *Bulgur:* Is a ground wheat that is available in three textures: coarse, medium and fine. It is used in tabouli and other dishes as a alternative to rice. Available in bulk or packaged. Requires little or no cooking and will soften to a palatable consistency after it is steamed or soaked in hot water. Store in cool, dry area and use within a month. (see page 265)

• *Butter:* Canned butter from New Zealand can be found in the island stores and some of the USA specialty stores. Requires no refrigeration.

Briny butter, first sterilize any wide-mouth jars and lids in boiling water. Cool down sterilized jars, and press in unsalted butter to within one inch of top, squeezing out any air bubbles. Add ¼ cup salt to 2 cups of boiling water, cool down and then add to butter in jars. Butter packed in brine will keep up to six months, store in cool dark place.

• *Cabbage:* Cabbage stores well without refrigeration in a netted bag.

Red or green, use alone or as a combination, in coleslaw, soups, stir-fry and stuffed cabbage.

Chinese celery cabbage, about 16 inches long, celery-like, leafy, broader than American celery. Green, yellow with white stalks. Crunchy, firm, moist, tender. bland, sold by the pound. Refrigerate in air-vent plastic bag.

Use in soups, stir-fried.

1 *pound* of cabbage will yield 5 firmly packed cups of shredded cabbage or three cups cooked.

• *Calabaza:* Also called West Indian pumpkin or Cuban squash. Fine grained, sweet, moist and bright orange in color.

Whole squash will keep for a month in a well-ventilated area. Usually sold in chunks because of its large size.

Keep cut calabaza covered tightly with plastic wrap, should stay fresh for a week or so in the refrigerator. When buying a cut chunk, look for the least fibrous, most close-grained flesh.

Can be baked, steamed, or used in soups, stews, purées, sauces, cakes, pies, custards, quick breads, cookies, puddings.

Substitute for pumpkin, butternut, acorn or Hubbards's squash.

Prepare an uncut whole calabaza, with a heavy cleaver, cut off the stem end, then cut the squash lengthwise. Scoop out and discard the seeds. Cut the squash into small chunks. Remove the rind with a paring knife or vegetable peeler.

Save seeds for toasting like pumpkin seeds. Boil 1 cup seeds in 2 cups water with ½ teaspoon salt, 10-12 minutes. Drain, toss with 1 teaspoon corn oil, spread on baking sheet. Bake at 350 degrees or until golden in color, 15-20 minutes, toss often.

• *Capers:* Capers are tiny flower buds about the size of peppercorns, with a big jolting flavor. Found in gourmet sections.

Use: add to salads, dressings, fish, tomato sauce, gravies, scrambled eggs, even place some in your meatloaf or meatball mixture.

• *Carob:* Fruit used as a substitute for chocolate. Contains natural sugar.

• *Carrots:* Wash, pat dry, wrap in white tissue paper, place in zip-lock bag, store in cool, well ventilated area. If you have room in refrigerator, store in the new air-vent plastic bags.

Use a potato peeler to cut carrots into fine thin shavings to serve with greens in tossed salads.

Add grated raw carrots to coleslaw, salads, meat-loaf mixtures, chicken or tuna salad, taco fillings and pasta sauces.

Stir finely grated carrots into cookie and cake batters.

Boil cut carrots along with potatoes and mash as usual.

Leftover cooked carrots can be added to homemade soup.

• *Cauliflower:* Look for an outer shell of fresh green stem and leaves, white or creamy white head. Avoid obvious small flowers in head or yellow withered leaves.

Keep white while cooking, add a little milk to the water.

• *Celery:* Wash well, cut leafy tops off first for your soups, stocks or salads. Store the remainder in vented vegetable plastic zip-lock bags.

1 large stalk of celery, diced will give you about ⅓ cup.

Substitution: use fresh bean sprouts, jícama, or green pepper.

• *Cereal:* (Hot) On those cold mornings make a bowl of hot cereal. Try Wheatena, Ralston, Rolled Oats and Quick Grits.

Top with your favorite nuts, raisins, brown sugar, honey, even some grated cheese on those grits. It's delicious, nutritious, economical.

Save the crumbs from cold cereal, mix different kinds in an airtight container, this makes a delicious coating for frying fish or chicken. Unsweetened cereal can be used as a filler for meat-loaf or ground beef. Sweetened cereals as a crumb topping for dessert.

• *Chayote:* **(shy-o-tay)** is a squash cultivated in tropical regions, also called Mango Squash, and Vegetable Pear because of its pear shape. In the Caribbean it's called Christophene; in Louisiana, Mirlition; Latinos call it Chayote. Light green, thin skin; delicate flavor.

Use: interchangeably with zucchini.

Select firm, smooth chayotes without blemishes

Uncooked: peel, seed, slice thin and chill for use as an appetizer with a platter of vegetables, crackers, and a bowl of dip; or chop and mix with flaked tuna, salmon, or cut-up cooked chicken salad as a substitute for celery.

Cooked: coarsely grate and cook with a little olive oil or butter. Season lightly with salt and pepper.

• *Cheese:* (cheese chart, see page 55)

Fresh block, hard cheese can be stored without refrigeration by covering cheese with cheesecloth soaked in vinegar. This prevents the growth of bacteria. The cheesecloth needs not be wet all the time; simply sniff it occasionally to make sure it still has a vinegary smell. If so, the cloth is still effective; if not, re-soak it. In places where the vinegar has come in contact with the cheese, a thin, dry rind will form which can be cut away and discarded. This method will allow you to store the cheese up to three weeks in warm climates.

Select your extra supply wax coated, which require no refrigeration.

Method for waxing cheese. First experiment with varieties you like before buying large quantities to put up. Crumbly types of cheese don't wax to well. After selecting the cheeses, cut large blocks into practical size squares.

Use equal parts of paraffin and beeswax, they are available at hardware and health food stores or from specialty houses mentioned below. Select a roomy, deep-sided melting pan, as wax spilled on the stove could cause a fire. Reserve the pan for waxing *ONLY,* do not use it for cooking. Heat the wax until it liquefies, then using a potato masher, lower the cheese into the wax mixture, dip until it is just covered, a few seconds. Place the cheese on a brown-paper covered rack to cool.

When it has cooled, you have preserved cheese. The cheese may weep a bit after waxing. This is part of the natural aging process. Wipe off the excess weeping oil and wrap the waxed chunks in anon-waxed butcher's paper, store in a cool, dry place. Should last up to one year, if any mold spots appear, just slice them away.

• *Make your own cheese:* Write to New England Cheese Making Supply Co. P.O. Box 85, Ashfield, MA. 01330 413-628-3808. They sell Direct Set Cheese Starter Cultures, that are freeze dried and sealed in packets that contain enough culture to set milk or cream to cheese.

Purchase canned cheese: The WSU Creamery Troy Hall 101, Pullman, WA.99164-4410, 509-335-4014 will provide information and prices on numerous varieties of canned cheese.

• *Cherimoya:* (chair-I-moy-a) Heart shaped and green when ripe, this delicious fruit has a rough skin with petal-like indentations. The texture of sherbet and a taste of strawberry, banana and pineapple at once. When fully ripe, tastes like a peach. Halve or quarter the fruit, remove seeds and eat raw by the spoonful. Or, cut it in pieces, remove skin and puree in a blender or food processor to mix into cold milk dishes or a topping for ice cream.

• *Chicken: Whole,* when chickens are on sale, purchase at least four. Making chicken breasts, wings, liver (keep adding to this frozen pack you'll soon have enough for a main dish), leg and thigh packs. After cutting the chicken for parts, use all the small pieces, bones for base to make chicken soup, strain for clear broth .

To clarify hot fat, consommé, broths, etc. Let drip through a paper coffee filter. Fit filter into a funnel with a narrow neck or a small strainer place on top of a bowl.

While roasting your chicken or turkey in the oven, place whole head of garlic (cut off tips) wrapped in aluminum foil. Remove roasted garlic cool slightly, then squeeze out the small cloves. Makes a great spread.

Canned chunk chicken is a quick source of chopped cooked chicken for salads, sandwich spreads and casseroles.

• *Chili paste with garlic:* Made from hot peppers, salt and garlic.

• *Chocolate:* Bittersweet and semisweet mean pretty much the same thing: slightly sweetened and without milk or cream. Domestic brands are usually called semisweet, while imported brands often use the term bittersweet.
Instant chocolate icing can be accomplished by placing chocolate chips in a heavy-duty ziplock bag. Immerse the bag in hot water to melt the chocolate. Snip off a small corner of the bottom of the bag, twist the bag and squeeze the chocolate out of the hole.
Lightly butter or grease the top pot of your double boiler in which the chocolate is to be melted. It will pour out easily.
Chocolate chips: 6-ounce package equals 1 cup.

• *Chutney:* Usually made from fruit, such as apples, mangoes, gooseberries, plums, and tomatoes. Flavorings are added in the form of spices, onions, garlic, and salt; the preserve is sweetened with sugar, or sugar and dried fruits.
Serve along with cream cheese and chopped walnuts, pecans or slivered almonds. Top with fresh chives.
Serve as a side dish accompaniment to main course.

• *Cinnamon sugar:* Use a small container for 1 cup white sugar and 1 tablespoon ground cinnamon. Stir thoroughly and you will have cinnamon sugar ready to use on pancakes, french toast, waffles.

• *Citrus fruit:* Store in a netted hammock or reed basket in a well vented area. Citrus fruit that has been refrigerated will go moldy after about two weeks. Fresh off the tree and stored properly, it will keep for a month (except honeybells and kumquats).
Preserve citrus flavor by drying the colored portion of the skin. Peel off only the colored portion of orange, lemon or lime skin, spread in the sun to dry. After a day of good hot weather, it can be crumbled and stored in a air-tight container.
Useful as in seasoning in fish, cakes, and cookie recipes.

• *Clams:* Clams in cans come in various sizes. Easy for making a chowder soup, cracker or vegetable spread, or in a sauce for pasta dishes.
Substitute for conch in conch recipes.

• *Cocoa:* Cocoa is chocolate with most of the fat removed. For those who can't eat chocolate or cocoa, the substitute is Carob powder which contains some natural sugar.

1-ounce of cocoa = ¼ cup; 1 pound of cocoa = 4 cups.

• *Collard greens:* The deep-green leaves are on fairly long and heavy stalks with the flavor between cabbage and kale. Sold by the bunch.

Wash thoroughly and cut in large strips; discard stem ends, place in pressure cooker alternately with diced onions and about ½ cup of small slices of uncooked bacon, finally top with a sprinkle of sugar. After well packed, pour in 1 cup water, secure cover, bring up to pressure, cook for 7 minutes. Remove from heat and let pressure drop of own accord. They will be soft and cooked down, open and stir. If they need more cooking; return to pressure and cook a few minutes longer. It's best to cook in less time, check and cook again then to overcook.

• *Concentrate:* Carry concentrate juice that comes in plastic containers. These concentrate juice containers take up little room; when ready to use just add the correct amount of water.

Tomato juice fan, buy tomato paste, (see tomatoes below).

• *Corn:* Nothing tastes better than corn in season. Lots of varieties.

When boiling, add a small amount of sugar to the water instead of salt. Salt in cooking water toughens corn.

Peel away husks, just down to the last layer, place corn in a plastic bag, lay flat and micro-wave your corn. Depending on size and amount, begin with 7 minutes and test.

Placing on the grill, peel away husk just to remove the silks. Push back husks and grill.

• *Couscous:* Made from recooked cracked millet or from coarsely ground semolina. Sold in bulk or packaged. Store in cool, dry, dark place.

Variation:, add a handful of one of the following after couscous is prepared: toasted pine nuts, raisins, dried currants, grated orange peel, chopped fresh parsley.

• *Cranberries:* Look for firm, plump berries but don't worry that the color varies from light to dark red. They also come canned and dried.

Uses: garnish hot cereals, in baked goods, dressings, sauces, and chutney.

Side dish for poultry, meats, fish and pork.

• *Cucumber:* Store individually wrapped in newspaper or tissue paper in cool dark area or netted bag. Should keep one week.

Try the new air-vent vegetable bags and place in refrigerator.

European hothouse hydroponic cucumber needs no peeling and has fewer seeds.

Leave skin on cucumber, scrape lengthwise with the tines of a fork across the outer skin to remove some skin. Wash, and slice.

• *Daikon:* A long Japanese white radish, a wonderful addition to any salad. Can vary in lengths, sold by the pound. Look for creamy white skin that's unbroken and unblemished.

Peel only a thin layer or scrub well before eating. Peel, serve raw, lightly sauteed, steamed or added to roasts and stews. Cut in julienne slices.

Once cut, wrap in plastic. Will keep refrigerated for several weeks.

• *Datil Pepper:* The Datil pepper is closely related to the Habero pepper, which it resembles in flavor and heat factor. The delightful pepper is grown in St. Augustine, Florida. Local legend says the datil pepper was brought to St. Augustine from Spain by the Minorcans in the mid-1700's. In all probability the datil pepper made its way to St. Augustine from somewhere in South America via the Spanish trade routes during the 18th & 19th centuries. Regardless of its origins, the datil pepper now belongs to St. Augustine, which remains the only known area in the New World for its cultivation. Dat'l Do-It makes hot sauce, relish, mustard, pepper jelly, vinegar, dried datil peppers, urban dressing, call 1-800-hot-datl.

• *Dehydrated/freeze dried foods:* Theses foods are lightweight, often packaged in a waterproof pack. A variety of foods for breakfast, dinner, lunch, desserts, soups, sauces. Good to have on board for those heavy weather, and emergency quick and easy meals.

• *Eggplant:* Most varieties of eggplant are available year-round. Whatever type selected, choose those firm, heavy for their size. The skin should be glossy, taut, the flesh firm, without soft spots.

Western eggplant, pear-shaped, deep purple skin and a green cap. Its flesh tends to be more bitter than that of other varieties.

Japanese eggplant, deep-purple exterior, but it is long and slender. The skin is thinner, the flesh smoother, with fewer, smaller seeds.

Chinese variety is similar to the Japanese, although slightly longer, lavender in color. The flesh tends to be sweeter, more tender than darker-skinned varieties.

Thai varieties, white eggplant, tends to be firmer, creamier and less bitter. The skin of some is tough and thick, requiring peeling. Some are small and round, some elongated. Their crisp texture makes them ideal for pickling. Another Thai variety resembles a miniature pumpkin bright red orange rather than gold or orange in color. It is used mainly in sweet-sour dishes, should not be substituted for other varieties.

Bake: Cut eggplant into ½ inch slices. Brush all side with olive oil, arrange in single layer in a shallow baking pan. Bake at 375 degrees for 20-30 minutes, until browned and tender when pierced.

Steam: Cut eggplant into cubes, steam on rack 4-5 minutes.

Grill: use miniature or small varieties. Cut tiny eggplants in half, larger ones in thick wedges. Grill over low coals until brown and tender when pierced, 10-12 minutes.

Fry: cut eggplant into ½ inch slices. Dip in a mixture of egg and water, then into bread crumbs. Heat safflower oil in a large skillet over medium heat. Cook eggplant in single layer, without crowding, not necessary to remove skin. Brown on both side 8-10 minutes and tender when pierced.

Leftover cooked eggplant: top with garlic butter or shredded cheese or sliced tomatoes or all three. Place under broiler and heat slightly.

Male eggplants have fewer seeds and are less likely to be bitter. To differentiate between male and female eggplant, inspect the flower end. The male has a small round and smooth end, the female is irregular and less smooth.

Avoid a watery eggplant casserole, remove excess moisture by salting eggplant slices and draining them on a rack prior to using. Rub slices with lemon juice to prevent discoloration.

• **Eggs:** breakfast section page 91 has additional information and recipes.

Keep 2 or 3 hard cooked eggs on hand to add to tuna, chicken, salmon, or ham salad spreads.

Cut a hard boiled egg into a fresh vegetable or potato salad.

Fresh eggs will keep without refrigeration about three weeks with just normal care. If you grease eggs with vegetable shortening and place right back in their cartons and store in a cool place you can extend their shelf life another three weeks. Some people use petroleum jelly to coat eggs. I like shortening myself, it's easier to apply. Turn eggs upside down in their containers every 2 or 3 days to keep the yolks suspended, especially in the tropics.

Freshness test: place raw eggs in salt water; fresh ones sink; spoiled ones float. Discard contaminated eggs and hard boil the survivors. Eggs that have never been refrigerated will last better than those that have. The usual supermarket eggs have all been refrigerated. Infertile eggs will keep longer than fertile eggs.

Wakefield Brand Scrambled Egg Mix, Wakefield, NE 68784. sells 30 6-ounce pouches per case. Each pouch is equal to approximately six to eight eggs. This egg mix is for baking, cooking, even scrambled eggs.

Breaking open eggs for omelet, etc: always open and place one at a time in a small cup. If one egg is bad, you have saved the opened fresh good eggs from the bad one.

Never beat egg-whites into an aluminum pan as it is sure to darken them.

When separating the yolk from the white of an egg, use the shell to easily pick part of egg yolk accidentally dropped into the whites.

• *Fish:* (Successful Fish & Seafood Secrets, see pages 245-252)

• *Flour:*
   All purpose flour is a mixture of hard-wheat and soft-wheat and comes bleached and unbleached.

Unbleached is a flour that has not been bleached or had maturing agents added.

Other types of flour: pastry, semolina, gluten, graham and cake. Read the specific instructions and uses for each on the package labels.

Self-rising flour is just all-purpose flour with baking powder and salt added to it. It is used primarily for biscuits, muffins, and other quick breads. To make self-rising flour, add ½ teaspoon salt and 1 ½ teaspoons baking powder to 1 cup of all-purpose flour.

Bread flour is made of the hardest wheat flours, which are generally considered most suitable for bread baking and pasta making.

Whole wheat flour makes a bread easily sliced for sandwiches or toast.

• *Fruits:* (Dried) Carry a variety of figs, dates, raisins, and tropical fruit.
   Use them in making your own granola, toppings, cakes, cookies, pies, or just snack on them. Dried fruits are often sold in bulk.

Canned or fresh sliced: add a couple of tablespoons of cordial or liqueur.

Add some thin slices of apple or pear into batter for muffins or pancakes.

Top thin slices of apple or pear on chicken, turkey breast and peanut butter sandwiches.

Layer granola, nonfat yogurt or low-fat cottage cheese with fresh or canned fruit of your choice for a light dessert.

• *Garam Masala:* A spice blend used in Indian cooking.
   Substitute an equal amount of curry powder.

• *Garlic:* Garlic varies in size and consists of several cloves enclosed in an outer skin. The entire cluster of cloves is called a garlic "head."

To peel a clove, give it a good whack with the flat side of a knife. The skin should come off easily. Chop the clove by hand with a sharp knife or put through a hand press.

Whole cloves of garlic: peel, store in olive or safflower oil, use as needed a tablespoon or two of this flavored oil in quick-fry or salad.

Roasted garlic: wrap a few heads in aluminum foil. Place in toaster oven, in the cavity of the roasting chicken or a quick cook in the pressure cooker.

The cloves pop out easily to spread on crackers or french bread.

Dry chips can be purchased in the oriental grocery. You can stir fry with them or take a small amount of chips and make crushed garlic.

• *Ginger:* Spicy and hot in taste. Look for plumb but firm pieces of Ginger root, light tan in color, with a tight skin. If the ginger shows wrinkled skin, it means dryness and shows age. Keeps well for several weeks wrapped in plastic wrap and refrigerated.

Store peeled ginger in a glass jar of sherry or vodka for several months.

Grate into salad, dressing, shrimp or vegetables dishes with all-purpose grater using the finest holes.

Slice: across the fibers thinly.

Sliver: stack slices and cut into slivers.

Mince: line up ginger root slivers on a cutting board, cut crosswise into small pieces.

• *Greens:* For a variety of greens see page 147.

Mild green: toss romaine with grilled shrimp and Parmesan, or roll up chicken salad in a tender leaf of Boston lettuce.

Spinach makes a healthy pizza topping.

Red -leaf lettuce adds texture when shredded over tacos.

Assertive greens: Use Belgian endive instead of crackers to hold a dip; use arugula, watercress to dress up a prosciutto, tomato and mozzarella sandwich; grill radicchio to accompany tuna steaks.

• *Guava:* Oval and about 4 inches in size. The skin is thin and light yellow-green. A ripe guava softens to the touch. The flesh color may graduate from white to pinkish-red, becoming juicy as it nears the center.

Eaten fresh, out-of-hand (discarding the seeds), sliced and served in fruit cups, or pureed as a base for mousse, pies, custard and cream desserts. Makes extraordinary jam.

• *Hoisin sauce:* A thick brown-red paste. Sweet and spicy condiment made from soy beans, wheat flour, red beans, ginger, garlic, salt, chili, sugar and spices. Refrigerated, it keeps almost indefinitely.

Use in sauces, gravies, marinating sauce .

• *Honey:* Store at room temperature in a dark area. If it crystallizes, place the jar in hot water to dissolve the crystals.

If recipe calls for both honey and oil, measure the oil first, that will make the honey not stick to the measuring cup and pour out easier.

• *Jícama:* (Hee-kah-ma) Large brown-skinned turnip with ivory-colored flesh. Taste something between a raw sweet potato and a water chestnut. Sweet and crunchy. Look for firm, smooth, relatively unblemished roots, although patchy is normal.

Store it unwrapped in the refrigerator. Once it's cut, cover tightly with plastic wrap and use within a couple of days.

*After peel*ed, dice, slice, cube or shred it.

Add to a stir-fry dish, or shred it and add to a batter of potato pancakes.

• *Kiwi fruit:* Light brown, furry-appearing, oval-shaped fruit about 2 ½-inches long, with tender, soft skin. Inside is bright green, soft and tangy.

Eat when it yields to slight pressure in your hand.

Ripen kiwi fruit by placing it in a brown paper bag at room temperature. Placing an apple or banana in the bag with it will hasten ripening. Ripened fruit will keep for several weeks in the refrigerator.

While its skin is edible, kiwi fruit is usually peeled before eating. The entire fruit, including tiny black seeds and lighter colored center is edible.

Top your favorite cheesecake with sliced kiwi.

Cut a whole kiwi in half, place one half in palm of hand and scoop out easily with a grapefruit spoon, for a quick individual serving.

• *Kohlrabi:* Delicious cabbage-related vegetable. Buy small heads called globes about 3 inches. Large globes tend to be woody. Avoid any that are cracked, bruised or split. Usually sold in bunches of three or four with stems and leaves. They are round, light green, crisp, and crunchy. Taste similar to turnip.

Cut off stems, pare with a swivel-blade peeler. Dice, cube, shred or julienne strips in salads or cut into wedges for dips.

Stir-fry quickly, steam or add to stews and soups toward the end of the cooking time. Overcooking makes their texture mushy and too soft.

• *Lamb:* If you buy a whole leg of lamb, have the butcher cut off some shoulder chops. This gives you two different lamb meals.

Roasting: pierce some slits on top and stick in a few whole cloves of garlic. Smear the top with brown mustard and roast.

• *Leeks:* Look for broad green tops and medium-sized necks that are whitish green 2 to 3-inches from root. Spring and fall are peak times for leeks, when you'll find them small and tender. Other times of the year, you'll find larger leeks, which tend to be tough. Leeks are usually packaged in bundles of three. They share the same family lineage as shallots, garlic, and onions but unlike its more-powerful siblings, the leek is just as much a vegetable as a seasoning. Leeks should yield slightly to pressure. Will keep 1 week in refrigerator.

Substitute leeks for onions in soups and stews.

Cook or purée with other vegetables for base of cream soup.

Preparation: cut off root end of leek. Cut off the tough, dark-green leaves, leaving the white and light-green portion. Slice leek in half lengthwise. Wash under cold running water to remove dirt and grit. Slice leek halves lengthwise, and then chop. For julienne-cut leeks, cut 2-inch pieces, and then slice lengthwise. Tie leeks in bunches and steam as you would asparagus, until fork tender.

Dress with a vinaigrette or cream sauce or just plain melted butter with lemon juice.

• *Lemons:* Pucker up, but the great taste is worth it. The heavier lemons are real juicy. Lemons will yield more juice when they are at room temperature.

Squeeze juice into a mug of hot water. It's a traditional tonic and a great substitute for coffee or tea. Squeeze fresh lemon juice over steamed zucchini just before serving.

Sprinkle steamed carrots with grated lemon rind and parsley.

Slices of lemon cooked with cauliflower keeps it white; eliminate odors.

Need only a few drops of juice? prick one end of a lemon, squeeze out the amount you need. Cover with plastic wrap and refrigerate.

For maximum storage time, wrap individually in aluminum foil and store in cool dark area.

Lemon juice is a fine tenderizer or marinade.

• *Limes: Key Lime,* great for baking, soups, fish, chicken, and in your mixed drink cocktails and even in beer. Bottled key lime juice is used in pies, cookies and cakes.

Persian limes:(fresh) Use on vegetables, soups, fish, chicken and in beverages.

• *Liqueurs: Use* orange and mint flavor to top off tea. Mix butterscotch flavor with some fresh milk and ice in a tall glass and sip.

Pour some on fresh sliced fruit for a quick and easy dessert.

• *Mangoes:* Select ones that are from orange-yellow to red in color and give slightly with finger pressure. The skins are not eaten, and the sap from the tree may be irritating to some folks. Mangoes ripen at room temperature. Once you start to see black spots on the skin, the fruit is getting over ripe. Never refrigerate a mango before it's ripe, you'll kill the flavor and it may never ripen. Once ripe, however, you can keep them in the fridge for two or three days. Green ones can ripen quickly in a brown paper bag.

Peeling: set the mango on a flat surface. It will usually sit with its oblong stone (the seed) flat. In a similar manner to filleting a fish, make a lengthwise cut into the deepest part of the fruit down along the stone, removing slab of the flesh from one side. Flip and repeat. Cut away the remaining flesh on stone. The little remaining meat on stone you get to gnaw off. To remove the skin, make careful cuts that do not penetrate the skin but leave the flesh cut like a checker board. Flex the skin inside out and push on skin with fingers to push the pieces off.

Freezing: like many fruits, you cannot freeze the whole fruit but sliced fruit freezes quite well. Squeeze a little lime juice on it as an aid, freeze in plastic freezer bags or containers.

• *Mayonnaise:* Make your own, (See page 196).

• *Milk:* There are two great powdered milks to select from, 2% low fat "Milkman" to whole milk Nestle's "Nido" and Borden's "Klim". Powdered milk is used not only for a beverage, but in everyday cooking or for instant puddings.

Various types of whole milk that has been sterilized and needs no refrigeration until opened can be found in local supermarkets.

Away from USA you can also find non-refrigerated Nestle's whipping cream in a can for the Fettuccine recipes.

Evaporated milk adds creaminess to foods such as mashed potatoes and cream sauces.

Leftover evaporated milk can be kept for up to a week in a covered container in the refrigerator.

Extended shelf life Parmalat, 1%, 2% low fat milk, whole milk and chocolate milk, will stay fresh six to twelve months without refrigeration. They come in quart and pint sizes.

Buttermilk powder: Saco Cultured Buttermilk Powder, comes in a 12 oz., 340 g, equivalent to 3.75 quarts of liquid buttermilk. Example: when recipe calls for 1 cup buttermilk, use 4 tablespoons of buttermilk powder and 1 cup of water.

• *Muffins:* Don't beat the batter smooth, leave some lumps just make sure the dry ingredients are all moistened. The result will be fluffier muffins.

Making a 12 muffin batch, pour ½ batter in each of the muffin cups, top with one or a variety of slices such as apples or dates or nuts, top with remaining batter. You can serve three different kinds from one batch.

• *Mushroom:* (black dried Chinese) They are sold by weight, packaged in cellophane bags. Keep almost indefinitely when you store them in an airtight container. When ready to use, soak in water and they return to normal size. They are a sweet full bodied mushroom. Don't discard water from soaking mushrooms, use it for recipes that call for water, such as rice.

Varieties; Portobello, Roman, Cremini or golden are the same mushroom. They are mature brown mushrooms with a richer, meatier flavor than their white button counterparts. Try marinating these mushrooms, grill or broil.

Chanterelle, Pumpkin-colored, has a distinctive aroma and flavor that bring apricots to mind. Use in stews, sauces for pasta and meat.

Enoki, small, mild in flavor. Sauté or eat raw in salads.

Morel, wild mushroom imported from Europe. Has a nutty flavor and a distinctive sponge-like cap. Sauté in butter, add to sauces, stews and pasta.

Shitake, fresh, rich and meaty in taste. They have over two inch caps and lend themselves to broiling or stir-frying over high heat.

Trumpet, also called false truffle, whether black or white, looks more like a velvety flower than a mushroom. The dried form (easily reconstituted in water) has a buttery flavor great in soups and sauces.

Preparation: don't wash fresh mushrooms. They tend to hold water and become spongy.

Store in a brown paper bag in the refrigerator. This prevents sweating, which causes them to turn brown. When ready to use, brush lightly with damp paper towel.

• *Mustard:* Dry mustard is the residue which remains after the oil is pressed from the seed. Ground seed varies from white, which is considered the finest, through brown, considered next best, to yellow.

• *Nuts:* Nuts keep better whole: store in a cool and dry area. If you need them chopped or ground, process only the amount you need.

Fine grinding: use a Mouli grinder or a four sided grater.

Coarser grinding or chopping: use a wooden mallet, after placing nuts in a plastic bag, or plastic wrap, place on a cutting board and hammer away. *Store* shelled nuts in a air-tight container in refrigerator.

• *Okra:* Green pods vary in shape and size from two to seven inches long. All should be relatively firm, bright and free of spots or mold. Red okra, should be firm, wine-colored, velvet pods. The taste is sweet and once cooked, the beautiful burgundy turns deep olive or spruce green. It keeps for a few days at most, if purchased in fine shape.

Store in a paper bag in the refrigerator.

Prepare: rinse, dry well before trimming, then cut off the stem and very top of the caps. Some fuzzy varieties may need rubbing with a paper towel prior to washing and trimming. For miniature okra, merely cut off the stems or slight protrusions. If larger okra is to be cooked whole, shave off the cap, taking care not to open the capsule and expose the seeds. When a recipe calls for sliced okra, simply cut off the whole top end, then slice the pod.

1 cup sliced pods for each 3 cups of liquid.

• *Oils:*

Extra-virgin olive oil, very pale yellow, comes from the first pressing of the olives. Heating this oil destroys the virgin flavors. Best use is on salads. Second and third pressings are progressively darker in color and heavier in flavor.

Sesame is made from roasted sesame seeds. It has a thick, nutty flavor and is light brown in color. Do not confuse it with the cold-pressed Middle Eastern sesame oil, which is light in color and not as aromatic. Chinese sesame oil is used more as a flavoring then in cooking. It comes in various bottle sizes and keeps almost indefinitely in cool place. Add 1 tablespoon near the end of cooking.

Peanut oil compliments best the flavor of the foods cooked in it. When a high-heat recipe as in stir-fry or tossed cooking peanut oil is used, it can withstand a high temperature without smoking and is not likely to burn. It's good for sauteing, mayonnaise, marinades, and general cooking.

Canola, safflower and sunflower oils are light, flavorless, and acceptable for frying, sautéing, baking.

Walnut oil is high in polyunsaturated fat and low in saturated fat. A small amount adds a lot of flavor. Watch the amount of oil you use rather than the type.

Use less oil when you sauté. The trick is to heat the skillet before you add the oil. Since the pan's heat causes the oil to become runnier and spread, you'll need less of it to coat the bottom of your skillet.

• *Old Bay seasoning:* Ingredients are celery salt, mustard, pepper, laurel leaves, cloves, pimento, ginger, mace, cardamom, cassia and paprika.

    Use: steamed crabs, sprinkle on fresh popcorn, potato-macaroni salad.

• *Olives:* The most common olives available in stores are green Spanish olives packed in brine. They come with pits, pitted, and pitted and stuffed with either pimentos, almonds or anchovies. Ripe olives can be either black or green . Black ones are very tender and delicate in flavor. Green ones (not Spanish olives) are meaty yet still delicate and good to marinate in a vinaigrette dressings for a few days. Greek and Italian black olives come marinated in flavored oil or are available partially dried and salted. There are many varieties of these wrinkled black olives.

    How to pit an olive: Lay olive on a work surface. Press down firmly on the olive with the side of a wide-blade knife. This splits the olive and loosens the pit, which then slips out easily.

• *Onions:* Flavorful, nutritious; consider them the foundation of almost all recipes. The storage onion has a thicker, darker, paper-like outer skin and a firm inside. The spring-summer onion has a thinner and lighter color skin and is more fragile.
The storage onion is more pungent than the spring-summer onion because it has a lower water and sugar content. It also does not bruise as easily. Its season begins in August and goes through March. Typical storage onions are available in red, yellow, and white varieties. Spring-summer onions are routinely sweeter and milder than storage onions. Their season begins in April and ends in August. Main varieties are: Carzalia, Maui, Sweet Imperials, Texas Sweet, Walla-Walla and Vidalia. Because of their high sugar content, the sweet onions are more perishable than ordinary varieties.

    Vidalia: this onion must be kept cool, dry and separate. Use the legs of old, clean sheer pantyhose. Tie a knot between each onion, and cut above the knot when you want an onion. Hang in a cool, dry well ventilated area. Store the Maui, Walla-Walla and Texas Sweet in the same manner.

Choosing an onion is simple. Look for outer skins that are dry, free of green sunburn spots or blemishes. The onion should be heavy for its size, with no scent. Avoid onions with strong odors, a sign of internal bruising.

High heat makes onions bitter. When sautéing, always use low or medium heat.

Reduce tearing when slicing onions, cut off the top, peel off the outer layers and leave the root end intact. The root end has the largest concentration of sulfuric compounds which make your eyes tear.

To get rid of onion breath, eat a piece of parsley.

Store onions where air can circulate around the, in like a netted bag. Potatoes and onions should not be stored together. The high moisture content in potatoes causes the onions to sprout prematurely.

Green onions or scallions are immature onions with small bulbs and long green stems. They have a mildly pungent flavor. Use them to top your salads, stir-fried rice, and cheese spreads.

Shallot is a petite member of the onion family formed with a head made of several cloves. The off white meat is tinged with green or purple and has a mild, delicate flavor that's sometimes described as being slightly like garlic.

• *Oriental foods:* Visit your Oriental food shop for some new food ideas: noodles, rice sticks, bean curds, dried ginger root, dried mushrooms, rice and black vinegars, plus many canned vegetables and vacuum sealed tofu.

Also chili paste, dry powdered mustard, candied ginger (eat a piece when you're sea sick), shrimp chips, egg and spring roll wrappers, variety of dried candies, sesame oil, soy sauces, water chestnuts, and bamboo shoots.

• *Pancakes/Waffles:* Add a small amount of sugar in the batter. This will make them brown quickly

• *Papaya:* Deep yellow or orange in color, flesh is slightly soft to pressure.

Raw: slice, dice or chop to add to other fresh fruit, such as pineapple, strawberry, orange, banana, coconut, or lime.

Halved: the fruit forms its own dish similar to cantaloupe.

Slivers of papaya go well with prosciutto or serve along with smoked meat, turkey, chicken, and seafood.

Purée papaya along with some ginger, cayenne, hot peppers. *Use* as a marinade, to tenderize and season meat.

If the fruit is not perfectly ripe, score the fruit lengthwise in quarters, cut delicately through the skin but not into the flesh. Turn the fruit onto its narrow stem end, set it in a glass so it won't tip, and leave it for a day. This slitting helps release the bitter papain enzyme present in green fruit. Papaya should be halved and seeded, remove the thin skin with a vegetable peeler.

Meat tenderizer has a papaya base, keep a jar onboard for stings from the sea. It seems to instantly lessen the pain.

• *Parsnips:* Choose smooth, creamy-colored roots free of cracks, cuts, nicks, or bruises.

Store parsnips in refrigerator, they have a long shelf life.

Scrub them clean of clinging dirt and peel as you would a carrot.

Use mostly in soups and stews.

Place alongside that roasting leg of lamb with whole potatoes and turnips.

• *Pastry:* Patch tears in pastry with a bit of pastry and a touch of water rather than rerolling it. Rerolling causes pastry to be tough.

Roll pastry between two sheets of wax paper. When the top paper is peeled off, the pastry may be easily turned into a pie pan and other paper removed.

• *Passion Fruit:* If I'm' wrinkled, that's the sign that I'm ripe and ready to eat! To eat one, simply cut the fruit in half crosswise, scoop out the perfumed pulp and edible seeds. It will take nearly a dozen small fruits to make a cup of pulp.

Passion fruit punch: Pour four cups of boiling water over one cup of passion fruit pulp. Let the mixture sit for one hour. Then rub the passion fruit pulp through a sieve to remove the seeds. Mix the juice with a squeeze of fresh lemon or lime, and add sugar or honey to taste.(1 cup of sliced pods for each 3 cups of liquid)

• *Pasta:* Additional information and recipes, (See page 267).

Use cooked vermicelli or spaghetti as a substitute for a regular pie shell when making a meat or vegetable pie.

• *Peaches:* Select firm bright colored ones, a few soft to touch for immediate eating. They ripen quickly.

Blanche to peel easily.

• *Peppers:* Sweet peppers are either yellow, green or red; they are interchangeable in any recipe unless specified.

• *Pimentos:* To make the unused portion of a can or jar of pimentos last longer, cover pimentos with salad oil and refrigerate in an airtight container

Add minced garlic, dash of red pepper flakes to chopped pimentos. Spread on toasted rounds of bread.

• *Pineapples:* Pineapples are usually picked green. As they ripen they turn yellow. Green picked pineapples will never ripen to the full flavor of field ripened ones. At the market, choose the ones showing the most yellow.

Crushed pineapple in the can is the closest to a field ripened pineapple. These pineapples when harvested were too ripe to go to the market place or even make pineapple slices, thus they were crushed for the can.

• *Plantain:* The very hard and bright green in color will take about 5-7 days before fully ripening with a skin that will turn black. When buying 3 or 4 at one time, select various stages of ripeness from green to yellow. Green ones usually fried with garlic have little banana flavor and no sweetness. When cooked in this stage they are like potatoes: thin-fried as chips or boiled in chunks, added to soups or stews; yellow ones used in baking; golden ones in custards, compotes, and cakes. When fully ripened (black), make a slit down the skin gently, with a paring knife peel skin away and slice then, sauté in butter on both sides, spoon honey on top and serve. Don't be turned off about the black color it will get. When sufficiently ripe, peel, wrap each tightly in plastic and freeze.

• *Pomegranates:* Look for richly colored, large fruits which will have a higher proportion of the clear red, juicy-crisp pulp. Heavy fruits promise more juice.

Store well in refrigerator for up to three months.

Extract them from their rubbery white chambers, cut out the blossom end and some pith, taking care not to pierce the red within. Score the skin in quarters, break the fruit gently, following the lines. Do this in a large bowl of water, the pith all floats, and the cleaned fruit sinks.

Used in vegetable, fruit salads, on top of fruit desserts, ice cream, tarts.

• *Potato:* New potatoes, thin-skinned red, pink, or pale tan can be boiled and sprinkle with parsley or dill, and a little butter. Use them with skins on to make hash browns. Old potatoes, dirt brown, are more substantial in size and come round or long. All purpose potato for potato salad; long Idaho for baking.

• *Prickly Pear:* Fruit skin ranges from medium green to dark magenta, while the inside is red-violet or ruby red.

Choose tender but not squishy, full and deep-colored. If fruit is very firm, let it soften at room temperature.

Prepare carefully: Jab a fork into the fruit and hold steady. Slice ½-inch from each end, then cut a lengthwise slit about ¼-inch deep. Get the knife under the thick underlayer and skin. Pull off the outer and under layers of skin by holding them down on a work surface with the knife blade as you roll the fruit with the fork. The fruit may have remains of some stinging, invisible hairs to irritate you. Be careful. Serve cubed or thinly sliced with other fresh fruit or in salads.

• *Pumpkin:* Look for golden orange color, hard rind, heaviness. Avoid soft spots.

Keep for one or two months in cool dark area.

• *Radishes:* Red with leafy bunches or clipped of their greens and packed in plastic bags. The long and slender white radish, called the Icicle, also comes both ways and has a crisp texture and zesty flavor.

Black radishes look exactly like huge black beets. When peeled, the flesh is ivory-white. Grate the radish, add finely chopped onion and a small amount of chicken-fat or olive oil, salt and serve as a appetizer along with black bread.

Black and red radish can be thinly sliced adding crunch to salads.

• *Rhubarb:* The early season rhubarb is the best to use when making pie. The more mature stalks are inclined to be tough and stringy in a pie.

To store rhubarb, first trim and discard the leaves; they contain oxalic acid, a toxic and potentially deadly poison. The stalks can be kept in the refrigerator, unwashed and wrapped tightly in plastic, for up to three days.

To freeze, chop into half-inch pieces, spread them on a sheet pan and place in the freezer. Once frozen, slide the rhubarb into a heavy-duty plastic bag. Seal tightly and put back in the freezer. Packed this way, rhubarb will keep up to four months.

Cooking rhubarb: use a paring knife to trim the ends and all brown or soft spots. Peeling the stalks is not necessary, but a vegetable peeler comes in handy for removing any tough or scaly parts. Wash and dry the stalks. Always cook this acidic fruit in nonreactive pans, such as stainless steel or Corning Ware.

• *Rice:* Grains, Legumes, Rice & Pasta, (see page 265)

• *Salami and Sausage:* There are several brands of smoked salami and sausage that need no refrigeration.

   Use in casserole dishes, topping on pizza, or a quick appetizer with cheese slices.

• *Shallots:* Hard, shiny coppery bulbs, greenish white or purplish varieties.

   They keep well for months in a dark, airy place loosely wrapped in white tissue paper.

   Cookeing: can be blanched, boiled, or roasted right in their skins.

   Use raw in salads and salad dressings. Sauté, simmer, or steam for a few minutes before adding to a cooked dish.

   Do not brown shallots deeply, unlike onion they will turn bitter.

• *Snow pea pods:* Wash, remove the strings by pulling from top down the sides. Cut in chunks or strips, stir fry or eat raw with favorite dip.

• *Soups:* (Can condensed) Great use as bisques, broths, and casserole dishes. Choose celery, mushroom, clear broth, green pea, asparagus and tomato.

   Try a combination: Tuna with cream of mushroom soup tossed with leftover pasta or rice. Salmon with tomato soup. Crabmeat with celery or asparagus soup. Ham with green pea soup. Shrimp with cheddar cheese soup. Diced chicken or turkey with broccoli soup. Potato soup, cream-style corn, with chunks of chicken.

   Split pea soup: after heating thoroughly, place a tbsp. of plain yogurt in each bowl with a pinch of ground basil.

   Tomato soup (canned), add life to it with ½ water and ½ milk.

   Add interest to your soups with a different garnish. Try shredded cheese, grated hard-boiled egg, lemon slices, sunflower or sesame seed, a dollop of sour cream or yogurt, alfalfa sprouts or roasted nuts.

• *Soy sauce:* (the Chinese is different from the Japanese.) This condiment is made from soy beans fermented with other grains. It comes in two varieties: one is the dark thick soy sauce, sweeter in taste (Chinese); the other thinner but salty (Japanese) soy sauce is also available in a lite and low sodium. I dilute the regular soy sauce with equal parts of water to make it light and less salty.

• *Spinach:* Look for large, fresh, green crinkly or flat leaf types.
1 pound of fresh spinach equals approximately 1 cup of cooked spinach.
For washing fresh spinach, add a little salt to the rinse water to help remove soil from leaves easily.
When frozen, just thaw well, squeeze dry.
Use in quiches or toss over hot pasta and olive oil.

• *Squash:* Acorn, Banana, Bohemian, Buttercup, Butternut, Hubbards, Kabocha, Pumpkin, Spaghetti and Turban, all store in a cool dark area. Keeps up to six months. See pages 316, 341, for easy preparation and recipes.
Acorn, the most popular winter squash is also called Table Queen. Shell is ribbed and usually dark gray-green with orange spots; flesh is orange, moist, nutty tasting. Bake or steam.
Banana, large, long and cylindrical; usually sold by the piece. Smooth shell ranges from gray to creamy white to yellowish-pink; flesh is orange.
Bohemian or Delicata, shaped like a thick cucumber; ridged ivory shell with green stripes. Yellow flesh is mild, moist and creamy; smells and tastes like fresh corn, excellent for stuffing.
Buttercup, dark green with grayish flecks and a turban-like crown. Flesh is orange and especially sweet, though slightly drier than other squash. Buy with stem intact to prolong freshness.
Butternut, resembles an oversize, elongated pear. Tan shell, richly flavored and dense creamy orange flesh. Bake, steam, serve mashed.
Hubbards, large, spherical; usually sold by the chunk. Ridged, warty shell can be gray-green, blue-green, or orange. Flesh may be yellow or orange; at its best it's firm textured and sweet. Good baked or steamed.

Kabocha, a round, slightly flattened Japanese squash with dark green shell mottled with white. Its golden flesh is richly flavored and sweet; the strands once it is cooked look like tangled spaghetti when fluffed with a fork. Mild flavored, ideal with pasta sauces.

Turban, large, round squash with a topknot resembling a turban; orange shell is streaked with green and white. Flesh is orange, dry and firm; good in soups.

• *Star Fruit:* Also called Carambola. Firm fruit from two to five inches long, with juicy-looking ribs. Can have some light brown spots and still taste good. If green in color let it ripen at room temperature until yellow. They will give you a floral-fruity aroma which indicates full ripeness.

Once ripe, use immediately or store in refrigerator, will keep 2 weeks.

Use in place of lemon or lime slices to garnish seafood, poultry or mixed drinks, fruit or vegetable salads, and purée to top ice cream.

Prepare by rinsing, cutting off both ends and edges of the five ribs, thinly slice, or eat like a peach. Cut into cross sections, it resembles a star and is used for garnish.

• *Stock:* The liquid in which vegetables, chicken, fish has been cooked in, is called for in many soup and entree' recipes. Preferable to water because of the flavor it contributes.

• *Sugar:* What's the difference between granulated, powdered or confectioners' sugar?

Powdered sugar comes from granulated sugar that has been crushed and screened. You can tell the degree of fineness of powdered sugar by the number of x's indicated on the package; fine powdered is 4x, very fine is 6x, ultra-fine is 10x.

Granulated sugar is available in regular, which is uniform in granulation, and extra-fine, which has smaller crystals resulting from additional processing.

Sugar in the raw or turbinado sugar comes from the initial pressing of sugar cane which permits some of the natural molasses to remain in the crystals. It's blond in color and has a distinct flavor. For information: Sugar in the Raw, 60 Flushing Avenue, Brooklyn, NY 11205. Packets, 2 pound bulk box.

Hardened or granulated sugar can be placed in warm oven for 10-12 minutes to soften.

Brown sugar: if it has already hardened, place in a plastic zip-lock bag with a few slices of fresh apple. Remove the apple once the sugar is soft, otherwise the sugar will spoil.

Other sweeteners: Cane syrup comes from sugar cane that has been boiled down to the consistency of syrup. Sorghum syrup comes from a coarse grass by the same name. This is processed until juice forms, which is concentrated by boiling until it becomes syrup. Maple syrup comes from the sap of the sugar maple tree. Like sugar cane, it's boiled down to the consistency of syrup.

Substitute honey, molasses, or maple syrup for sugar in a recipe. Honey, molasses and syrup are about 20-30% water. 1 cup of honey equals 1¼ cups granulated sugar. Molasses in place of granulated sugar: use the same amount of molasses as sugar, and reduce the liquid by ¼ cup for each cup of sugar used in the recipe.

• *Sweet potato:* Yellow-brown, orange-brown, bright orange, yellow-red. Most taste sweet, but the degree of sweetness varies from variety to variety. Their shape goes from round to oval to long, slender and tapered on the ends. Select firm, bright, smooth skins. Odd shapes will be hard to peel and cut without waste unless you will be baking them.

Store them in a cool, dry, dark and well ventilated area.

Can be baked, fried, sautéed, mashed or scalloped .

• *Tofu:* Low in calories, rich in calcium and iron, and cholesterol-free. Fresh tofu is always the best. After purchasing, rinse and drain, then refrigerate in fresh water. Change water daily and tofu will remain fresh for 6-10 days. Tofu also comes sterilized and packaged for no refrigeration.

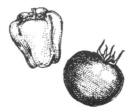

• *Tomatoes:* Purchase in various stages from green to ripe.

Store green ones in a brown paper bag, they will slowly turn from pink to red; remove the pink ones as they ripen to the fresh air basket or net.

Sun-dried, they are sold by weight and have a wonderful concentrated tomato flavor. Also available packed in oil and in dried form in cellophane packaging. To bring back to life place equal parts of boiling water and wine vinegar and let soak 1 hour, turn once. Then drain and pat dry with paper towels.

Tomato paste is now available in tubes as well as cans. So when a recipe calls for less than a full can there's no waste. If you love tomato juice, don't stock up on those heavy large cans. Purchase the name brand of the supermarket tomato paste, because this is tomato concentrate without salt (read ingredient label carefully). Beside the use for your spaghetti sauce, use this concentrate to make your tomato juice by adding enough water to bring it to the consistency of juice.

Tomato sauce: one can of tomato paste plus two cans of water.

Unless tomatoes are fully ripe, canned peeled Italian plum tomatoes, and tomato puree are preferable in cooking.

To peel and seed, drop the tomatoes into boiling water gently. Return the water to a boil and drain into colander, cool slightly. The tomato skin will then slip off easily. To core the tomatoes, halve them crosswise, holding each half cut side down, gently press with your hand, making the seeds fall out.

• *Tortillas:* Flour, corn and whole-wheat tortillas. Warm them in a nonstick skillet on low heat. Spread tortillas on a nonstick cookie sheet, lightly sprinkle or spray tortillas with water, cover with foil, then warm in a moderate 350-degree oven until heated through. You can purchase a Styrofoam tortilla holder, or choose a heavy covered casserole. Place a cotton tea towel, dampened and well wrung out, over the tortillas, then cover with lid.

• *Tree ears:* (cloud ears, edible fungi) They come curled, shriveled, black-gray and dried. Thin and brittle when dry, they expand when soaked in boiling water. They do not have a flavor of their own but take on the flavor of other ingredients, have a crunchy, chewy texture. Keep in an air-tight container or zip lock bag almost indefinitely.

Use in a soup or stir-fry recipe.

• *Turnips:* White, red, or gray; long, round or flat. White flesh, with a green or purple band across top of skin. Can be very sweet. Look for crisp green tops, firm roots. The yellow turnip is also known as Rutabagas which have a yellowish color, slightly elongated shape and thick neck. Avoid dark, soft spots.

Wash, peel the skins and prepare to eat raw or cook.

Boil, mash with butter and nutmeg.

1 pound diced will give you about 4 cups.

Add raw to salads; shredded to garnish soups or fish dishes.

Reduce odor by adding a little sugar to the water when cooking.

Add some turnips to the pork roast during the last 30 minutes of roasting.

Stores for weeks in a plastic bag in the refrigerator or in a cold dark well ventilated area.

• *Vinegars:*

Balsamic, rich and sweet, use in salads, as a marinade for beef and onions. Balsamic and herb-flavored vinegars enhance the flavor of poached chicken without adding salt.

Black, dark in color, made with vinegar, sugar, water, fired rice and spices. Great with a mixture of greens or onions.

Cider, distilled from apple cider. Good in banana bread. Add 1 teaspoon to 1 tablespoon in a glass of cold water for a healthy drink.

Distilled (white), mostly used for non-cooking purposes. Harsh.

Rice, a light amber-colored vinegar, is neither as sharp or as sour as malt vinegar but is actually sweet. Very mild, perfect for cooked vegetables, spinach salad; add one tablespoon per serving in your favorite bean soup. Found in most stores, but in the oriental groceries we find the larger sizes at low cost.

Varieties: raspberry, cider, tarragon, sage vinegars on fruit, chicken and toss salad vinaigrette. Save white vinegar for those steamed crabs.

➤ *Note:* The secret of fine salad dressing is in the choice of vinegars.

• *Wheat Germ:* Flaked or as a coarse meal, raw or toasted. Keep in refrigerator after opening jar.

Filler for meatloaf.

• *Yams:* The flesh is white or yellow and the texture similar to the white potato. Yams grow up to very large sizes. Use in recipes as you would a sweet potato.

• *Yogurt:* Great plain or flavored.

Use yogurt as an ingredient in a recipe or combined it with another food.

Substitute for sour cream, use in baking, dips, instead of mayonnaise.

Flavor pea soup with a tablespoon of plain yogurt on top and a pinch of ground basil.

Let yogurt reach room temperature before heating. This will prevent separation.

Make your own yogurt and yogurt cheese from scratch (see page 420).

• *Wasabi:* (powdered Japanese horseradish) This has the pugent flavor of horseradish. It comes in a small can and has a long shelf life.

• *Whipping Cream:* The dry package of powdered cream whips up nicely for topping.

Can be found in a small can, needs no refrigeration, makes great fettucini or other light cream sauces.

Cheese Chart

Cheese is made from milk that has separated into curds(soft, white, lumps) and whey (the thin liquid that remains after the curds have been removed). The curds are drained, flavored in any number of ways, pressed into molds and left to cure through the action of harmless bacteria. They ripen, or grow stronger, with age.Uncured cheeses are cottage cheese, cream cheese, and Neufchâtel.

• *Anfrom:* (Quebec) A round, flat cheese similar to Oka, a Port Salut type. Robust and slightly creamier than Port Salut.

• *Appenzeller:* (Switzerland) Raw milk; firm texture; fruity taste from wine or cider wash during curing.

• *Asiago:* (Italy) Partly skimmed milk; cylindrical. Semisoft and mild when aged two months; firm texture, zesty flavor when aged a year.

• *Austrian Monastery:* (Austria) Buttery, semisoft; mild flavor.

• *Banon:* (France) Raw goat's molk; soft texture, mild, lemony taste.

• *Bel Paese:* (Italy) Creamy white, yellow wax covering. Dessert cheese.

• *Boursault:* (France) Soft, smooth texture; buttery taste.

• *Brick:* (United States) Resembles Cheddar with a light Limburger flavor. A wax coating contains its increasingly strong aroma. The cheese is slightly firm, ideal for slicing.

• *Brie:* (France) Delicate, creamy, soft-ripening, edible white crust.

• *Bucheron:* (France) Raw goat's milk; log shaped, creamy, slightly tangy flavor.

• *Camembert:* (France) Soft ripening cheese is stronger than its cousin, Brie. Mild to pungent, edible crust. Dessert or snack.

• *Canadian Cheddar:* Made from raw milk, slightly nuttier than U.S. Cheddars.

• *U.S. Cheddars:* When young it is delicate and moist; longer aging results in a sharper taste and a drier, more crumbly texture. Cheddars made in Wisconsin range from very mild to very sharp, and vary widely in quality; Tillamook, made in Oregon, less aging and a milder cheese. Coon Cheddar is full-bodied and crumbly.

• *Cheshire:* (England) Slightly tart flavor, dry, melts well.

• *Colby:* (United States) A variation of Cheddar, milder, moister.

• *Comté:* (France) Dense, nutty cheese similar to Switzerland's Gruyère.

• *Cottage:* (United States) Soft, moist, mild, white, good in fruit salads, cooking.

• *Edam:* (Holland) Mild flavor when young, slight rubbery consistency. Encased in a red wax rind. Edam is similar to its cousin, Gouda in flavor. Edam, is made from partly skimmed milk, Gouda is made from whole milk. Used for dessert, snack.

• *Emmentaler:* (Switzerland) Part-skim raw or pasteurized milk. Firm texture; mild, nutlike flavor, small holes. The original Swiss cheese.

• *Feta:* (Greece) Made from Ewe's milk, unveined and pure white. Pickled in brine, salty, flavor, tangy, crumbly. Used in salad, cooking.

• *Fontina:* (Italy) Smooth and creamy, with the flavors of Port Salut and Gruyére. (Danish) softer flavor, similar to Gouda.

• *Gjetost:* (Norway) Sweet, caramellike flavor. Served in wafer-thin slivers on crisp cracker.

•*Gorgonzola:* (Italy) Firm Gorgonzola resembles blue cheese, has more mold and less sharpness. Creamy Gorgonzola, also blue-venined, less salty, delicate flavor when young. As it matures, it becomes more aromatic, shaper and very soft.

• *Gournay:* (France) A member of the French Neufchâtel family; soft, flavored with either pepper or garlic and herbs. Also called Boursin, La Bourse.

• *Gouda:* (Holland) Mild cheese, higher butterfat than its cousin, Edam. Young Gouda has a red wax rind, nutty flavor.

• *Gruyère:* (Switzerland) Firm texture; small, nutty flavor. Widely dispersed holes. (French) Studded with large, round holes and has a nut-sweet flavor.

• *Havarti:* (Denmark) similar to Tilsit, a savory, straw-colored aromatic cheese, flecked with small irregular holes.Cream Havarti, has added cream moist, with a buttery flavor, often enlivened with carawy seeds..

• *Jarlsberg:* (Norway) Fine textured, nutty flavor, and is flecked with large holes.

• *King Christian:* (Denmark) Spiced with caraway seeds.

• *Liederkranz:* (United States) Soft-ripening cheese, becomes more mellow and aromatic as it ripens. When young it is delicate and semisoft; at maturity it it soft, creamy and aromatic. Edible light orange crust

• *Limburger:* (Belgium) Soft, smooth, white, robust, aromatic.

• Livarot: (France) Raw, partly skimmed cow's milk. Soft; similar to Camembert but spicier and stronger in aroma.

• *Mimolette:* (France) Flattened ball, firm, mild Cheddar flavor.

• *Monterey Jack:* (United States) Skim or part-skim Jack is hard and used for grating; high moisture Jack is semi-soft used in Mexican dishes, ideal for cooking.

• *Mozzarella:* (Italy) A soft, spongy Italian curd cheese, bland taste, white.

• *Muenster:* (Germany) Semisoft, mild, light orange rinds.

• *Oka:* (Canada) Semisoft texture; similar to French Port-Salut tangy, fruity flavor.

• *Parmesan:* (Italy) Hard, brittle, sharp, and light yellow.

• *Petit-Suisse:* (France) Creamy, fresh, unsalted cheese made from whole milk with cream added. Soft, faintly sour flavor; dessert cheese.

• *Port Salut:* (France) Semi-soft, pale yellow with a bright orange rind.Creamy and and fairly mild.

• *Provolone:* (Italy) Salty, smoky, mild to sharp, hard.

• *Raclette:* (Switzerland) Wheel shaped, firm texture; mellow flavor.

• *Ricotta:* (Italy) Soft, creamy, bland, white. Used for cooking and fillings.

• *Rondelé:* (France) A soft spiced cheese flavored with garlic and herbs.

• *Romano:* (Italy) Hard grating cheese made from sheep's milk, similar to Parmesan in appearance but somewhat strong in flavor.

• *Roquefort:* (France) Semi-soft, blue-venined, crumbly, salty but piquant flavor.

• *Sage Derby:* (England) Firm; Cheddar flavor enlivened sage leaves.

• *Saint Marcellin:* (France) Crumbly cream cheese made from goat's milk, salty.

• *Saint Nectaire:* (France) Semi-soft, pale yellow, mottled yellow-brown crust, earthy flavor.

• *Sap Sago:* (Switzerland) Mixture of whey, skim milk and buttermilk. Small cone shape; flavored with mountain herbs.

• *Stilton:* (England) Semi-soft, sharp, has a Cheddar base and is blue-veined, with a dry brown crust.

• *Taleggio:* (Italy) Raw milk; squarish shape, semi-soft texture, creamy flavor.

• *Wensleydale:* (England) Crumbly in texture, color varies from white to creamy yellow, mild taste. Served with apple pie, excellent for use in cooking.

Seafood Cheddar Quiche

Serves 8-10

cooking spray
2 cups cooked shrimp or crabmeat
4 ounces cream cheese, cut in small cubes
1 cup cheddar cheese, shredded
2 cups milk
1 cup biscuit mix (see page 407)
3 eggs
¼ teaspoon nutmeg

• Lightly spray quiche or deep pie pan, set aside. Preheat oven
to 350 degrees.
• Spread evenly seafood of your choice, then cheese on top.
• Mix together remaining ingredients in a medium mixing
bowl. Pour liquid mixture on top of seafood.
• Bake 40 minutes or until lightly brown.
• Let cool 5 minutes before cutting.

➤ *Hint:* Quick and simple Cajun Popcorn. Cajun seasoning mix, (see
page 395). Sprinkle mixture over freshly popped popcorn, tossing until
evenly coated.

Smokey Vegetable Dip

Serves 12

1 (16oz.) carton sour cream
1 package dried green pea soup mix
1 cup sharp Cheddar cheese, grated
dashes of hickory smoke liquid to taste

• Combine all ingredients in a medium bowl.
• Chill until serving time.
• Serve with crackers or assorted raw vegetables.

Beer Hot Dogs (KISS #1)
1 lb. hot dogs cut bite-sized
½ C BBQ sauce
½ C brown sugar
½ C beer

Boil all ingred → simmer 3"

Zucchini Quiche Triangles

Yield 4 dozen

3 cups unpeeled zucchini, thinly sliced
1 cup biscuit mix (see page 407)
½ cup onion, chopped
½ cup Parmesan cheese, grated
2 tablespoons fresh parsley
½ teaspoon sea salt
½ teaspoon seasoned salt
½ teaspoon dried marjoram
1 teaspoon hot pepper sauce
dash of ground black pepper
2 cloves of garlic, finely minced
½ cup vegetable oil
4 eggs, slightly beaten

• Lightly grease 9x13 baking pan, set aside. Preheat oven to 350 degrees.
• Mix all ingredients gently spread evenly in pan.
Bake 25 minutes, remove from oven.
• Cool 5 minutes, cut into squares, then triangles.

Artichoke Hot Spread

Yield: 3 cups

1 cup mayonnaise
1 cup grated Parmesan cheese
1 (6oz.) jar artichoke hearts, drained and chopped
1 (7oz.) can chopped green chilies
1 small can mushrooms, drained and chopped

• Combine all ingredients in a medium mixing bowl.
• Preheat oven to 350 degrees; Spoon into an 8-inch baking dish.
• Bake 20-25 minutes or until bubbly.
• Serve hot with whole wheat crackers or tortilla chips.

Oven Fried Quesadillas

Yield: 32 wedges

2½ cups (10oz.) Monterey Jack cheese, shredded
1 (6oz.) jar marinated artichoke hearts, drained and chopped
½ cup green stuffed olives, thinly sliced
⅔ cup picante sauce
½ cup toasted almonds, chopped
¼ cup fresh cilantro, chopped
8 flour tortillas
3 tablespoons butter, melted

• Combine cheese, artichokes, olives, picante sauce, almonds
and cilantro, mix well, set aside. Preheat oven to 350 degrees.
• Brush lightly one side of 4 tortillas with butter, place tortilla
buttered side down on baking sheet.
• Spread 1 cup cheese mixture onto each tortilla to within ¾
inch of edge. Top with remaining tortillas, pressing firmly
around edges Brush tops of tortillas with remaining butter.
• Bake 10 minutes or until tops are lightly browned.
• Remove from oven, let cool 5 minutes. Cut each tortilla into
eight wedges.

➤ *Hint:Goat cheese easy pita pizza.* Crumble 8oz. goat cheese onto 4
(split) rounds of pita bread, sprinkle with salt free herbs mixture, page
394. Heat in a 325 degrees oven about 10 minutes, or until cheese melts.
Serves 4.

Black Bean & Salmon Spread

Yield: 2½ cups

1 (7oz.) can pink salmon, drain, discarding bones and skin
1⅔ cups (16oz.) can black beans, drained and rinsed
½ teaspoon grated lime rind
¼ cup fresh lime juice
2 tablespoons olive oil
¼ cup fresh parsley, chopped
1 tablespoon onion, minced
1 tablespoon celery, minced
2 teaspoons garlic, minced
¾ teaspoon cumin
¼ teaspoon hot red pepper flakes
¼ teaspoon pepper

• Flake the salmon with a fork lightly in a medium bowl.
Add remaining ingredients, combine well.
• Chill, serve with crackers or tortilla chips.

➤*Hint:* For tomato juice lovers why buy and carry water? Use your own source of concentrate. Purchase the super market brand of tomato paste, the generic kind that has no salt added, read the labels. Tomato paste is really just concentrate tomatoes. Use your empty 1 liter plastic adult beverage bottles to reconstitute your tomato paste into tomato juice or tomato sauce as needed. Flavor to suit your taste (add just a touch of Tabasco or your favorite red hot sauce).

Smoked Oyster Dip

Yield: 2 cups

1 (8oz.) package cream cheese, softened
1 (4oz.) can black olives, drained and chopped
1 (3¾oz.) can smoked oysters, drained and chopped
½ cup sour cream
½ cup mayonnaise
6 dashes of hot pepper sauce
1 tablespoon fresh lemon juice

• Combine all ingredients in a medium bowl, mix well.
• Chill until serving time.
• Serve with crisp firm cracker.

Ezy-Pâté

Yield: ½ cup

1 small can liverwurst
1 small onion, grated
1 teaspoon, brandy

• Combine all ingredients in a medium bowl, blend well.
• Serve on whole wheat cracker or rounds of toasted bread.

➤ *Hint:* Celery stalks filled with peanut butter make a quick and easy appetizer.

Salmon Ball

Yield: 2 cups

1 (15oz.) can salmon, drain, discarding skin and bones
1 (8oz.) package cream cheese, softened
¾ teaspoon dillweed
½ teaspoon liquid smoke
1 tablespoon fresh lemon juice
½ cup pecans, chopped
¼ cup fresh parsley, chopped
garlic salt and black pepper to taste

• Combine cream cheese, dillweed, liquid smoke, garlic salt, pepper and lemon juice in a large mixing bowl.
• Add salmon and blend well. Shape into ball or log on a piece of wax paper.
• Mix pecans and parsley together. Coat salmon well.
• Chill until serving time.

➤ *Hint:* Preparations tips on roasted peppers using the oven broiler. Place peppers on a rack as close to the flame as possible. Keep the oven door open and turn the peppers often until the skins are charred on all sides. Place the charred peppers in a brown paper bag and close. After 45 minutes, remove the cooled peppers from the bag. Peel and de-seed them. Placing the peppers in a paper bag once they are charred allows moisture to develop between the flesh and skin, which makes peeling them so much easier. Use your stove top smokeless grill for roasting pepper as well, (see page 11).

Sardine Spread

Yield: 2 cups

1 (3 ¾oz.) can water-packed sardines with bones, drained
2 tablespoons plain nonfat yogurt
2 tablespoons grated Parmesan cheese
1 tablespoon scallion, chopped
1 ½ teaspoons Dijon-style mustard
1 teaspoon grated lemon rind
3 teaspoons fresh lemon juice
ground pepper, to taste
dash cayenne, to taste
1 teaspoon sesame seeds toasted

• Combine all ingredients except sardines and sesame seeds in a medium bowl.
• Add sardines and blend well. Place the mixture in a serving bowl. Sprinkle with sesame seeds. Chill until serving time.
• Serve with crackers, or stuff some celery stalks.

➢ *Hint:* Quick and easy: thin slices of prosciutto around melon slices for an elegant appetizer.

Ricotta & Blue Cheese Spread

Yields ¾ cup

2 ounces blue cheese
½ cup ricotta cheese
2 tablespoons non-fat plain yogurt
2 tablespoons chopped fresh dill or
1 teaspoon dried dill

• In hand food chopper, combine all ingredients until creamy and smooth.
•Serve with assorted crackers or stuff into celery stalks.

Tofu Guacamole

Yield: 1½ cups

1 large ripe avocado
2 cakes (½ pound) medium-soft tofu
½ teaspoon salt
dash black pepper
dash cayenne
2 cloves of garlic, crushed
¼ teaspoon cumin
3 tablespoons fresh lemon juice
1 tablespoon fresh parsley, chopped

• Place all ingredients except parsley in a medium bowl. Mash well with a potato masher. Sprinkle with parsley, chill slightly.
• Serve with party rye or rye crackers.

➢ *Hint:* For dips and spreads: substitute part-skim ricotta cheese, low-calorie Neufchatel or low-fat farmer's cheese for cream cheese and regular mayonnaise.

Shrimp Dip

Serves 8

16 ounces cream cheese, softened
1 (6oz.) can small shrimp, minced
2 tablespoons grated onion
1 tablespoon lemon juice
¼ teaspoon sea salt

• Blend cream cheese and shrimp in medium bowl.
• Add remaining ingredients, mix well.
• Serve with assorted crackers.

Feta Cheese Pâté

Yields: 2¾ cups

1 cup feta cheese, drained and crumbled
2 tablespoons extra virgin olive oil
⅓ cup milk
1 cup walnuts, chopped
1 teaspoon paprika
dash of cayenne pepper

• Combine in hand food chopper 3 tablespoons milk, oil,
⅓ cup feta cheese, ⅓ cup walnuts. Blend for 6 seconds.
• Add remaining ingredients, blend till almost a smooth paste.
• Chill until serving.

➢ *Note:* Hand food chopper: (see page 9)

Herb Goat Cheese

Yield: ⅓ cup

3 ounces semisoft goat cheese
2 teaspoons fresh basil, chopped or
½ teaspoon dried basil and
¼ teaspoon onion powder
dash ground black pepper

• In a small bowl combine goat cheese, basil, onion powder and
pepper. Blend thoroughly, if dry: stir in a little milk 2 or 3
teaspoons or drizzle in some extra-virgin olive oil.
• Cover with plastic wrap, chill until ready to serve.
• Spread on toast or firm cracker.

Chutney Spread

Yield: ⅔ cup

8 ounces cream cheese, cut in half lengthwise
4 tablespoons walnuts, chopped
4 tablespoons chutney, (see page 185-187)

• Place one half cream cheese on serving plate.
• Spread gently 2 tablespoons chutney. Sprinkle with 2
tablespoons nuts.
• Place second half cream cheese on top, repeat procedure of
chutney and nuts.
• Serve with crackers or stuff celery ribs.

Chili Peanut Dip

Yield: ⅔ cup

⅓ cup peanut butter (smooth or crunchy)
3 tablespoons water
2 tablespoons soy sauce
2 tablespoons lemon juice
2 teaspoons honey
3 cloves garlic, minced
1 tablespoon chili powder
dash of crushed dried red pepper flakes

• Stir peanut butter and water into a paste.
• Add remaining ingredients and blend well. Add more water if
peanut butter is too firm.
• Serve with carrot and celery sticks.

➢ *Note:* Keep a variety of food in small jars on hand. Such as pimento,
water chestnuts, gherkin or dill pickles and olives, chutney, corn relish,
pickled onions and mushrooms, artichoke hearts and chilies, stuffed
olives with anchovies or capers. Cut cubes of cheese and alternate on a
toothpick with one or more of these toppings for a quick and easy
hors d'oeuvre.

Yogurt Hummus

Serves 6-8

1 (16oz.) can chickpeas, drained
¼ cup yogurt
2 cloves garlic, minced
¼ cup tahini
⅓ cup fresh lemon juice
2 tablespoons chopped parsley
½ teaspoon salt
½ teaspoon olive oil

• Purée all ingredients except olive oil and parsley in a hand food chopper or blender. The dip should be about the consistency of guacamole, additional lemon juice or yogurt can be added to thin it.
• Spread dip in a flat serving dish, using a spoon to spread out. Drizzle with olive oil, and sprinkle with chopped parsley.
• Serve with triangles of pita bread.

Crescent Crab Rolls

Serves 4-6

vegetable cooking spray
1½ cups (6½oz.) can crab meat, drained and shredded
1 cup broccoli, cooked and diced
¼ cup mayonnaise
½ cup Swiss cheese, grated
1 large container of refrigerator crescent rolls
¼ cup red pimento, diced

• Lightly spray baking sheet with cooking spray, set aside. Preheat oven to 375 degrees.
• Combine broccoli, crab meat, mayonnaise and cheese.
• Separate crescent rolls, spread crab mixture on each roll, roll up starting at wide edge. Place rolls up on baking sheet.
• Bake 20 minutes or until golden brown, serve hot.

Hot Imitation Crabmeat Dip
Yield: 1½ cups

½ pound imitation crabmeat, chopped
½ cup mayonnaise
2 teaspoons Old Bay Seasoning
½ cup grated Parmesan cheese

• Blend mayonnaise and seasonings well. Pour into baking dish, top with cheese. Preheat oven to 375 degrees.
• Bake 10-15 minutes or until heated through. Serve hot.

Ham'N Cheese Nut Log
Serves 4-6

1 cup ham, chopped
1 cup (4oz.) cheddar cheese, shredded
1 (3oz.) package cream cheese, softened
1 tablespoon white horseradish
½ cup pecans, chopped

• Combine ham, cheeses, horseradish and blend thoroughly.
• On a piece of wax paper form into a roll. Roll in chopped nuts. Chill until ready to serve.
• Serve on nutty cracker or Triscuit.

➤*Hint:* Quick and Easy: cut a small section of each garlic bulb you will use, wrap it in aluminum foil and place garlic on rack in pressure cooker, pour in water up to rack. Bring up pressure for 2 minutes. Let pressure drop of own accord. Remove garlic, pinch out each clove. Proceed with recipe. Next time you are roasting a chicken, place foil wrapped garlic bulbs in cavity of chicken and roast away. Peel roasted garlic and spread on rounds of bread or mashed into a dish of mashed potatoes.

Anchovy Spread

Yield: 1¼ cups

1 cup cottage cheese
½ cup butter, softened
4 anchovies, finely chopped
1 tablespoon capers, chopped
1 tablespoon chives, chopped
1 tablespoon caraway seeds
1 tablespoon dry mustard
1 tablespoon Hungarian paprika
½ teaspoon celery salt.

• Mash all the ingredients in a medium bowl, sprinkle with extra paprika on top. Chill until ready to serve.
• Serve with black or rye bread.

Cheezy Vegetable Spread

Yield: 1½ cups

1 cup (4oz.) farmer cheese
3 tablespoons plain yogurt
1 teaspoon lemon juice
1 teaspoon soy sauce
¼ cup apple, pared, cored and chopped
¼ cup carrot, chopped
2 tablespoons celery, chopped
2 tablespoons pecans, chopped
2 tablespoons currants
1 tablespoon tasted wheat germ
½ teaspoon curry or more to taste

• Place cheese, yogurt, lemon juice and soy sauce in hand food chopper fitted with a steel blade. Blend until smooth.
• Combine remaining ingredients in a medium bowl, stir in yogurt cheese mixture and blend well.

➢*Note:* When serving spreads, use party slice breads, small pita pockets, variety of assorted crackers.

Pizza Cold & Sassy Squares

Serves 6-8

1 package crescent rolls
½ cup green pepper, diced
½ cup carrots, diced
½ cup tomato, diced
1 (8oz.) package cream cheese, softened
2 teaspoons garlic powder
2 tablespoons mayonnaise
dash of salt and pepper to taste

• Open rolls, place on cookie sheet making a large square, press edges softly together. Preheat oven to 350 degrees.
• Bake until golden brown, remove and let cool completely.
• Combine cream cheese, mayonnaise, garlic powder, salt and pepper, blend well. Spread cheese mixture evenly on baked cooled crust.
• Combine remaining vegetables in a medium bowl, sprinkle on cheese mixture. Cut into squares and serve immediately.

Spicy Tuna Spread

Yield: 2 cups

1 (12½oz.) can tuna, drained
1½ to 2 jalapeño chilies, seeded
1 small onion, cut in quarters
1 rib of celery, cut in chunks
¼ cup mayonnaise
1 to 2 shakes Worcestershire sauce
1 teaspoon curry powder
sea salt and pepper to taste
⅛ teaspoon cilantro

• Chop tuna, jalapeños, onion and celery in hand food chopper. Add remaining ingredients, blend.
• Add additional mayonnaise if you want a real smooth spread.
• Place in serving bowl, chill until ready to serve.

Guacamole Dip

Serves 4

1 ripe avocado, peeled, seeded and mashed
1 tomato, peeled and finely chopped
1 small onion, finely diced
1 cup plain low-fat yogurt
½ teaspoon dried dill
¼ teaspoon black pepper
2 tablespoons red wine vinegar

• Combine all ingredients in a medium bowl, mix well. Chill until ready to serve.

➤*Hint:* If you are not serving guacamole instantly, place pit in center of bowl to prevent darkening, remove when ready to serve.

Bacon-Guacamole Dip

Yield: 2½ cups

8 slices of bacon, cooked and crumbled, set aside
2 medium ripe avocados, peeled seeded and mashed
⅓ cup mayonnaise
¼ cup pimento-stuffed olives, diced
2 tablespoons lemon juice
1 tablespoon onion, grated
¼ teaspoon chili powder
dash of cayenne

• Combine all ingredients except bacon. Mix well.
• Add ½ of bacon, combine well. Place in serving bowl, top with remaining bacon.

Spicy Conch Fritters

Yield: 50 fritters

2 pounds conch, finely chopped
1 cup lime or lemon juice
¼ cup olive oil
1 large green bell pepper, finely chopped
1 large red bell pepper, finely chopped
1 large onion, finely chopped
4 eggs, beaten
2 cups all-purpose flour
1 teaspoon sea salt
1 teaspoon Cajun seasoning
6 dashes hot red sauce
3 teaspoons baking powder
canola oil for frying

• Marinate conch in olive oil and lime or lemon juice for
30 minutes, drain and pat dry.
• Place chopped conch in large mixing bowl. Add remaining
ingredients, blend well.
• Pour about 1 inch of oil into wok or deep skillet. Heat oil,
place one tablespoon of conch mixture into hot oil at a time. As
soon as one sets, add another tablespoon. Do not crowd, turn
once. When golden brown, remove fritters and place on paper
plate to drain well. Add oil as needed to complete frying.

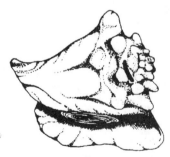

Carrots Cayenne

Serves 6-8

1 pound carrots, peeled and cut in quarters
water to cover
3 tablespoons olive oil
1 tablespoon vinegar or lemon juice
kosher salt and freshly ground pepper to taste
½ teaspoon cumin seed
1 teaspoon cayenne
2 tablespoons fresh chopped parsley for
garnish

• Simmer the carrots in water until fork
tender. Remove, drain and place in
medium bowl, coat with olive oil and
vinegar.
• Season with remaining ingredients.
Serve cool or chill.
• Garnish with parsley before serving
with pita bread halves.

Scallop Seviche

Serves 4

1 pound raw bay scallops, cut in quarters
1 cup lime juice
1 small onion, chopped
2 jalapeño chilies, chopped
2 tablespoons chopped parsley
½ cup virgin olive oil
sea salt and ground black pepper to taste

• Place scallops and lime juice in large bowl. Marinate 2 hours.
• Add remaining ingredients, blend well, serve.

Tacos Stuffed with your choice of fillings

• *Cheese Tacos:* slices of Monterey Jack, diced jalapeño chilies, chopped tomatoes, salt and pepper.
• *Ham Tacos:* diced cooked ham, diced onion, cream cheese, chopped jalapeño chilies.
• *Sweet Pepper Tacos:* chopped bell peppers, onions diced, chopped tomatoes, sour cream, dash of ground black pepper.
• *Bean Tacos:* refried beans, shredded cheddar cheese, lettuce, diced jalapeño chilies.
• *Picadillo Tacos:* shredded cooked beef, diced onions, jalapeño chilies, sour cream.
• *Chicken Tacos:* diced cooked chicken, onion, tomatoes, shredded lettuce, sour cream, and diced jalapeño.
• *Steak Tacos;* sliced cooked steak, picante sauce, sour cream, shredded lettuce and cheddar cheese.

➢ *Note: Tacos are tortillas corn or flour, usually fried and then stuffed with fillings. Lightly mash or toss one of the fillings then stuff tacos and eat away.*

Artichoke Dip
Yield: 1½ cups

1 (12oz.) can artichokes, drained
1 cup mayonnaise
1 cup grated Parmesan cheese

• In a hand food chopper place artichokes, chop fine.
• Place chopped artichokes in bowl, stir in mayonnaise, Parmesan cheese. Spoon mixture into shallow casserole dish, bake at 350 degrees for 20 minutes or until bubbly and heated through.
*Garnish with bacon bits.

Eggplant Caponata

Yield: 6 cups

1½ pounds or 3-4 cups unpeeled eggplant, wash and cut into
¾-inch cubes. Do not peel.
1 tablespoon coarse (kosher) salt
½ cup olive oil
⅓ cup green bell pepper, cut into small squares
1 cup coarsely diced onion
1 cup coarsely diced celery
3 cloves of garlic, crushed
½ cup mushrooms, chopped
1 can tomato paste, plus 2 cans water or 2 cups tomato purée
2 tablespoons red wine vinegar or more to taste
¼ cup Spanish olives, sliced
¼ cup pitted sliced oil-cured black olives
½ teaspoon sugar
2-3 tablespoons capers with juice
salt and ground black pepper to taste

• In large skillet, sauté the onion, peppers, celery in olive oil,
over medium heat for 5 minutes, stirring often.
• Add the eggplant, garlic, mushrooms, and stir for 5 minutes.
• Add remaining ingredients except capers and olives, stir for
5 minutes, cover and cook for 20 minutes or until eggplant is
fork tender. Stir occasionally.
• Add olives and capers, cook for 5 minutes, stir in well.
Remove from heat, cool completely, store in airtight container.
Will keep for two weeks in the refrigerator.
• Serve at room temperature with crackers.

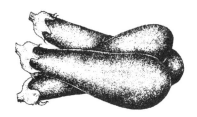

Bollos

Yield: 24

1 pound black eye peas soaked in water overnight,
or 2, 1 pound cans rinsed and drained.
3 cloves of garlic, minced
dash of sea salt, ground red pepper flakes
water as needed

• In a hand food chopper, grind all ingredients except water.
Slowly add water to get the consistency of a thick cake batter.
• In a nonstick skillet, drop batter from a teaspoon into deep
medium hot fat and brown. Keep turning so they will brown
evenly. If batter begins to thicken hard, add a small amount of
water.

Curry Peanuts

Yield: 2 cups

2 cups salted peanuts
2 teaspoons curry powder

• Preheat oven to 350 degrees. In a brown paper bag combine
and shake well peanuts and curry powder.
• Spread the coated nuts on a cookie sheet and bake
20 minutes. Cool, then store in an airtight container.

Hot Cheddar Nachos

Serves 2

5oz. bag of tortilla chips
1 pound Cheddar cheese, grated
⅓ cup chopped green chilies, peeled
½ cup finely chopped onion

• Preheat oven to 400 degrees; place chips on cookie sheets.
In a bowl toss cheese, chilies and onion, sprinkle over chips.
• Bake 5 to 7 minutes or until the cheese has melted.

Sandpipers Onion Tart

Serves 4-6

Shell: 1 cup flour
　　　1 cup sharp cheddar cheese, grated
　　　½ cup melted butter
Filling: 3 large or 4 medium onions, chopped
　　　　¼ cup butter
　　　　¼ cup flour
　　　　1 cup milk
　　　　1 egg, beaten
　　　　¼ cup sharp cheddar cheese, grated
　　　　dashes sea salt, pepper and paprika

• Preheat oven to 350 degrees, use large pie plate or quiche dish.
• Mix shell ingredients to form a soft dough and press into pie plate or quiche pan.
• In a nonstick skillet, sauté onions in butter till translucent, sprinkle with flour to give a coated look. Add a little milk to the beaten egg, then the remaining milk to the onions. Slowly cook to make a white sauce, stir often.
• Add egg and milk mixture to onions and cook for 1 minute on low heat. Add cheese, salt, pepper and mix well.
• Remove from heat and pour into prepared pie shell. Sprinkle with paprika, bake for 30 minutes. Serve warm.

➢*Optional;* to above recipe, add a topping of one of the following: ½ cup broccoli florets chopped or cauliflower just before baking.

Zucchini Squares

Serves 4-6

3 cups zucchini, thinly sliced
½ cup onion, chopped
2 cloves garlic, minced
2 tablespoon fresh parsley, chopped
½ teaspoon sea salt
4 eggs, slightly beaten
1 ½ cups biscuit mix (see page 407)
½ cup Parmesan cheese, grated
½ teaspoon oregano or basil
dash of ground black pepper
½ cup canola oil

• Combine all ingredients well, spread in 9x13 baking pan. Preheat oven to 350 degrees.
• Bake 25 minutes or until golden brown. Cool slightly and cut into squares.

Cucumbers & Radish Yogurt Dip

Serves 6

½ cup low fat yogurt, well drained (see page 420)
½ cup sour cream
¾ teaspoon ground cumin
¾ teaspoon ground coriander
sea salt and ground black pepper, to taste
½ tablespoons fresh mint, finely chopped
2 cucumbers, unpeeled, scored and cut into ¼ inch slices
10-12 radishes, washed and trimmed

• In a medium mixing bowl, combine the yogurt, sour cream, cumin, coriander, salt and pepper, mint until well blended.
• Chill, serve with cucumber sticks and whole radishes.

Spicy Refried Beans

Yield: 2 cups

1 cup canned refried beans
⅓ cup minced red onion
⅓ cup finely diced sweet red peppers
3 cloves garlic, minced
2 teaspoons chili powder
2 tablespoons chopped fresh parsley
2 tablespoons non-fat plain yogurt
2 teaspoons lemon juice
3 tablespoons crushed wheat bran breakfast cereal
 * chopped parsley for garnish (optional)

• In a large bowl combine all ingredients, stir until well blended.
• Place in serving bowl, garnish with fresh parsley sprigs.
• Serve with crackers, assorted fresh vegetables or pita bread.

Ezy-Clam Dip

Yield: 2 cups

1 (8oz.) package cream cheese
1 (6½oz.) can minced clams, drain slightly
1 tablespoon minced onion
1 teaspoon chopped parsley
1 teaspoon Worcestershire sauce
1 tablespoon mayonnaise
½ teaspoon brown mustard

• Blend cheese with mayonnaise and Worcestershire sauce.
Add remaining ingredients blend well. Chill until serving time.
• Serve with assorted crackers or carrot and celery sticks.

Garlic Bagel Thins

Serves 6

2 bagels, slice each bagel into 6 very thin rounds
1 tablespoon butter, melted
2 cloves garlic, minced
½ teaspoon grated Parmesan cheese
1 tablespoon chopped fresh parsley

• Combine butter, garlic, cheese and parsley until well mixed.
Brush over bagel rounds. Preheat oven at 350 degrees.
• Place bagel thins on baking sheet, bake 10-14 minutes, or
until bagel chips are well browned.

Chee-zy Mushrooms

Yield: 10 mushrooms

10 medium size button mushrooms, remove stems
6 tablespoons unsalted butter
1 large clove of garlic, minced
3 tablespoons shredded Monterey Jack cheese
2 tablespoons dry white wine
1 teaspoon soy sauce
⅓ cup fine cracker crumbs

• Melt 2 tablespoons of butter, mix well with mushroom caps.
• Thoroughly blend remaining ingredients in a small bowl,
place mushrooms, cavity side up, in a 8-inch baking pan. Fill
each mushroom cap, press lightly.
• Broil for 3-4 minutes until bubbly and browned.

Hot Cranberry Punch
Yield: 3 quarts

1 (48oz.) bottle cranberry juice cocktail
1 cup water
½ cup firmly packed brown sugar
¾ teaspoon ground cloves
½ teaspoon ground allspice
½ teaspoon ground cinnamon
¼ teaspoon ground nutmeg
1 (46oz.) can pineapple juice

• Combine first 7 ingredients in saucepan, mix well. Bring to a boil, stirring occasionally.
• Add pineapple juice, return to a boil, reduce heat and simmer 5 minutes. Serve hot.

Hot Mocha
Yield: 1 cup

1 envelope (1oz.) hot cocoa mix (see page 402)
½ teaspoon freeze-dried coffee
¾ cup hot boiling water

• Pour coffee and cocoa in mug.
• Add boiling water, stir and sip.

Hot Lemon Kiss
Serves 1 (use large mug)

½ small fresh lemon
boiling hot water

• Squeeze lemon juice from lemon directly into a mug, then place lemon piece in mug.
• Add boiling water, let sit a moment, then sip. It's a real thirst quencher.

International Coffees

Serves 1, use coffee mug

Brazilian
2 tablespoons cocoa
cinnamon stick
whipped cream

Irish
⅔ cup hot coffee
⅓ cup Irish whiskey
whipped cream

Italian
1 teaspoon sugar
freshly ground nutmeg
shaved chocolate

Viennese
1 teaspoon sugar
freshly ground nutmeg
whipped cream

Mexican
½ hot coffee
¼ cup Kahlua
¼ cup rum
whipped cream

• For each, start with one cup hot coffee or as given.
• *Brazilian:* add cocoa, stir with cinnamon stick, top with whipped cream.
• *Irish:* add whiskey, top with whipped cream.
• *Italian:* add sugar, sprinkle with nutmeg, top with shaved chocolate.
• *Mexican:* add Kahlua and rum, top with whipped cream.
• *Viennese:* add sugar, top with whipped cream, and sprinkle with nutmeg.

➤*Note:* In starter section (see page 402), how to make your own hot drink mix.

Hot Apple Cider

Yield: 12 cups

8 cups apple juice
3 cups water
½ cup honey
3 cinnamon sticks
½ teaspoon ground allspice
12 whole cloves
½ teaspoon ground nutmeg
1 cup lemon juice
1 orange, sliced (remove pits)

• Combine apple juice, water, honey and spices in saucepan.
Bring to a boil, reduce heat. Simmer for 20 minutes.
• Let stand overnight; strain.
• Add citrus to spiced apple drink. Reheat before serving, but
do not boil.

➤ *Hint:* broth's, keep a generous supply of beef, chicken, and fish
bouillon cubes or dried packaged broth on hand. They make a quick and
healthy hot drink. Please read ingredient labels carefully.

Tomato Juice Cocktail

Serves 2

8 ounces tomato juice, chilled
½ teaspoon Old Bay seasoning
2 thin slices of lemon

• Combine all ingredients except lemon. Stir well, top each
drink with lemon slice.

➤ *Note:* Powdered Drinks: many powdered or concentrated drinks
usually thought of as cold drinks can be successfully used as hot drinks.

Pineapple Coconut Flip

Serves 4-6

1 (46oz.) can pineapple juice
1 (15.5oz.) can cream of coconut
8 cups water
1 (12oz.) concentrate orange juice, thawed and undiluted
1 small orange thinly sliced, remove seeds

• Combine all ingredients in large pitcher. Stir well. Pour into tall glasses with ice cubes.
• Top each drink with a slice of fresh orange, stir and sip.

Mediterranean Sipper

Serves 4

8 cups vegetable juice
4 teaspoons lemon juice
1 teaspoon olive oil
¼ teaspoon dried oregano leaves, crushed

• Combine all ingredients in pitcher.
• Pour over ice cubes in tall glass, stir and sip.

Mock Champagne Punch

Serves 20

1 (2 liter) bottle ginger ale
1 large can frozen apple juice, thawed (no water added)

• Mix both ingredients in a large pitcher, pour over crushed ice.

Low-Cal Egg Nog

Serves 2

2 cups skim milk
½ cup powdered egg substitute
sugar substitute equal to 2 tablespoons sugar
1½ teaspoons vanilla extract
pinch of freshly grated nutmeg

• Combine all ingredients in hand food chopper and blend well.
• Pour in chilled glasses and serve. Top with nutmeg.

Citrus Spray

Serves 4-6

4 large oranges, squeeze well
2 large limes, squeeze well
1 bottle (24oz.) white grape juice
3 cups of sparkling water

• Combine fruit juices and grape juice in a large pitcher, mix well.
• Add sparkling water, stir and pour into glasses filled with crushed ice.
• Top each glass with a slice of lime.

MangoYogurt Chill

Serves 4

1¼ cups plain non-fat yogurt
½ teaspoon lemon juice
½ cup fresh ripe mango
⅓ cup cold water
4 tablespoons honey
10 standard-size ice cubes, crushed

• Put all ingredients except ice cubes into hand food chopper, whirl 2 minutes or until thoroughly blended.
• Add crushed ice to glasses and pour mixture on top.

Banana Nog Crunch

Serves 1

1 ripe banana
1 cup crushed pineapple with juice
3 tablespoons plain non-fat yogurt
1 egg
4 ice cubes, crushed

• Place all ingredients except ice in hand food chopper, blend well.
• Place ice in glasses, pour mixture on top.

➤*Hint:* Place ice cubes in a plastic bag, bang with wooden crab mallet for crushed ice.

Pineapple Coco

Serves 2

½ cup crushed pineapple
4 ounces pineapple juice
4 tablespoons canned cream of coconut
½ teaspoon lemon juice
7 ounces of water

• In a hand food chopper (see page 13) blend all ingredients.
• Place ice in glass, pour mixture on top.

Orange Mamie

Serves 2

4 tablespoons orange preserves
4 tablespoons powdered orange drink
2 tablespoon powdered sugar
3 cups water
* garnish with slices of orange or lemon (optional)

• In hand food chopper (see page 13) blend all ingredients.
• Place ice in glass, pour mixture on top.
• Garnish with fresh fruit.

➢ *Hint:* Whipping cream: to a dry package of powdered cream,
add confectionery sugar in place of granulated sugar. The cream will fluff
easier and hold up longer.

Quick & Easy Refreshing Drinks

• Shake equal amounts of yogurt or sour cream with tomato juice, dash of salt and pepper. Pour into a glass filled with ice cubes.

• Leftover beet juice? Shake equal amounts of juice and sour cream, dash of salt and pepper. Pour into a glass filled with ice cubes.

• Shake equal amounts of skim milk and apple juice. Pour into a glass filled with ice cubes, dash of nutmeg on top.

• Combine whole fruit with fruit juice. Start with a banana, orange, apple or berries, use one or mix and match. In a hand food chopper, chop the fresh fruit. Pour chopped fruit into a large pitcher, add fruit juice. Stir well, pour into a glass filled with ice cubes.

• In a hand food chopper blend well 1 medium banana, 1 cup plain non-fat yogurt, ½ teaspoon vanilla, ¼ cup skim milk. Pour into a tall glass.

• Combine ½ cup cranberry juice, 2 cups club soda. Pour into a tall glass with ice cubes. Top with slice of lemon.

• Combine ingredients in a large pitcher: 1 (4oz.) can frozen orange juice concentrate, ¼ cup lemon juice, 1 (46oz.) can unsweetened pineapple juice, 1 (28oz.) bottle of raspberry soda. Mix orange, lemon and pineapple juice in a large pitcher. Add bottle of soda. Pour into glasses filled with ice. Yield: 8 servings.

• Combine ingredients in a large pitcher: 1 (6oz.) can frozen lemonade concentrate, 1 (6oz.) can grenadine, 6 cans water. Pour all ingredients into a large pitcher, stir well. Pour into glasses filled with ice. Yield: 8 servings.

Rum Russian

Serves 1
1 ounce dark rum
2 ounces Tía María
ice
• Fill glass with ice, pour on ingredients. Stir and sip.

Butterscotch Milk

Serves 1
2 ounces, butterscotch liqueur
1 cup milk
ice
• Fill glass with ice, pour on ingredients. Stir and sip.

Cranberry Vodka

Serves 1
1 ounce vodka
½ cup cranberry juice
club soda
ice
• Fill glass with ice. Pour in vodka and juice. Top off with club soda. Stir and sip.

Bourbon Amaretto

Serves 1
2 ounces bourbon
2 oz. amaretto
ice
• Place ice in glass. Pour ingredients on ice. Stir and sip.

Roses Lime

Serves 1
1 oz. roses lime juice
club soda
ice

• Fill glass with ice, pour on ingredients. Stir and sip.

Party Sangría

Serves 4-6

1 (750ml) 25.4oz. bottle chilled dry red wine
1 (12oz.) can chilled club soda
juice of whole lemon
2 tablespoons sugar
1 peach, peeled and thinly sliced
1 apple, peeled and diced
1 lemon, thinly sliced
ice (12 cubes)

• Place ice, lemon juice, sugar and sliced fruit in pitcher.
• Add wine and soda. Stir gently, serve immediately.

Hot Apple Toddy

Serves 6 (use mugs)

4 cups apple juice
2 tablespoons brown sugar, packed
12 whole cloves
3 inches of stick cinnamon
⅛ teaspoon ground nutmeg
2 large apples, peeled, cored and quartered
1 cup brandy
¾ cup dark rum
pats of unsalted butter

• In large saucepan, mix apple juice, sugar, and spices. Simmer covered 20 minutes. Add apples, cover, simmer 10 minutes more. Scoop out apple slices and put into mugs.
• Add liquors to hot juice and heat through.
• Place a pat of butter in each mug, pour hot juice on top.

Grand Marnier (KISS #1)

1 c sugar
½ c H2O
3 c brandy (cheap)
2 tsp orange extract

Mix sugar + H2O together →
heat 3 min, stirring. Let cool.
Add brandy & orange. Pour in tight lidded bottle, shake QD x 3 wks.

EGGS

I use fresh large eggs in all of my recipes, in fact whenever possible I prefer brown eggs. Listed below are a few other sources using eggs.

• *Eggs in a can*: you can measure out powdered eggs and reconstitute with water. Three tablespoons combined with ⅓ cup water makes the equivalent of 2 eggs. It has half the calories and protein value of real eggs. Purchased from Chicago Dietetic, Inc., La Grange, IL, Brand name Cellu.

• *Eggs in an envelope:* pre-measured packets of powdered egg that equal two whole eggs when mixed with water. Tillie Lewis Foods, Stockton, CA, Brand name Eggstra. Eggstra has a protein content nearly as high as real eggs, some cholesterol, but a lot fewer calories.

• *Eggs from the freezer:* This is a frozen liquid you simply defrost and pour, ½ cup equals 2 eggs. Eggbeaters contain extra oil, so they're more fattening than real eggs. Fleischmann, Standard Brands, NY, Brand name Eggbeaters.

	Cholesterol	Protein	Calories
2 large eggs	550 mg.	14 gr.	176
Cellu brand	none	7.6 gr.	78
Eggstra	114 mg.	11 gr.	86
Eggbeaters	none	13.30 gr.	200

➤*Hint:* Cut down on cholesterol by using fewer whole eggs and more egg whites. For every two eggs in a recipe, substitute 1 whole egg and 1 egg white.

• *Soft cooked eggs:* The soft cooked eggs should show only a slight congealing of yolk and albumen. I soft-cook eggs in the shell by placing the eggs in a saucepan with sufficient room temperature water to cover them. (If you put them directly into boiling water, they have a tendency to crack!) Bring to a rolling boil. Boiling time depends on your taste. If you like them very soft, they will be that way about the time the water boils freely. For medium, or fully congealed, boil an additional 2½ minutes and 5 minutes more gets them hard-boiled. Add an extra minute of boiling time for very large or newly laid eggs. Be careful not to overheat or boil too rapidly because you might overcook the layer next to the shell.

I enjoy eating soft-cooked egg from a whisky glass or egg cup, eating the egg directly out of its shell. Use a sprinkle of salt and a little demitasse spoon (taught to me when I was a child by Grandfather Nathan).

• *Hard cooked eggs:* After boiling, place in cool water, making them easier to shell. Take one egg at a time and roll it gently on counter top or side of sink cracking the shell into tiny pieces. Pinch up the shell at the egg's large end (air pocket usually forms here) use the membrane to strip away the shell.

• *Poached eggs:* The egg is simmered in a liquid after being removed from its shell. The liquid should cover the egg completely. You can add a few drop of vinegar to the water before poaching. Poaching can be done in other liquids such as broth, stock, or wine.

• *Fried eggs:* Just enough butter should be used to coat the skillet's bottom, or lightly spray the skillet with cooking spray if you prefer. Cook on medium/low heat until whites set, yolks soft. For fried eggs over lightly, slide a spatula far enough under the eggs to support the yolk when turning them over.

➢ *Note:* When poaching or frying eggs, slide them directly from your test cup into the boiling liquid or skillet.

• *Omelet:* Omelets are made by making a mixture of eggs, milk, cream or water, salt, pepper and butter. The lightly beaten egg mixture is carefully poured into a pre-heated and coated skillet. Use low-medium heat to prevent drying out your omelet. As the mixture sets along the outside edges of the skillet, pull the cooked egg towards the center with a fork, while allowing the uncooked egg to replace the set egg. When the entire omelet is set, fold it in half and slide it out of skillet onto plate.

• *Scrambled eggs:* Use up to a teaspoon of water per egg or use evaporated milk, cream or milk for a richer mixture. Add seasoning. Use one teaspoon of butter for each egg for cooking. Add eggs, seasonings and liquid together, beat lightly. Pour egg mixture into coated skillet on medium/low heat. Stir cooking eggs continuously using a wooden spoon. Keep stirring, especially from skillet bottom and sides until eggs are no longer runny.

➤*Note:* To insure you do not accidentally break a bad egg into your mixture, test your eggs first, by breaking them into a small cup, before adding them to the larger amount.

Scrambled eggs for 1

2 eggs
salt, freshly ground black pepper
1 or 2 dashes of hot pepper sauce
1 teaspoon water (for lighter scrambled eggs, creamier use evaporated milk or 2% non-fat milk)
2 tablespoons butter

• Break the eggs into a bowl, add salt, pepper, water (or milk) and hot sauce and beat lightly with a fork.
• Melt butter in a nonstick skillet over medium-low heat, pour in the eggs. As soon as the eggs begin to coagulate, start making pushing strokes with a wooden spoon so you get curds. Continue doing this until all small curds.

➤ *Hint:* I like evaporated milk best of all at about ½ tablespoon per egg. Many just use ¼ teaspoon water per egg. You can use skim milk or eliminate the milk entirely.

Omelet for 1

2 large eggs
½ teaspoon salt
pinch of ground black pepper
1 tablespoon water
1 tablespoon butter

• Break the eggs into a bowl, add the seasonings and water, and beat lightly with a fork, don't over-beat, only enough to blend yolks and whites.
• Using a nonstick skillet melt butter on medium-low, add egg mixture. As soon as the eggs have begun to set, push eggs toward center of pan with wooden spoon to allow remaining loose egg to cook until almost completely set. Add one of the fillings suggested below and heat thoroughly.
• Take your fork and loosen one end of the omelet, rolling it over onto itself.
• Tip the skillet over your plate and the omelet will roll out.

Fillings For Omelets

• Smoked ham, mushrooms, green pepper, onion, cheddar cheese
• Crumbled crisp bacon, green chilies, Jack cheese, salsa
• Cheddar cheese, Jack cheese, green chilies, mozzarella cheese
• Crumbled crisp bacon, avocado, diced tomatoes, Jack cheese
• Spicy capicola ham, diced tomatoes, mozzarella
• Tomatoes, sprouts, avocado, mozzarella and Jack cheese
• Crabmeat, nutmeg, onions, Jack cheese
• Broccoli, cauliflower, onions, green pepper
• Just herbs, parsley, chives, tarragon, cheddar cheese
• Asparagus, mushrooms, sprouts, Jack cheese
• Cooked flaked fish, tomatoes, basil, green pepper
• New cooked potatoes, crisp bacon, green chili strips, Monterey Jack cheese
• New cooked potatoes, ham, onion, green pepper, mushrooms, tomatoes cheddar cheese
• Sliced pineapple, strawberries and apricot jam
•Slices of kosher salami or sliced sausage (brown first in nonstick skillet on both sides; do not coat skillet), then add egg mixture on top

➢*Note:* Omelets can be served anytime for breakfast, lunch or dinner.

Breakfast Sandwiches

Serves 2

2 eggs
1 tablespoon water
2 tablespoons Boursin cheese
4 slices whole wheat bread, toasted

• Beat eggs and water in bowl with wire whisk until fluffy.
• Lightly spray skillet, cook eggs until slightly dry.
• Spread Boursin cheese on 2 slices toast.
• Top each with half the cooked egg mixture and remaining toast.
• Cut sandwich in half, and serve.

French Bread Bake

Serves 6

1 loaf French bread, sliced
1 (8oz.) package cream cheese
10 eggs or egg substitutes
1 pint half & half
maple syrup, spread lightly
1 stick unsalted butter, melted
1 tablespoon cinnamon

• Spread slices of French bread with cream cheese. Place in layers into 9x12 baking dish. Pre-heat oven to 350 degrees.
• Mix together eggs, half&half, maple syrup, butter, pour over bread. Press down with a spatula until well saturated with liquid. Sprinkle cinnamon on top. Bake 45-60 minutes, or until set.

Egg Scramble

Yield: 6 servings

⅓ cup chopped onion
¼ cup chopped green pepper
¼ cup butter
2 medium potatoes, peeled, cooked and cubed
1½ cups julienne fully cooked ham
6 eggs
2 tablespoons water
dash ground black pepper

• In a large nonstick skillet, cook onion and green pepper in butter until crisp and tender.
• Add potatoes and ham; cook and stir for 5 minutes.
• In a medium bowl, beat eggs, water and black pepper. Pour over ham mixture.
• Cook over low heat, stirring occasionally. Once eggs set, serve.

Poached Buttery Egg

Serves 1

2 tablespoons melted butter
1 slice of toast
1 poached egg, (see page 92)
sprinkle with fresh dill

• Spread a small amount of melted butter on toast.
• Add the cooked poached egg, pour remaining butter on top and sprinkle with dill.

➢ *Note:* Variation; 1 English muffin, halved, 2 poached eggs, 2 slices of tomatoes, ¼ cup deviled ham. Spread ham on muffin top with tomato slice, place muffins under broiler until heated thoroughly. Remove from broiler, top with poached eggs.

Egg Casserole

Serves 6

6 hard-boiled eggs, sliced
1 pound hot bulk sausage, cooked and drained
1½ cups sour cream
½ cup dry bread crumbs
1½ cups cheddar cheese, grated
dash sea salt and ground black pepper

• Preheat oven to 350 degrees; place eggs in buttered 9x13
baking dish or casserole, sprinkle with salt and pepper.
• Spread cooked sausage, sour cream over eggs.
• Combine crumbs and cheese, sprinkle on top.
• Bake 40-45 minutes or until cheese is bubbly.

Muffy Cottage Cheese

Serves 6

1 cup cottage cheese
¼ to ½ cup chopped dates or figs or prunes
¼ cup mixed slivered almonds and sesame seeds
1 teaspoon honey
½ teaspoon ground cinnamon
grated peel from 1 orange
3 English muffins, split or whole grain bread

• Mix first 6 ingredients in bowl.
• Spread over English muffin halves.
• Place on baking sheet, broil until
bubbly.

Peachy Granola

Serves 4

1 (21oz.) can peach halves
granola (see starter page 413, 414)
brown sugar
butter

- Place peach halves in baking dish.
- Fill center cavity with granola.
- Sprinkle with brown sugar. Dot a pat of butter on each.
- Pour peach juice in bottom of baking dish.
- Bake 10 minutes basting once with juice.

Kasha Delight

Serves 2

1 cup cooked bulgur (see pages 28, 265, 275)
½ cup shredded Swiss cheese
sesame or sunflower seeds to taste

- Place bulgur and cheese in a buttered saucepan.
- Stir constantly over low heat until cheese melts.
- Remove from heat, top with sesame or sunflower seeds.

➤*Hint:* Enjoy good old fashioned breakfast consisting of cooked hot oatmeal, wheatena or oatbran cereal. Please follow package directions.

➤ *Hint:* Try garlic-seasoned cheese or add chopped green chilies to add zip to a grits casserole.

Pickled Eggs

Yield: 2 dozen

2 dozen eggs, hard boiled and peeled
1 cup white vinegar
¼ cup water
½ cup sugar
¼ teaspoon salt
4 whole cloves
1 small bay leaf
1 medium onion, thinly sliced

• Place eggs in a tall, narrow sterilized glass jar.
• In a medium saucepan combine remaining ingredients except onion, bring to a boil. Reduce heat and simmer for 5 minutes.
• Pour hot solution over eggs, making sure eggs are completely covered. Place onions on top.
• Secure lid, refrigerate and let stand several days.
• Serve whole or halved, or sliced egg sandwich for breakfast, hors d'oeuvres, topping for salad.

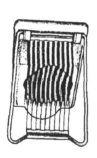

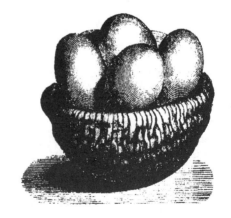

Nutty French Toast

Serves 4

½ cup peanut butter
½ cup raisins
2 tablespoons apricot preserves
cinnamon to taste
12 slices whole grain bread
2 eggs
½ cup milk
2 tablespoons butter

• Combine peanut butter, fruit, preserves and cinnamon in medium bowl.
• Spread 6 slices of bread with mixture. Top with remaining bread.
• Beat eggs with milk in shallow bowl.
• Dip sandwiches in mixture, draining excess.
• Melt butter in nonstick skillet on medium heat. Brown lightly on each side.

Eggs Pronto

Serves 4

1 (6oz.) can hash
4 eggs
¼ cup grated cheddar cheese
vegetable cooking spray

• In a nonstick skillet, spray lightly with cooking spray.
• Spread hash in skillet, set on medium flame. Top hash with egg and sprinkle with grated cheese.
• Cover and cook until eggs are done.

➢ *Note:* Variation: In a nonstick skillet, spray lightly with cooking spray. Spread hash in skillet, set on medium flame. Make four depressions and break an egg into each hole. Top each egg with a dash of catsup, sprinkle with cheddar cheese. Cover, steam until the eggs are set.

Zucchini Quiche

Serves 4

1 9-inch unbaked pie crust (see page 364)
1 cup peeled and shredded zucchini
2½ cups shredded sharp Cheddar cheese
½ cup Monterey Jack cheese with jalapeño peppers
3 eggs, beaten
4 teaspoons dry minced onion or ¼ onion, chopped
4 slices bacon, crisply fried and crumbled
½ teaspoon sea salt

• Combine zucchini, cheeses, eggs, onion, bacon, and salt.
• Pour into unbaked 9-inch pie shell.
• Bake for 45 minutes.

Artichoke Frittata

Serves 4

4 eggs, beaten
6 soda crackers, crumbled
½ pound grated sharp Cheddar cheese
2 jars (6oz. each) artichokes
3 green onions, chopped
1 tablespoon chopped parsley
1 clove garlic, finely chopped
salt, pepper, and red hot sauce to taste
canola or safflower oil

• Lightly oil 8x10 baking pan, set aside. Preheat oven to 325 degrees.
• Combine all ingredients in large bowl and mix gently. Pour mixture into pan, bake 35-40 minutes.
• Cool slightly before serving.

➤*Note:* A frittata is an Italian version of an omelet and usually has the filling mixed into the eggs before they are cooked.

Salmon Quiche

Serves 6

1 9-inch unbaked pie crust (see page 364)
1 (15½oz.) can red sockeye salmon
3 large eggs
1 cup cottage cheese
2 teaspoons Dijon mustard
¾ teaspoon salt
½ cup half-n-half
1 cup sliced mushrooms
½ cup shredded carrots
¼ cup thinly sliced green onions
fresh parsley, chopped

• Partially bake pastry shell on lower rack of oven for 12 minutes.
• Drain salmon, reserving 2 tablespoons liquid. Place salmon in a small bowl, break salmon into chunks, remove skin and bones. Set aside.
• In a medium bowl, beat eggs with cottage cheese, mustard, and salt. Add half-n-half, salmon liquid and mushrooms; stir once. Add carrots, onions, and salmon; blend well.
• Pour mixture into partially baked pastry shell; bake 45-60 minutes or until set in center.
• Remove from oven; garnish with parsley, let stand 5 minutes before serving.

➤*Note:* A dab of cottage cheese and a pinch of rosemary will spruce up your scrambled eggs.

Morning Rice Pudding

Serves 4

1 cup cooked brown rice
½ cup cottage cheese
½ cup plain yogurt
1 ripe banana, mashed
honey

• Mix cooked rice, cottage cheese and yogurt in bowl.
• Sweeten with a little honey or ripe banana.

➢*Optional*: For additional toppings use raisins, shredded coconut, chopped walnuts.

Pepperoni Quiche

Serves 4

2 cups (½ pound) diced pepperoni
1 cup shredded mozzarella cheese
1 cup shredded or diced Muenster cheese
2 eggs, lightly beaten
2 cups milk
1 ½ cups all-purpose flour

• Preheat oven to 400 degrees; lightly grease 8-inch baking pan.
• Mix all ingredients together, pour mixture into prepared pan. Bake 15-20 minutes; cool slightly before serving.

Cheddar Cheese Topper

Serves 4

1 small onion, chopped
1 tablespoon unsalted butter
2 tablespoons water
1 (10oz.) can tomato soup
8 ounces Cheddar cheese, shredded
1 tablespoon Worcestershire sauce
hot red pepper sauce to taste
French bread slices or toasted English muffins

• Sauté onion with butter in a nonstick skillet until golden.
• Add water, soup; simmer till heated through.
• Add cheese, stirring until melted; add remaining ingredients
heat thoroughly.
• Serve over French bread or muffins.

Spinach Soufflé

Serves 4

1 (10oz.) package frozen spinach, thawed and drained
3 tablespoons unsalted butter, melted
¼ cup all-purpose flour
12 ounces cream cottage cheese
3 ounces Cheddar, Parmesan or Swiss cheese, grated
3 eggs, beaten

• Preheat oven to 350 degrees; lightly
grease 2-quart casserole dish.
• Combine butter, flour and cheeses and
add to beaten eggs. Fold in spinach.
Pour into prepared casserole dish.
• Bake, uncovered, for 1 hour. Cool
slightly before slicing.

Clam Quiche

Serves 4-6

1 9-inch unbaked pie shell, lightly pricked
½ pound bacon, cooked and crumbled
1 (15oz.) can New England clam chowder
4 eggs, slightly beaten
½ cup finely chopped onion
½ cup plain yogurt
2 tablespoons chopped fresh parsley
¼ teaspoon ground black pepper
dash of sea salt
4 slices of American cheese

• Preheat oven to 400 degrees; bake pie shell for 8-10 minutes, remove pie shell. Reduce oven to 325 degrees.
• Combine remaining ingredients except cheese in a medium bowl; mix well. Pour ⅔ of the chowder mixture into baked pie shell. Arrange cheese slices on top.
• Cover with remaining chowder mixture; bake 1 hour or until knife inserted near center of quiche comes out clean. Let stand for 15 minutes before slicing.

Hot Apple Rice

Serves 2

1 cup minute rice
1 cup water
½ teaspoon sea salt
1½ cups finely diced, unpeeled apple

• Place apple and water in a medium saucepan; bring to a boil then simmer for 2-3 minutes.
• Add rice and salt, reheat until bubbly, cover and remove from heat. Let sit 5 minutes before serving.

Couscous & Eggs

Yield: 6 servings

1½ cups milk
¼ cup unsalted butter
1½ cups couscous
1½ cups (6oz.) shredded Swiss cheese
2 cups spaghetti sauce
6 large eggs
¼ teaspoon ground black pepper

• Place milk and butter in a large saucepan, bring to a boil, add couscous, cover and remove from heat. Let sit for 4-5 minutes. Stir with a fork and spoon into a 2-quart shallow baking pan, spread evenly.
• Sprinkle with 1 cup of cheese; spoon on spaghetti sauce. Bake covered in a 400 degree oven until sauce is very hot, 15-20 minutes.
• Remove from oven, make 6 deep wells in couscous, slide 1 egg into each. Sprinkle with remaining ½ cup cheese. Return to oven and bake uncovered, until whites of eggs are firm, about 10 minutes. Remove, sprinkle with pepper.

Shredded Wheat & Peaches

Serves 1

2 shredded wheat biscuits
canned peach slices with juice
brown sugar
cinnamon
milk

• Place biscuits in bowl, top with fruit, sprinkle with sugar and cinnamon. Pour in milk and serve.

Bread Baking Guide

The pleasure of baking homemade bread is matched only by eating it, except when something goes wrong. Most problems can be determined and easily avoided the next time.

Problem . . .	Cause . . .
Bread or biscuits are dry	Too much flour; too slow baking; over-handling
Bread has too open texture or uneven texture	Too much liquid; over-handling in kneading
Strong yeast smell from baked bread	Too much yeast; over-rising
Tiny white spots on crust	Too rapid rising; dough not covered properly while rising
Crust has bad color	Too much flour used in shaping
Small flat loaves	Old yeast; not enough rising or much too long; oven temperature too hot
Heavy compact texture	Too much flour worked into bread when kneading; insufficient rising time; oven temperature too hot
Coarse texture	Too little kneading
Crumbly texture	Too much flour; under mixing; oven temperature too cool
Yeasty sour flavor	Too little yeast; rising time to long
Fallen center	Rising time too long
Irregular shape	Poor technique in shaping
Surface browns too quickly	Oven temperature too hot
Bread rises too long during baking and is porous in center and upper portion of loaf	Oven temperature too cool

Basic Beer Bread

Yield: 1 loaf

3 cups self-rising flour
3 tablespoons sugar
1 (12oz.) can of beer, room temperature

• Lightly grease loaf pan, set aside.
• Preheat oven to 350 degrees.
• Mix all ingredients together, pour into pan.
• Bake at 40-50 minutes or until a cake-tester or a toothpick inserted in the center of the loaf comes out clean.

➤ *Hint*: 3 cups all-purpose flour, 3 teaspoons baking powder, 1 teaspoon salt makes self-rising flour for above recipe.

Basic Beer Bread Variations:

• *Herb bread*: Add 1 teaspoon caraway seeds, ½ teaspoon freshly ground nutmeg, and ½ teaspoon powdered sage.

• *Onion Bread*: Add ½ cup finely chopped onion.

• *Whole Wheat Bread*: Decrease white flour to 2 cups, and add ¾ cup of whole wheat flour and ¼ cup bran flakes.

➤*Hint:* To knead bread dough, fold the dough toward you, then push it away with the heels of your hands in a rocking motion. Rotate it a quarter turn and repeat until dough is springy and blistered with tiny bubbles under the surface and smooth on top.

Yogurt Bread

Yield: 2 loaves

1 tablespoon yeast, dilute with ¼ cup warm water, set aside
2 cups warm water
2 tablespoons of honey
1 cup of plain yogurt
2 teaspoons of sea salt
1½ cups rye flour
7 to 9 cups of all-purpose flour

• Preheat oven to 350 degrees, lightly grease and flour two loaf pans, set aside.
• Combine all ingredients in a large bowl, less 2 cups of all purpose flour.
• Mix until the dough is elastic, slowly adding remaining flour. Divide the dough into two halves. Place dough in loaf pans. Let rise once until ½ to ¾ inch above pans.
• Bake 45 - 50 minutes or until golden brown.
• Remove bread from oven, invert on a wire rack. Cool slightly before removing breads.

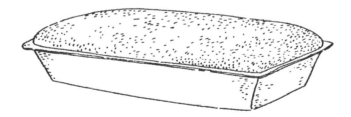

➤ *Hint:* Quick and easy bread sticks: Cut 12 hot dog buns into quarters lengthwise. Spread with a mixture of 1 cup softened butter, 1 teaspoon basil, 1 teaspoon dillweed and ¼ teaspoon garlic powder. Bake at 250 degrees for 1 hour or until golden brown.

Amish Friendship Bread

Yield: 2 loaves

2 cups sourdough starter (page 423)
⅔ cup canola oil
3 eggs
1 cup sugar plus 1 tablespoon sugar
2 cups flour
1 teaspoon vanilla extract
1 teaspoon ground cinnamon
1¼ teaspoons baking powder
½ teaspoon baking soda
½ teaspoon salt

• Preheat oven to 350 degrees, grease 2 loaf pans, sprinkle each pan evenly with ½ tablespoon of sugar, set aside.
• Mix all ingredients together, pour into prepared pans.
• Bake 40-50 minutes or until bread is golden brown.
• Remove, cool 10 min. before removing bread from pans.

➤ *Note: Variation:* For above recipe add ½ cup nuts, raisins, chocolate chips or 2 mashed bananas. Slivered almonds may be sprinkled on top before baking.

Sour Cream Corn Bread

Yield: 16 servings

1½ cups self-rising cornmeal
2 tablespoons sugar
1 cup cream-style corn
1 medium onion, chopped
½ cup canola oil
2 eggs
1 cup sour cream

• Combine all ingredients; fill greased muffin cups ¾ full. Bake at 400 degrees for 20 - 25 minutes. Serve hot.

Cornbread
Yield: 1 bread or 12 muffins

2½ cups cornbread mix (see page 406)
2 eggs
1 cup milk
4 tablespoons unsalted butter, melted

• Grease a square 8 inch pan or 12 muffin cups, set aside.
Preheat oven to 450 degrees.
• Place cornbread mix in a large bowl.
• Beat eggs and milk in medium bowl, then add butter blend
well.
• Stir egg mixture into dry ingredients, mix only until
moistened, don't over-mix.
• Spoon batter into prepared pan or cups.
• Bake 20 minutes for muffins, 35-30 minutes for bread.

➤*Optional addition:* Add ½ cup corn kernels (fresh, or
drained canned corn), 1 jalapeño pepper, finely chopped.

Mincemeat Bread
Yield: 1 loaf

2½ cups all-purpose flour
2 teaspoons baking soda
1 (28oz.) jar mincemeat
2 eggs, beaten
1 ounce dark rum

• Grease a medium-size loaf pan, set aside.
• Mix together the dry ingredients, then add remaining
ingredients. Spoon into loaf pan. Bake at 300 degrees for 1½
hours. Remove, let cool 10 minutes before removing it from
the pan.

Onion Flat Bread

Yield: 1 flat bread

1⅓ cups all-purpose flour
¼ teaspoon salt
2 teaspoons baking powder
¼ cup plus 2 tablespoons water
2½ tablespoons oil
Topping:
2 tablespoons butter
¼ cup minced onion
1 egg, beaten
1 tablespoon water
1 teaspoon poppy seeds
1 teaspoon sesame seeds

• Lightly grease pizza pan, set aside.
• Combine flour, salt and baking powder in a small bowl, mix well.
• Mix together water and oil in a large bowl. Add the dry ingredients. Blend well, pour mixture on a lightly floured board and knead for 1 minute. Pat out dough on pan, set aside.
• Melt butter in a nonstick skillet, add onions, cook on low heat until onions are golden. Set aside.
• Beat egg and water in cup, brush on dough. Spread the onion mixture evenly on dough. Sprinkle the poppy and sesame seeds on top.
• Bake 8-10 minutes, or until nicely browned.

➢ *Hint:* Spread some low-fat yogurt cheese on a freshly baked muffin or biscuit, (See page 421). To the basic cheese recipe, add some finely shredded carrots, chopped radishes, chopped green onions, dill, cilantro, parsley or a combination of two or more, dash of salt and pepper.

Poppyseed Lemon Bread

Yield: 1 loaf

1 lemon
1 cup all-purpose flour
¾ cup sugar, divided
⅓ cup poppy seeds
1½ teaspoons baking powder
1 egg
⅔ cup milk
⅓ cup canola oil
½ teaspoon vanilla extract

• Grease pan lightly, set aside. Preheat oven to 350 degrees.
• Grate the rind from the lemon; squeeze out the juice and reserve, set aside.
• Stir together the flour, ½ cup sugar, poppy seeds and baking powder in a medium bowl.
• Beat the egg, milk, oil, vanilla and half the lemon rind in a small bowl. Add mixture to the dry ingredients and mix until smooth. Pour batter into pan.
• Bake 45-50 minutes or until a cake-tester or a toothpick inserted in the center of the bread comes out clean. Let bread cool 3 minutes, place a piece of wax paper under wire rack, invert bread on top of rack.

* While the bread is baking, make the GLAZE. Stir together the lemon juice and remaining lemon rind and ¼ cup sugar. Drizzle over the loaf, any glaze that dribbles off will land on wax paper.

Buttermilk Bread (KISS #1)
2 C buttermilk
1 tsp salt
4 c. self-rising flour

Honey Carrot Date Muffins

Yield: 12 muffins

¼ cup butter, melted
½ cup honey
½ cup milk
2 eggs
1½ cups all-purpose flour
1 heaping teaspoon baking powder
1 teaspoon sea salt
1 cup grated carrots
1 cup pitted, chopped dates

• Grease muffin pan, set aside. Preheat oven to 375 degrees.
• Combine butter and honey in large bowl. Stir in milk, eggs, and beat well.
• Place dry ingredients in large strainer and sift directly into egg mixture. Stir thoroughly.
• Fold in carrots and dates. Spoon mixture into muffin cups, ¾ full. Bake 15-20 minutes or until lightly browned.

➤ *Hint:* For a sweet treat, toast bread slightly and then cut into strips. Spread 1 side with butter, sprinkle with confectioners' sugar, shredded coconut and cinnamon. Brown lightly on a cookie sheet in the oven.

Cranberry Nut Bread (KISS #1)
2 C flour
1 C honey
1½ tsp baking powder
½ tsp baking soda
1 tsp salt
¼ C shortening
3/4 c OJ
1 Tbsp grated orange rind
1 egg, beaten
½ c chopped nuts
1 C fresh cranberries, halved & wshed.

In lg. bowl, sift dry ingred. Add shortening & blend. In small bowl combine OJ, rind, egg. Pour into dry ingred. Blend just until damp. Fold in nuts & berries. Bake in lg. baking pan or 2 loaf pans. Bake 350° 35-40 min

Zucchini Apple Muffins

Yield: 12 muffins

1 ¼ cups all-purpose flour
½ cup quick-cooking rolled oats
2 teaspoons baking powder
½ teaspoon baking soda
1 teaspoon cinnamon
⅓ cup packed brown sugar
¼ cup safflower oil
1 egg
1 medium tart apple, peeled and shredded
1 medium zucchini, grated

• Line muffin cups with paper baking cups, set aside.
• Combine flour, oats, baking powder, baking soda and cinnamon in a medium bowl.
• In a large bowl combine brown sugar, oil and egg. Whisk until well blended, stir in apple and zucchini.
• Add dry ingredients all at once into egg mixture. Stir only until moistened; the batter should be slightly lumpy.
• Spoon evenly into baking cups ¾ full.
• Bake 20-25 minutes or until golden brown. Remove muffins on to a wire rack to cool.

➤ *Hint:* Leftover crusts and hollowed-out bread make a great filler for that next meat loaf.

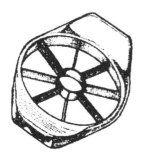

Blueberry Muffins

Yield: 12 muffins

½ cup plus ⅓ cup sugar
½ teaspoon allspice
2⅔ cups all-purpose flour
½ cup butter, softened
1 egg
4 teaspoons baking powder
½ teaspoon vanilla extract
1½ cups fresh blueberries, rinse and pat dry

• Grease muffin pan, set aside. Preheat oven to 375 degrees.
• Sift 2⅓ cups of flour, baking powder and salt onto a piece of wax paper, set aside.
• Mix ½ cup sugar, allspice, ⅓ cup flour and ¼ cup butter in medium bowl until crumbly. Set aside.
• Cream remaining ⅓ cup sugar and ¼ cup butter in large bowl. Blend very well.
• Add egg to butter and sugar mixture blend well. Alternate dry flour mixture and milk into the egg mixture, beginning and ending with flour mixture.
• Add vanilla and mix well; fold in blueberries gently. Spoon mixture ¾ full into muffin cups, top with crumb mixture.
• Bake 20-25 minutes or until golden brown. Serve warm.

➤*Hint*: Muffins can be easily removed from a hot pan it is placed on a damp towel first for 2 minutes.

Biscuit Mix
1 C shortening
4.5 C flour
½ Tbsp salt
2 Tbsp baking powder

Mix & store in tightly covered container

Cheddar Pepper Muffins
Yield: 12 muffins

2 cups all-purpose flour
3½ teaspoons baking powder
1 cup shredded Cheddar cheese
1 teaspoon paprika
½ teaspoon sea salt and ground black pepper
1 egg, beaten
1 cup whole or skim milk
¼ cup melted butter

• Lightly grease muffin pan, set aside. Preheat oven to
425 degrees.
• Combine flour, baking powder, cheese, paprika, pepper and
salt in a large bowl. Make a well in center, set aside.
• Combine egg, milk and butter in small bowl, mix well.
Pour egg mixture into well, mix just until moistened.
• Spoon ⅔ batter into each of the prepared muffin cups.
• Bake 20 minutes.

Butter Corn Sticks
Yield: 2 dozen

⅓ cup unsalted butter
2¼ cups sifted all-purpose flour
4 teaspoons baking powder
2 tablespoons sugar
1 teaspoon sea salt
¼ cup milk
1 cup cream-style canned corn

• Melt butter in a 13x9 baking pan. Sift flour with baking
powder, sugar and salt. Stir in milk and corn.
• Mix, then turn out on floured board. Knead lightly, roll to
about ½-inch in thickness. Cut in 1-inch strips. Lay each strip
in the melted butter, turning to coat each side.
• Bake at 450 degrees, 15-18 minutes or until brown.

Dillweed Ring

Serves 10

¼ cup butter, melted
¼ cup Parmesan cheese
1 teaspoon dillweed
¼ teaspoon garlic powder
2 (10oz.) cans Hungry Jack flaky biscuits

• Preheat oven to 350 degrees.
• In a small bowl, combine butter, cheese, dillweed and garlic powder.
• Separate each can of dough into 10 biscuits. Cut each biscuit in half.
• Randomly place 10 pieces in a ungreased bundt pan; spoon ½ cheese mixture on top. Make a second layer with the remaining cut biscuits and cheese.
• Bake 20 to 30 minutes or until golden brown.
• Cool 2 minutes, remove from pan.

Oatmeal Muffins

Yield: 1 dozen

1 cup buttermilk
1 cup quick oatmeal
½ cup light brown sugar, packed
1 cup all-purpose flour, sifted
½ teaspoon sea salt
½ teaspoon baking soda
2 teaspoons baking powder
1 egg, beaten
¼ cup melted shortening

• Preheat oven to 375 degrees; grease 12 muffin cups.
• Combine buttermilk, oatmeal, brown sugar, let stand 10 minutes. Sift flour, salt, baking soda and baking powder.
• Add beaten egg to oatmeal mixture, then add shortening, mixing well. Stir in flour mixture, just to moisten ingredients. Bake 20-25 minutes.

Banana-Chocolate Chip Muffins
Yield: 24 muffins

4 cups all-purpose flour
2 tablespoons baking powder
¾ teaspoon baking soda
⅝ cup sugar
3 eggs
1 cup safflower oil
2 cups mashed banana
1½ ounces milk
½ cup chocolate chips

• Lightly grease muffin pan, set aside. Preheat oven to 375 degrees. Mix dry ingredients in a large bowl.
• Add eggs, oil, milk and banana. Mix just until moistened.
• Fill muffin cups, bake 20-30 minutes or until browned.

Big Bread Sticks
Yield: 8 bread sticks

½ cup unsalted butter, melted
½ cup minced green onions, including tops
¼ teaspoon dry thyme leaves
3 cloves garlic, minced
2 baguettes (½lb. each), cut lengthwise into quarters

• Blend together all ingredients in a small bowl. Brush over cut sides of bread quarters. Place pieces buttered side up in a 9x13 baking pan. Broil about 4-inches below heat until golden, about 5 minutes.

➢ *Hint:* Make Easy Beer Bread by mixing 3 cups self-rising flour and 3 tablespoons sugar with one 12-ounce can of beer at room temperature. Place in greased loaf pan, let rise for 30 minutes. Bake at 350 degrees for 1 hours.

Sweet Potato Biscuits

Serves 8-12

2 cups self rising flour
¼ cup shortening
1 cup sweet potato purée
¾ to 1 cup buttermilk

• Place flour in large bowl, make a well in center.
• Blend shortening and sweet potato in small bowl.
• Pour into well in flour, add enough buttermilk to make a soft dough.
• Roll about 1 inch thick on a lightly floured surface. Cut with biscuit cutter.
• Arrange on baking sheet. Bake at 400 degrees for 10-12 minutes or until golden brown.

Quick & Easy Bread

Yield: 1 loaf

1¼ cups lukewarm water
1 package dry yeast
1 egg
2 tablespoons sugar
2 tablespoons melted shortening
¾ teaspoon sea salt
3 cups all-purpose flour

• Mix all ingredients in a large bowl. Cover and let rise until doubled in bulk, about 1-2 hours.
• Stir down, pour into greased 1½-quart bread pan. Let rise, uncovered, until doubled, about 1 hour.
• Bake at 350 degrees for 45-50 minutes.

Hush Puppies

Yield: 15 servings

2 cups cornmeal
½ cup all-purpose flour
1 tablespoon baking powder
½ teaspoon baking soda
2 teaspoons sea salt
1 egg
1 medium onion, minced
¼ cup shredded Cheddar cheese
1 cup buttermilk
canola oil for deep frying

• Combine first 5 ingredients in a large bowl. Add egg, onion and cheese, mix well. Add enough buttermilk to make batter of consistency to drop from spoon. Drop by spoonfuls into hot oil. Fry until golden brown, turning frequently. Drain on paper plate.

➤*Hint:* Any type of crushed herb from thyme to rosemary to sage to parsley adds an extra dimension to biscuits. Add the herb when you are mixing the batter.

Cream Biscuits

Yield: 12 biscuits

2 cups all-purpose flour
½ teaspoon sea salt
3 teaspoons baking powder
1 cup heavy cream

• Sift flour, salt, baking powder. Whip cream until stiff. Combine cream and flour mixture with fork. Place dough on a lightly floured board, knead for one minute. Pat dough ½ inch thick, cut with biscuit cutter. Bake in oven at 450 degrees, for about 12 minutes.

Cornmeal Batter Tortillas

Yield: 2 dozen

½ cup yellow cornmeal
½ cup all-purpose flour
3 eggs
3 tablespoons unsalted butter, melted
¾ cup milk
¾ cup water
1 teaspoon salt
vegetable oil for frying

• In a hand food chopper (see page 13), blend all ingredients except oil for 3 minutes. Pour mixture into a large bowl, cover and let rest at room temperature for an hour before using. Stir the batter just before making the tortillas.
• Brush the bottom of a 6-inch skillet with a little oil, on medium heat drop 1½ tablespoons of batter, tilt and rotate the skillet to coat the bottom evenly. Cook until the underside of the tortilla is light brown, turn it with a spatula and quickly brown the other side.
• Remove the tortilla from the skillet and store in a covered tortilla holder or clean dish towel. Repeat the process with the remaining batter.

➤ *Hint:* Batter breads are made from very soft yeast doughs that are beaten vigorously, but not kneaded. You can bake these loaves in 1 or 2 lb. coffee cans. The can gives the loaf its distinctive shape: tall, round, and domed. The plastic lid is placed on and pops off when the dough is ready to bake. If the lid pops off before the dough reaches the top of the coffee can, just place the lid back on until the dough pushes it off.

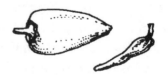

Baking Powder Biscuits

Yield: 12 biscuits

2 cups all-purpose flour
1 tablespoon baking powder
½ teaspoon salt
¼ cup unsalted butter
¾ to 1 cup skim milk
cooking spray

• Lightly spray baking sheet, set aside.
• Sift flour, baking powder and salt in medium bowl, mix.
• Cut butter into flour mixture until crumbly. Stir in enough milk to form dough that holds together.
• Knead on lightly floured board until smooth. Roll ½ inch thick; cut with biscuit cutter.
• Bake 12 minutes or until golden brown.

➤ *Hint*: For light biscuits, roll dough thick and place biscuits close together on the baking sheet. For crusty biscuits, cut dough thin and place biscuits far apart on the sheet.

Quick Apricot Coffeecake

Yield: 1 dozen

1 package refrigerated crescent dinner rolls
½ cup apricot jam
1 cup dairy sour cream
1 tablespoon sugar
½ teaspoon vanilla

• Unroll crescent rolls and pat into a greased 13x9 baking pan. Preheat oven to 425 degrees.
• With fingertips draw edges together to form a sheet. Spread with jam and bake 15 minutes. Remove from heat.
• In a small bowl, blend sour cream, sugar and vanilla, spread over pastry. Reduce heat to 350 degrees, bake 5 minutes more. Cool slightly and cut in squares.

Whole Wheat Bread

Yield: 2 loaves

1 cup honey
3 cups hot water
2 envelopes dry yeast
¼ cup canola oil
1 tablespoon sea salt
1 cup all-purpose flour
9 cups whole wheat flour

• Blend honey and hot water in large bowl, cool to lukewarm.
Add yeast; stir until dissolved.
• Add oil, salt, and flours; mix well. Knead on floured board.
Place in greased bowl, turning to coat surface. Cover to let rise
until doubled in bulk.
• Punch dough down; shape into 2 loaves and place in greased
loaf pans. Cover to let rise until doubled in bulk. Bake at 350
degrees for 45-50 minutes.

Baked Brown Bread

Yield: 1 loaf

1 egg, slightly beaten
4 tablespoons sugar
1 cup light molasses
⅔ cup buttermilk
1 cup all-purpose flour
½ teaspoon sea salt
1 teaspoon baking soda
1 cup whole wheat flour
⅔ cup raisins

• Preheat oven to 350 degrees; grease loaf pan lightly.
• In a large bowl, blend egg, sugar then add molasses and
buttermilk.
• Sift flour with salt and baking soda, add whole wheat flour
and raisins. Combine the wet and dry mixtures, stir only to wet
ingredients; don't beat. Bake 1 hour, cool on wire rack.

Pumpkin Corn Bread

Serves 6
2 teaspoons safflower oil
⅓ cup honey
2 eggs
2 teaspoons vanilla
1 cup mashed cooked pumpkin
¼ cup cornmeal
2 teaspoons baking powder
½ teaspoon salt
⅔ cup dry milk powder

• Grease a 5x9 inch loaf pan, set aside.
• Combine oil, honey, eggs and vanilla in large bowl. Stir in pumpkin.
• Combine cornmeal, baking powder, salt and dry milk powder in a small bowl. Add to egg mixture, stirring to moisten.
• Pour into prepared pan. Bake at 350 degrees, for 40 minutes. Cool in pan for 15 minutes; invert onto wire rack to cool completely.

Irish Tea Bread

Yield: 1 loaf

1 cup strong brewed tea
1 cup light brown sugar, pack
2 cups golden and dark raisins (1 of each)
½ cup dried currants
1 egg, beaten
2 cups all-purpose flour
1 teaspoon baking powder

• Preheat oven to 300 degrees; grease loaf pan then layer it with wax paper.
• Combine tea, sugar, raisins, currants, and let stand overnight. In the morning stir in egg, sift the flour, and baking powder, add to batter. Mix well, turn into prepared pan. Bake 1½ hours. Turn onto a wire rack, cool, remove wax paper, and slice.

Upside-Down Pizza

Yield: 1 medium pizza

1½ lbs. ground beef or hot sausage
1 medium onion, chopped
1 (15½oz.) jar pizza sauce
½ teaspoon garlic salt
¼ teaspoon dried oregano
8 ounces mozzarella cheese, grated
2 eggs
1 cup milk
1 tablespoon canola oil
½ teaspoon salt
1 cup all-purpose flour
½ cup grated Parmesan cheese

• Grease 9x13 baking pan lightly, set aside. Preheat oven to 350 degrees.
• Brown ground beef or sausage, onion; pour off fat. Blend in pizza sauce, garlic salt and oregano.
• Pour sauce in baking pan, sprinkle with mozzarella cheese.
• Mix eggs, milk, oil, salt and flour in a small bowl, pour over meat mixture, then sprinkle with Parmesan cheese.
• Bake 30 minutes.

➤*Note:* To the above recipe you could add mushrooms, bell pepper slices just before adding the mozzarella cheese.

Tea Scones
2 C flour
2 tsp sugar
2.5 tsp. bak. powder
½ tsp salt
⅓ c milk
⅓ c shortening
2 eggs (save 1 white)
raisins (handful)

Save some egg white to coat tops. Sift dry ingred. Mix eggs & milk. Cut shortening into dry ingred. Add raisins, then eggs & milk all @ once. Roll on floured board. Mix ī fork. Cut dough into triangles. Place on greased sheet. Coat ī egg white. Bake 450° 12 min.

Whole-Wheat Pizza Crust

Yield: 2 (12-inch) round crusts

½ teaspoon honey
1 cup warm water
1 package active dry yeast
¾ cup whole wheat flour
2 cups all-purpose flour
½ teaspoon sea salt
1 tablespoon olive oil

• Add honey to warm water, stir. Add yeast and stir until yeast dissolves. Set aside.
• Place flours, salt and oil in large bowl, stir once. Pour in yeast mixture, mix ingredients until smooth, slightly sticky dough is formed in about 3 to 5 minutes.
• Place dough on lightly floured surface, knead until smooth. If dough is too sticky, add flour by the tablespoon until it reaches desired consistency.
• Place dough in large bowl, cover and let rise until double in bulk, about 50 minutes to 1 hour.
• Preheat oven to 500 degrees.
• Punch dough down, let stand 5 minutes. Knead a few minutes more on lightly floured board, then press out onto pizza pan(s).
• Top with your favorite sauce and toppings. Bake for 10-12 minutes or until edges of crust are brown and crisp.

Pizza Crust

Yield: 2 (12-inch) round crusts

½ teaspoon honey
1 cup warm water
1 package active dry yeast
2¾ cups all-purpose flour
½ teaspoon salt
1 tablespoon olive oil

• Stir honey into warm water. Add yeast, stir once, set aside.
• Mix flour with salt and oil in a large bowl.
• Add yeast mixture into flour, mix until smooth, slightly sticky dough is formed, about 3 minutes.
• Knead dough by hand on a lightly floured surface until smooth. If dough is too sticky, add flour by the tablespoon until it reaches desired consistency.
• Place dough in large bowl, cover and let rise until double in bulk, about 50 minutes to 1 hour.
• Preheat oven to 500 degrees.
• Punch dough down, let stand 5 minutes. Knead a few minutes more on lightly floured board. Press into pizza pan(s). Top with your favorite sauce and toppings.
• Bake for 10-12 minutes or until edges of crust are brown and crisp.

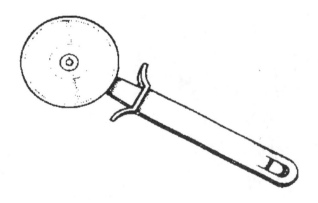

Toppings for Pizza

After your favorite red sauce goes onto pizza dough, and before the cheese, try one of the following toppings.

• Slices of pepperoni, crushed garlic, extra cheese
• Chunks of tomatoes, green and red peppers, black olives, onions, broccoli, cauliflower, carrots, extra cheese
• Chopped spinach (cooked and drained), mushrooms, onions, black olives, extra cheese
•Ham chunks, pineapple, black olives
• Tomato chunks, onions, black olives, mushrooms
• Shrimp, celery, red bell pepper, onions, black olives
• Italian ground sausage (browned and well drained), black olives, mushrooms, green pepper
 • For the anchovy lover: black olives, onions, green peppers and slices of anchovies
• Artichoke hearts, drained and quartered, mushrooms, cooked skinless chicken strips, onions
• Goat cheese, assorted fresh mushrooms, such as Portobello, Cremini, Shiitake, or Cèpes
• Eggplant, zucchini, plum tomatoes, onions
• Cheddar and Monterey Jack cheeses, chunky salsa
• Cheddar cheese, mango chutney, onions, sweet pickles
• Sausage, black olives, onions, garlic, green pepper
• Minced clams, black olives, onions, mushrooms
• Cooked spinach, feta cheese, black olives, onions
• Cooked shrimp and lobster, onions, black olives
• Green and red peppers, onions, mushrooms
• Broccoli, cauliflower, mushrooms, black olives

Corn Muffins

Yield: 12 muffins

1 cup all-purpose flour
1 cup yellow cornmeal
3 teaspoons baking powder
½ teaspoon salt
1 cup skim milk
1 large egg, lightly beaten
2 tablespoons honey
2 tablespoons unsalted butter, melted

• Preheat oven to 400 degrees; lightly grease muffin pan.
• In a large bowl, mix flour, cornmeal, baking powder and salt.
• In a small bowl, whisk together milk, egg, honey, and butter.
Add liquid mixture to dry ingredient, stir just until the dry
ingredients are moistened. Spoon batter into muffin cups.
• Bake 15-20 minutes, or until a toothpick inserted in the center
of a muffin comes out clean.
• Cool muffins in pan for 3 minutes, remove, and cool on wire
rack.

Quick Corn Fritters
1 med. can creamed corn
2 eggs
¼ tsp salt
2 Tbsp flour
2 Tbsp butter (melted)
1 Tbsp honey
Mix all. Drop by
spoon into skillet
c 1" oil. Fry
both sides.

French Roll Pizza

Serves 6-12

¾ pound sharp Cheddar cheese, grated
½ cup canola oil
1 (6oz.) can olives, chopped
4 green onions with tops, chopped
5 hot chili peppers, chopped
2 cloves garlic, pressed
½ teaspoon salt
4 to 6 French rolls, thinly sliced

• Mix all ingredients together except French rolls in medium bowl. Slice French rolls, spread mixture on.
• Place slices on a baking sheet and broil until cheese melts.

Cheese Biscuits

Serves 6

2 cups biscuit mix, (see page 407)
¼ cup shredded Cheddar cheese
½ teaspoon garlic powder, divide in half
⅔ cup milk
¼ cup melted butter, divide in half

• Combine baking mix, cheese, garlic in large bowl. Stir in milk. Drop by spoonfuls onto ungreased baking sheet. Bake 8 to 10 minutes. Brush hot biscuits with remaining butter and garlic powder.

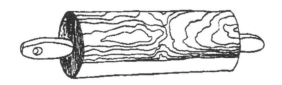

Spoon Bread

Serves 4

½ cup white cornmeal
½ cup grits
1½ cups boiling water
¼ cup unsalted butter
3 egg yolks, beaten
3 egg whites, lightly beaten
1 cup buttermilk
¼ teaspoon baking soda
⅛ teaspoon sea salt
1 tablespoon sugar
1 cup shredded Cheddar cheese

• Combine cornmeal and grits in a large bowl; stir in water,
cool. Add butter, egg yolks; mix well. Add buttermilk, baking
soda, salt and sugar; mix well.
• Fold in egg whites and cheese. Pour into greased 1½-quart
baking dish. Bake at 375 degrees for 45-50 minutes or until set
and golden brown.

Quick Gingerbread | (KISS # 1)

1½ c flour
1 tsp ginger
1 tsp baking powder
3/4 c H2O
¼ c. oil
¼ c honey
+ raisins & nuts
(optional)

Mix all in bowl.
Bake in greased
loaf pan.   375°   20 + 30"

Scotch Shortbread | (KISS # 1)

½ lb butter
½ c sugar
2½ c flour
pinch salt

Cream butter & sugar. Add rest.
Bake in ungreased pan. 350°   30"

SANDWICH IDEAS

• *Bread*: The foundation of the sandwich. Sandwiches vary in size, shape, texture and tastes. There are many types of bread to use as this foundation: French, Cuban, Italian, whole wheat, multi-grain, pita pockets, cheese, Jewish rye, Russian pumpernickel, raisin, nut, croissant, sweet , spiced and fruit breads, English muffins, bagels, sourdough, tortillas, assorted hard rolls and onion rolls.

• *Types:* Open-faced, grilled, club, triple decker, stuffed pita pockets, fajitas, tortillas.

• *Spreads:* Flavor and moisten the sandwich. Use a variety of: mayonnaise, mustards (Dijon, horseradish, dill, honey-mustard, peppercorn),honey, Russian and Thousand Island dressings, mango chutney, jellies and jams, butter blends, tartar sauce, barbecue sauce, peanut butter, yogurt sauce .

• *Toppings:* Gherkins, jalapeño peppers, sauerkraut, coleslaw, cranberry sauce, bread and butter pickles, apple and pear slices.

• *Side Dishes:* To accompany sandwiches. Three bean salad, baked beans, pretzels, tossed green salad, hot or cold soup, coleslaw, chips, hot or cold potato salad.

• *Fillings:* Ah, the heart of it all. They can be simple or complex, delicate or hearty, cooked or uncooked. Here are a few suggestions:

For Russian Pumpernickel Bread:
• Cold meat-loaf, red onion slices, sprouts.
• Corned beef or pastrami, Swiss cheese, sauerkraut.
• Chopped chicken liver, lettuce, hard boiled egg slices.
• Herring salad, tomato, sweet red onion.
• Cream cheese and capers, onion slices, sardines.
• Sliced tomatoes, chopped basil, sprouts.

For hard rolls or onion rolls:
• Cold steak slices, shredded Cheddar cheese, sprouts.
• Chicken breast, green chili strips, Jack cheese, lettuce, tomato.
• Roast lamb, mint jelly, cucumber slices, Jarlsburg cheese.
• Shrimp or crab salad, cold cooked asparagus.
• Avocado slices, raw mushrooms slices, sprouts, cheese.
• Liverwurst, cream cheese, greens.

For sourdough, Italian or French Bread:
• Thinly sliced roast beef or grilled steak slices, sweet red onion slices, greens or sprouts.
• Grilled salami and egg.
• Salami, bologna, liverwurst, tomato, pitted black olives and cream cheese
• Sausage, grilled peppers and onions.
• Thinly sliced brisket of beef, sweet red onion.
• Turkey breast, ham, cucumber, sweet red onion.
• Turkey breast, tomato, avocado slices, crisp bacon.
• Honey-ham, prosciutto, hard salami, provolone cheese, artichoke hearts.
• Sliced hard-boiled egg or egg salad, watercress, red onion, anchovy slices.

For Jewish Rye Bread:
• Thin slices smoked tongue, dill pickle, chutney, sprouts.
• Turkey breast, whole cranberry sauce slices, sprouts.
• Provolone, Muenster, Colby and Fontina cheeses.
• Bacon, lettuce, avocado and tomato slices.

For Whole Wheat Bread:
• Bacon, lettuce, tomato, dill cream cheese.
• Turkey breast, provolone cheese, sprouts, tomato.
• Sardines (deboned and mashed), cream cheese, sprouts, onion, cucumber.
• Cream cheese, chopped walnuts or sunflower seeds, seedless raisins.

For Assorted Bread:

• Cold meat-loaf, chili sauce, shredded carrots, on croissant.

• Smoked or baked ham slices, tomato, shredded cheese, on croissant or English muffin.

• Shrimp or crab meat salad, sprouts, slices of avocado on croissant rolls.

• Smoked salmon, dill cream cheese, sweet red onion, tomato, on toasted bagel.

• Chicken breast, romaine lettuce, anchovy slices, yogurt sauce, on a croissant or toasted bagel.

• Chicken or beef, quick stir-fry with green bell pepper, onions, on top of a floured tortilla and rolled becomes a fajita.

• Chunks of chicken, almonds and apple, yogurt sauce stuffed into pita pockets.

• Chicken or turkey salad, stuffed into pita pockets.

• Cottage cheese, chopped pitted olives, gherkin, onion, red peppers, sprouts, into pita pockets.

• Assorted crisp raw vegetables, (bell peppers, onions, carrots, and zucchini diced) into pita pockets.

• Sautéed chicken livers with crisp bacon, stuffed into pita pockets.

• Slices of grilled pork, shredded lettuce, black beans, diced tomato, bell pepper, green onion, stuffed into whole wheat pita pockets.

• Capicola ham, green peppers, onions, mozzarella cheese on Cuban bread.

• Cold roast pork, thinly sliced apple, sprouts, on Cuban bread.

• Peanut butter, apple or pear slices, Cheddar cheese on multi grain bread.

• Grilled cheese (at least 3 of your favorite kinds), slices of tomato on multi grain bread.

• Curried tuna salad, avocado slices, sprouts, Cheddar cheese on multi grain bread.

• Peanut butter, crisp bacon, slices of banana, honey, on nut bread.

• Sprouts, tomato, avocado slices, Cheddar and Monterey Jack cheese on fruit bread.

For assorted bread: continued,
• Chive cream cheese, slices of cucumber, sprouts, mango chutney, on raisin nut bread.
• Mashed cooked black beans, refried beans or pinto beans wrapped in whole-wheat tortillas, and dressed with cilantro, sprouts, salsa, grated cheese.
• Grated carrots, sprouts, lettuce, radish slices, tomato, on spice bread.
• Cream cheese, chopped olives, sprouts, on spice bread

Salmon Broil

Serves 4

1 (16oz.) can pink salmon
1 cup grated Cheddar cheese
½ cup mayonnaise
1 tablespoon minced onion
1 (4½oz.) can black olives, chopped
1 teaspoon mustard
paprika
4 English muffins

• Remove bone and skin from salmon and flake. Reserve liquid.
• Combine salmon and salmon liquid, cheese, mayonnaise, onion, olives and mustard.
• Spread on muffin halves. Place on baking sheet, sprinkle with paprika and broil for 7 minutes, (3 inches from heat) or until lightly browned.

➤ *Hint*: Canned chunk chicken or turkey is a quick source of chopped cooked poultry for salads, sandwich spreads and casserole dishes.

Chicken Spread

Serves 2

1 cup minced cooked chicken
2 strips bacon, crisp and crumbled
2 tablespoons diced pared apples
¼ teaspoon salt
dash of pepper
¼ cup mayonnaise

• Combine all ingredients in a small bowl.
• Serve on toast, crackers, or on a bed of lettuce.

➤*Hint*: Add the zesty taste of horseradish to a small amount of mayonnaise or mustard for an extra kick for your sandwich spread topping.

Oriental Hot Turnovers

Serves 4

½ lb. ground beef
1 envelope dried onion soup mix
½ cup diced water chestnuts
½ cup diced mushrooms
1 cup bean sprouts
2 tablespoons chopped onion
2 packages refrigerated crescent rolls

• Sauté beef lightly.
• Stir in soup mix, water chestnuts, mushrooms, bean sprouts, and onion; remove and cool mixture.
• Separate each package of rolls into 4 squares and press perforations together.
• Place ¼ of filling on each, fold over and crimp edges. Place turnovers onto baking sheet.
• Preheat oven to 375 degrees; bake 10-15 minutes or until golden brown.

Reuben Sandwich

Serves 4

8 slices rye bread
6 thin slices of cheddar, Swiss or other hard cheese
16 to 20 thin slices cooked corned beef or canned corned beef,
shredded
1 cup drained sauerkraut
⅓ cup thousand island dressing (see page169)
4 tablespoons butter

• Spread a thin layer of the dressing on each of the 8 slices of
bread. Place the cheese on 4 slices of bread.
• Top four pieces of bread with corned beef and sauerkraut.
Close the sandwiches.
• Melt ½ the butter in skillet, place two whole sandwiches and
cook on medium heat for four minutes, spread remaining butter
on sandwich top, turn sandwich to the other side and brown
another four minutes.

➢*Note*: Here's another way of making a corned beef sandwich in a
nonstick skillet, called Lazy Corned Beef. Grease skillet lightly, evenly
spread out a can of shredded corned beef, add sauerkraut, next cheese.
Cover and cook on medium heat for about 4 minutes or until cheese
begins to melt. Line up slices of bread with dressing, spoon out cooked
corned beef.

Coconut Peanut Butter Bagel

Yield: 2 halves

1 bagel, cut in half
4 tablespoons crunchy peanut butter
½ banana, sliced
2 teaspoons coconut

• Spread bagel halves with peanut butter, top with banana
slices and sprinkle with coconut.

Pumpkin Applesauce Soup

Serves 4

2 tablespoons butter
1 tablespoon Canola oil
½ cup chopped onion
1 cup finely sliced celery
1 (16oz.) can puréed pumpkin
1 cup unsweetened applesauce
4 cups chicken broth
1 teaspoon marjoram, crushed
1 teaspoon sea salt
* garnish: ½ cup sour cream, mixed with grated lemon peel

• In a large deep saucepan, sauté onion and celery in butter and oil, until the onion is translucent.
• Stir in pumpkin, applesauce, chicken broth and seasonings. Cook, covered, over low heat 15-20 minutes. Stir occasionally.
• Serve in individual bowls. *Garnish with sour cream and lemon peel.

Shrimp Bisque

Serves 6

2 (10¾oz.) can cream of shrimp soup
1 small can shrimp, mince, do not drain
1 soup can whole milk
¼ - ½ soup can dry sherry or to taste

• Combine all ingredients in a large saucepan; heat on simmer, stir often.

➢*Hint:* By refrigerating fresh homemade hot soup or stew of the day overnight, you can easily remove any excess fat that solidifies on the top.

Shrimp Curry Soup
1 sm. can shrimp
1 Tbsp flour
2 Tbsp butter
2 c milk
1 Tbsp. parsley
¼ tsp curry powder
¼ tsp onion salt
dash pepper
Make paste of ¼ c milk + flour. Combine rest in pan. Cook med. heat. Add flour paste, stir til thickened.

Sailors Rarebit
1 c tomato soup
1 tsp. worcestershire
½ lb cheese — grated.
Heat all.
Serve very hot on toast.

Butternut Squash Soup

Serves 4-6

1 large butternut squash
½ cup butter
½ cup powdered milk
salt and pepper to taste
1 teaspoon red hot pepper sauce
cooking water from squash
* garnish with chopped chives

• Peel, seed and cut squash into cubes. Place in large deep saucepan with just enough water to cover, bring to boil.
• Simmer squash until soft, then drain (reserving liquid); mash with salt, pepper and butter until smooth.
• Blend in powdered milk, until the mixture is paste-like. Add some squash water to make a cream soup consistency, add hot sauce to the soup, simmer 10 minutes.
* Garnish with chopped chives.

Easy Creamy Crab Soup

Serves 4

1 (10¾oz.) can cream of celery soup
1 soup can of milk
½lb. flaked cooked crab meat
salt and pepper to taste
*optional 1 tablespoon of sherry

• Place all ingredients except sherry in a saucepan, simmer soup until thoroughly heated. Add sherry, stir and serve.

➢*Hint:* Any leftover clear broth can be used to poach your morning egg instead of water.

Cold Broccoli Soup

Serves 6

1 large bunch fresh broccoli, cut up and cooked
½ cup liquid from cooked broccoli
1 cup chicken broth or bouillon
½ cup finely chopped onion
1 (10¾oz.) can cream of mushroom soup
3 tablespoons butter
1 cup sour cream or plain yogurt
1 teaspoon capers, drained and mashed
2 tablespoons chopped pimento

• Drain cooked broccoli saving ½ cup of cooking liquid.
• Chop cooked broccoli, place in large deep saucepan with reserved cooking liquid.
• Add broth and onion, bring to a boil, then simmer for 2 minutes.
• Add mushroom soup, butter, sour cream or yogurt, capers and pimento, stir until well blended.
• Remove from heat, chill then serve.

Easy Crab Soup

Serves 6-8

2 (10oz.) cans cream of mushroom soup
2 (10oz.) cans cream of asparagus soup
1 soup can milk
2 cups cooked crab meat
½ cup dry white wine

• Combine soups, milk and crab meat in a large deep saucepan. Stir over low to medium heat.
• Add wine and heat throughly before serving.

Cream of Corn Soup

Serves 4

3 tablespoons unsalted butter, melted
1 small onion, diced
3 tablespoons all-purpose flour
1 teaspoon sea salt
3 cups milk
dash of ground black pepper
1 (16oz.) can cream-style corn

• In a large saucepan, melt butter and simmer onions until translucent. Blend in the flour, salt, and pepper.
• Add 1 cup of milk, and stir over low heat until smooth and thick, add remainder of milk and corn. Continue to cook until heated thoroughly. Do not boil.

Hot Broccoli Soup

Serves 4-6

3 cups broccoli florets
1 medium onion, chopped
1 carrot, shredded
¼ cup butter
2 cups milk
1 (10¾oz.) can cream of chicken soup
ground black pepper and paprika to taste

• Sauté broccoli, onion and carrot in butter in large saucepan; until vegetables are fork tender.
• Stir in milk and soup. Cook just until heated through. Sprinkle with pepper and paprika. Serve immediately.

Easy Tuna Chowder

Serves 2

2 tablespoons butter
1 medium onion, chopped
1½ cups potatoes, peeled, diced
1 cup milk
1 (6½oz.) can tuna, flaked, do not drain
¼ teaspoon sea salt

• In a medium saucepan; sauté onion in butter until golden.
Add potatoes and milk, simmer until potatoes are fork tender.
• Add tuna and salt, stir and heat through.

Buttermilk Borscht

Serves 6-8

1 (14oz.) can of whole beets
1 quart buttermilk (see page 371,388)
1 small onion, chopped
2 tablespoons lemon juice
2 tablespoons tomato paste
¼ teaspoon sea salt
½ teaspoon sugar
* Garnish; with a dollop sour cream or plain yogurt, a sprinkle
of chopped chives or chopped dill.

• Place beets with their juice in hand food chopper, chop fine.
Put chopped beets and juice in a deep container that has a lid.
Add buttermilk, onion, lemon juice, tomato paste, salt and
sugar. Secure lid, shake and refrigerate until well chilled.
• Shake, before serving.
 Garnish: top each bowl of soup with a dollop of sour cream or
yogurt, sprinkle with chopped chives or dill.

King Crab Bourbon Bisque

Serves 4-6

1 (10¾oz.) can green pea soup
1 (10¾oz.) can tomato soup
1 soup can milk
1 soup can light cream or half and half
2 cups flaked cooked crab meat
½ cup Bourbon

• In a deep large saucepan combine soups and milk, stir over low to medium heat. After well blended, add crab meat and reheat.
• Slowly add in cream, continue to simmer, stir often. Add bourbon, stir once. Serve immediately.

Fruit Gazpacho

Serves 6

1 small orange, peeled, cut into sections
1 cup seedless grapes, halved
¾ cup fresh blueberries
½ cup diced pineapple
½ cup diced strawberries
1 cup apple juice
½ cup orange juice
sprinkle of ground black pepper

• In a large bowl, combine all ingredients except pepper.
• Divide into 5 servings, sprinkle with pepper.

Gazpacho Zing

Serves 2

1 large or 2 plum ripe tomatoes, cut in half
1 small onion, cut in half
1 small cucumber, peeled, cut in chunks
½ medium green pepper, cut in chunks
6 leaves fresh basil
1 teaspoon fresh parsley
2 cloves garlic, peeled
1 (11.05oz.) can V-8 juice
3 tablespoons red wine vinegar
1 tablespoon lemon juice
1 teaspoon Worcestershire sauce
dash of red hot sauce, sea salt and pepper
* Garnish with a handful croutons and chopped scallions.

• Place first seven ingredients in a hand food chopper, chop
fine (see page 9).
• Place mixture into large pitcher. Add remaining ingredients
to vegetable mixture, stir and chill thoroughly.
*Garnish with croutons and scallions at serving time.

Zucchini Corn Soup

Serves 2-4

1 (15½oz.) can corn kernels
1 large onion, diced
2 cloves garlic, chopped
4 medium tomatoes, peeled and chopped
4 cups chicken stock
4 medium zucchini, chopped
3 tablespoons fresh basil, chopped
dash of red pepper flakes, and sea salt

• Place all ingredients in a large deep saucepan and bring to a
low boil, simmer 20 minutes.

Clear Mushroom Soup

Serves 6

2 pounds mushrooms, washed and thinly sliced
3 tablespoons butter
6 cups chicken broth
4 tablespoons sherry
*Garnish with chopped parsley

• In a large deep saucepan melt butter; add mushrooms and coat well. Add broth and simmer for 25 minutes.
• Add sherry, stir and serve, garnish with parsley.

➤*Hint:* For a clearer and more flavorful broth, bring soup slowly to a boil while carefully skimming off any foam or residue that rises to the top.

Cream of Potato Soup

Serves 4

1 medium onion, diced
⅔ cup water
1 cup seasoned mashed potato
2 cups milk
¼ cup cream
1 tablespoon unsalted butter
1 chicken bouillon cube
dash of sea salt and ground black pepper
grated Parmesan cheese

• Cook onion and water in a large saucepan, until onion is tender. Remove from heat and stir in mashed potato, then put the mixture through a sieve or whirl in a hand food chopper.
• Add milk, cream, butter and bouillon cube; heat very hot but do not boil. Season with salt and pepper; serve with Parmesan cheese.

Green, Greener, Greenest

Belgian Endive	White, yellow-edged crunchy leaves with Bitter bite.
Bibb Lettuce	Small heads, pale-to-medium green tender leaves that have a sweet, subtle taste.
Boston Lettuce	A loose head with soft, pale green leaves that have a buttery flavor.
Cabbage, green *Chinese*	Pale green, crisp leaves with a bite. Very light green, crinkly leaves on an elongated head.
Chicory (curly endive)	Curly and crisp green leaves with pale center.
Escarole	Green leaves with a pale heart; the crisp, light-colored leaves are best for salads. The dark leaves are good to cook.
Frisée	The sweetest in the chicory family, with pale green to almost white curly leaves; mildly bitter.
Iceberg	Crisp, cool leaves; very mild flavor.
Arugula/Rocket	Dark greens with a peppery taste; small leaves are mildest.
Dandelion	For salads, pale young leaves are best, while the larger, darker, more pungent leaves are good cooked.

Green, Greener, Greenest, cont.;

Loose-leaf Lettuce	Young, soft red or green leaves are sweetest.
Mâche	Sweet-nutty taste; best when young. (Also know as lamb's lettuce, corn salad, field lettuce).
Mesclun	Mixture of very young tender greens; may include arugula, chervil, dandelion, mâche, nasturtium, oakleaf lettuce, and herbs.
Romaine	Long, crisp, succulent medium green or red leaves, sweet, nutty flavor.
Red Cabbage	Crisp, purple leaves.
Cress	Hot, peppery taste.
Kale	Dark red or green robust leaaves; young and small are good for salads, others can be braised.
Radicchio	Brilliant, ruby-colored leaves with a cabbagelike tender head; slightly bitter, peppery taste.
Spinach	Long, heart-shaped smooth leaves with a spicy taste.
Watercress	Tiny round, dark green, glossy leaves; spicy, peppery taste.
Yuca	The white petals of the yucca or century plant have the texture of Belgian endive but milder taste.

Spinach Salad Supreme #1

Serves 4-6

1½ pounds fresh spinach
½ pound fresh mushrooms, thinly sliced
½ cup feta cheese, crumbled
2 hard-boiled eggs, sliced
3 slices cooked crisp bacon, crumbled

• Wash spinach thoroughly; break away large stem ends. Tear large leafs in half. Let spinach drain in colander.
• Combine all ingredients into large salad bowl.
• Add creamy caper vinaigrette (see page 168, or 174) toss lightly to coat.

Spinach Salad Supreme #2

Serves 4

1 pound fresh spinach
4 slices bacon, cooked, crumble, reserve grease
¼ cup apple cider or red wine vinegar
* Optional: ¼ cup Feta cheese crumbled

• Wash spinach thoroughly; break away large stem ends. Tear large leaves in half. Let spinach drain in colander, pat dry with paper towel.
• Cook bacon until crisp, remove and save half of the bacon dripping. Place spinach in large salad bowl, top with crisp bacon bits.
• Heat up bacon dripping on medium flame. Pour vinegar slowly into skillet; bring to a boil. Pour hot mixture directly on spinach. *Add cheese, toss and serve immediately.

Spinach Shrimp Salad

Serves 4-6

½ pound fresh spinach
2 cups cooked boiled shrimp
2 cups fresh broccoli florets
1 (8oz.) can water chestnuts, drained and thinly sliced
1 cup fresh bean sprouts
3 slices bacon, cooked and crumbled

• Wash spinach thoroughly; break away large stem ends and tear spinach in bite-size pieces.
• Wash bean sprouts and broccoli, let drain and pat dry.
• Combine spinach, shrimp, broccoli, water chestnuts, bean sprouts, and bacon in a large salad bowl.
• Toss with Honey Vinaigrette (see page 168)

Tomato Onion Salad

Serves 2

3 plum tomatoes, cut in chunks
1 small red onion, thinly sliced
1 tablespoon fresh basil, cut into snips

• Combine tomatoes, basil and onion, toss with apple vinaigrette (see page 172)

➤*Hint:* Pour ⅓ cup olive oil in a square shallow dish. Sprinkle with crushed red pepper flakes. Serve with slices of French, Italian or sourdough bread slices. Serve with slices of tomato and mozzarella cheese.

Green Bean Pea Salad

Serves 4-6

1 (16oz.) can French-style green beans
1 (16oz.) can tiny peas
1 (7oz.) jar pimentos, chopped
2 ribs celery, chopped
1 medium green pepper, diced
1 cucumber, diced
1 medium red onion, thinly sliced
1 cup safflower oil
1 cup apple cider or red wine vinegar
¾ cup sugar

• Drain beans and peas; combine all ingredients in a medium bowl.
• Mix oil, vinegar and sugar; pour onto bean mixture. Toss gently.

Ginger & Green Papaya Salad

Serves 4

1 medium very green papaya, seeded, peeled and grated
2 teaspoons sea salt
1 tablespoon fresh ginger, minced
2 tablespoons cider vinegar
2 tablespoons canola oil
ground black pepper to taste

• Put grated papaya and salt in a bowl; cover with water and soak 10 minutes. Rinse and squeeze to remove salt.
• Combine remaining ingredients in a large bowl, whisk well. Add papaya, toss thoroughly; let sit 15 minutes before serving.

Spicy Cucumber Salad

Serves 2

3 tablespoons rice vinegar
2 to 3 drops hot pepper sauce
¼ teaspoon sea salt
⅛ teaspoon freshly ground black pepper
1 small cucumber

• Mix all ingredients except cucumber in a medium bowl, set aside.
• Peel the cucumber and cut in half lengthwise; remove seeds. Slice cucumber, add to vinegar mixture, mix thoroughly.

Artichoke Salad

Serves 4

1 jar (6oz.) marinated artichokes
1 small Bermuda onion, sliced thin
4 cups mixed salad greens
¼ cup black olives, chopped
grated Romano cheese, salt and ground black pepper

• Pour the marinade from artichokes in a large salad bowl; slice up artichokes and add to bowl.
• Add remaining ingredients to salad bowl, toss well.

➤ *Hint:* Salad topping mixtures: Croutons, Parmesan cheese, ripe olives; avocado, croutons, anchovies; sliced Mandarin orange, red onion, pine nuts; baby corn, chopped walnuts, golden raisins; broccoli, black olives, diced tomato.

Chutney Chicken Salad

Serves 4

2 cups diced cooked chicken breast
1 medium apple, cored and diced
1 small can pineapple chunks, drained
½ cup seedless raisins
1 rib celery, thinly sliced
2 green onions with top, thinly sliced
½ cup unsalted peanuts, crushed
⅔ cup mayonnaise (see page 196)
½ cup mango chutney (see page 185)
½ teaspoon curry powder

• In large salad bowl toss together chicken, apple, pineapple, raisins, celery, green onions and nuts.
• In a small bowl, stir together mayonnaise, chutney and curry powder.
• Add dressing to salad, toss till well coated.

➢*Note*: Serve above recipe on a bed of Boston lettuce. Garnish with one or more of the following: artichoke hearts, avocado slices, black and green stuffed olives or serve on toasted wheat bread for a sandwich.

Salmon & Potato Salad

Serves 4-6

1 (8oz.) can salmon, drained, deboned and flaked lightly
½ cup diced cucumber
1 small onion, minced
3 medium potatoes, cooked and diced
½ cup sliced stuffed olives
¼ cup sour cream
¼ cup mayonnaise
1 teaspoon cider vinegar
¼ teaspoon sea salt

• Combine all ingredients in a medium bowl, toss lightly. Chill until ready to serve on a bed of mixed salad greens.

Apple Carrot Salad

Serves 4

2 cups shredded carrots
1½ cups diced, unpeeled apples
½ cup raisins
¼ cup chopped walnuts
½ cup chopped celery
½ cup mayonnaise (see page196)
1 tablespoon lemon juice
1 tablespoon honey

• Combine first five ingredients in a large bowl; set aside.
• Blend mayonnaise, lemon juice and honey; pour mayonnaise
mixture onto carrot mixture. Toss until coated.

➤*Hint:* The seeds of fresh papaya are edible. Use them as a garnishin
sauces or salad dressing.

Jícama Orange

Serves 6

1 (11oz.) can Mandarin oranges, drained
1 medium red onion, thinly sliced
2 cups jícama, peeled and cut into julienne strips
2 cups assorted greens
1 tablespoon lime juice
1 tablespoon orange juice
1 tablespoon finely chopped cilantro
2 tablespoons olive oil
sea salt to taste

• In a large bowl, combine oranges, onion, jícama and greens.
• In a small bowl, combine remaining ingredients, blend well;
toss with salad mixture.

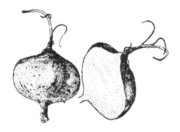

Curried Chicken Salad

Serves 2

1 cup diced cooked chicken
¼ teaspoon curry powder
½ teaspoon dried mustard powder
1 celery rib, diced
1 tablespoon fresh lemon juice
1 tablespoon non-fat yogurt or mayonnaise
½ cup seedless grapes

• Combine all ingredients in a medium bowl, blend well.
• Serve in pita pockets.

Chinese Kasha

Serves 6

3 cups cooked kasha (coarse or whole groats)
1 cup shredded Chinese (nappa) or regular cabbage
1 large carrot, shredded
½ cup cooked green peas
¼ cup diced water chestnuts
¼ cup sliced almonds
2 green onions, thinly sliced
½ cup mint dressing (see page 171)

• Prepare kasha according to package directions, using chicken broth. Cool kasha, then combine salad ingredients in a large bowl.
• Toss lightly with salad dressing.

Flaked Fish Salad

Serves 4

1 cup chopped cooked fish flakes
1 cup shredded crisp cabbage
½ cup chopped celery
2 tablespoons chopped sweet pickle
1 hard-cooked egg, mashed
2 tablespoon chopped onion
½ cup mayonnaise
dash of sea salt, ground black pepper

• Mix all ingredients in large bowl; toss lightly.

Spanish Onion Orange Salad

Serves 4

¼ cup safflower oil
3 tablespoons red wine vinegar
3 medium oranges, peeled and sliced thin
½ cup thinly sliced red onion
8 cups crisp mixed greens
¾ teaspoon sea salt
½ teaspoon coriander
⅛ teaspoon ground fresh pepper
¼ cup ripe olives, sliced
2 tablespoons toasted almonds or pine nuts for topping

• Combine all ingredients except greens in a large bowl; toss well.
• Add mixed greens, toss lightly and serve immediately.

Seafood Macaroni Salad

Serves 4-6

1 pound imitation crab meat, cut in chunks
2 lemons, squeezed
2 cups uncooked elbow or seashell macaroni
1 small unpeeled zucchini, cut lengthwise, thinly slice
Old Bay seafood seasoning to taste (see page 43)
½ cup yogurt thousand island dressing (see page 169)

• Cook macaroni to package directions; set aside.
• Combine all remaining ingredients in large bowl; add cooked macaroni, toss.

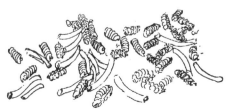

Ham & Potato Salad

Serves 6

4 medium potatoes, cooked and diced
1½ cups finely chopped celery
2 tablespoons finely chopped green pepper
½ teaspoon prepared horseradish
1½ cups cooked diced ham
¼ cup mayonnaise or salad dressing
2 hard-cooked eggs, sliced

• In a large bowl, mix potatoes, celery, green pepper, horseradish and ham.
• Fold in mayonnaise; top with eggs.

Ham & Orange Salad

Serves 6-8

2 cups cubed, cooked ham
1½ cups orange sections
1 cup chopped celery
½ cup chopped nuts
⅓ cup minced onion
½ cup mayonnaise
2 tablespoons cream
1 tablespoon apple cider vinegar
dash of ground black pepper

• Combine all ingredients; mix well.

➤*Hint:* Serve chicken or seafood salad with avocado, melon, or pineapple slices.

Salmon Chick-Pea Salad

Serves 4

3 cups canned or cooked chick-peas, drained
½ cup finely chopped onion
½ cup finely chopped celery
1 (14¾oz.) can pink salmon
1 teaspoon finely minced garlic
4 tablespoons finely chopped fresh parsley
4 tablespoons finely chopped fresh dill
3 tablespoons red wine vinegar
½ cup extra virgin olive oil
salt and black pepper to taste

• In a large bowl combine the chick-peas, onion, celery, garlic, parsley and dill.
• Add the vinegar, oil, salt, and pepper, toss lightly.
• Drain the salmon, remove bones and soft skin.
• Add salmon to vegetables mixture, toss lightly.

Pizza Tomato Salad

Serves 8-10

6 large beef tomatoes, thickly sliced
1½ ounces pepperoni, thinly sliced and diced
7 pitted black olives, sliced
½ medium green bell pepper, diced
5 small green onions with tops, thinly sliced
1 tablespoon chopped fresh basil
4 tablespoons caper vinaigrette (see page 168)
1 cup shredded mozzarella cheese

• In a shallow oven-proof pan, overlap tomatoes slightly.
• Distribute evenly pepperoni, olives, green pepper, onions and basil.
• Drizzle with dressing; top with cheese.
• Place under broiler, remove just as cheese begins to melt.

Avocado Papaya Salad

Serves 6-8

3 medium avocados, peeled and sliced
3 medium papayas, peeled and sliced
3 tablespoon lemon juice
½ cup honey poppyseed dressing (see page 173)
½ cup toasted slivered almonds
1 large head lettuce

• Place papayas, avocados in a large bowl; sprinkle with lemon juice, set aside.
• Place lettuce leaves on individual salad plates.
• Drain off lemon juice from papayas and avocados. Add dressing toss lightly.
• Spoon mixture onto lettuce; top each with almonds.

Raisin Couscous

Serves 4

2 teaspoons olive oil
½ cup chopped green onions with tops
2 large cloves garlic, minced
⅔ cup chicken broth
⅓ cup lemon juice
¾ cup couscous
½ cup raisins
¼ cup chopped fresh parsley
½ teaspoon dried oregano
¼ teaspoon sea salt

• Heat oil in medium saucepan, add onions and garlic. Sauté, stirring for 2 minutes.
• Add broth and juice, bring to a boil. Stir in remaining ingredients; remove from heat and cover.
• Let stand 5 minutes, stir once and serve.

➢*Note:* Serve as a side dish with grilled chicken or fish.

Curried Tuna Salad

Serves 2

1 (3oz) can tuna fish, drained and mashed
1 small apple, cored, peeled and diced
2 tablespoons chopped sweet onion
1 small celery rib, diced
1 teaspoon curry powder
½ teaspoon ground cumin
¼ cup jalapeño jelly

• In a medium bowl combine the tuna, apple, onion, and celery.
• Stir together in a small bowl, curry, cumin and jelly.
• Add to tuna mixture and mix well.

➢ *Note:* Can also be served on bed of lettuce or stuff in pita bread pockets.

Tabbouleh Salad

Serves 6

1½ cups boiling water
1 cups bulgur wheat (see page 28)
1 teaspoon salt
¼ cup lemon juice
1 clove garlic, pressed
¼ cup olive oil
2 tomatoes, diced
1 cup chopped fresh parsley
4 green onions with tops, chopped

• Pour boiling water over bulgur and salt, cover for 30 minutes.
• Stir in lemon juice, garlic and oil; chill slightly.
• Add remaining ingredients toss gently, serve on leaf lettuce.

➢*Hint:* Toast a handful of sesame seeds in a dry nonstick skillet for 1 or 2 minutes; sprinkle over a tossed salad.

Black Bean & Corn Salad

Serves 8

1 (16oz.) can black beans, rinsed and drained
1 (16oz.) can garbanzo beans, drained
1 (8¾oz.) can whole kernel corn
12 ripe stuffed green olives, sliced thin
1 small onion, diced
2 tablespoon capers with juice, mashed
6 black olives, slice thin
½ cup finely chopped green bell pepper
1 large plum tomato, diced
2 tablespoons extra virgin olive oil

• Place beans and corn in colander; rinse once, drain well.
• Place bean mixture into a large bowl; add remaining
ingredients, toss lightly. Let sit for 5 minutes before serving or
chill until serving time. (This salad stays fresh up to 3 days in
the refrigerator).

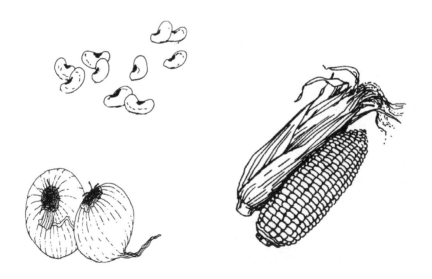

Buckwheat Feta

Serves 4-6

1 cup whole buckwheat groats
1 cup water
1⅓ cups honey vinaigrette (see page 168)
1 cup diced plum tomatoes
1 (6oz.) jar marinated artichoke hearts, drained and coarsely chopped
1 cup pitted oil-cured black olives
⅓ cup sliced green onion
⅓ cup diced, red or green sweet pepper
⅓ chopped, fresh basil
⅓ cup minced parsley
1 cup diced feta or mozzarella cheese
3 cups fresh spinach, washed thoroughly
½ cup raddichio leaves

• In two-quart saucepan, boil water and 1 cup cider vinaigrette. Stir in buckwheat groats; reduce heat, cover and simmer for 15 minutes or until liquid is absorbed.
• In a large salad bowl, toss cooled buckwheat groats with remaining ingredients.

➤ *Hint:* Make a quick salad of canned marinated artichoke hearts, tomato wedges; place on Romaine lettuce leaves. Garnish with anchovy fillets and black olives. Top with a vinaigrette.

Bean Sprout Salad

Serves 2

1 cup bean sprouts
¼ cup grated carrots
1 tablespoon minced onion
1 tablespoon soy sauce
3 tablespoons safflower oil

• In a medium bowl, combine all ingredients.

Macaroni & Cheese Salad

Serves 4

3 ounces cooked macaroni, drained and cooled
1 (12oz.) can ham, cut in strips
1 cup cheddar cheese, cubed
½ cup celery, thinly sliced
¼ cup pickle relish
½ cup mayonnaise
1 tablespoon Dijon mustard
¼ teaspoon sea salt

• Combine all ingredients in a large bowl.

Shrimp Apple Salad

Serves 6

2 cups cooked diced potatoes
2 cups chopped cooked shrimp
½ cup finely shredded carrot
¼ cup grated onion
¾ cup diced tart apples
¾ cup mayonnaise
dash of sea salt and ground black pepper
2 tablespoons Dijon mustard
1 tablespoon lemon juice

• Mix all ingredients in a large bowl, chill.

➢ *Hint:* Sliced toasted almonds; heat a small amount of oil in a nonstick skillet and sauté almonds until golden brown. Drain on paper towels and sprinkle with sea salt. Toss into a mixture of salad greens, vinaigrette dressing.

Greek Salad

Serves 4

3 tomatoes, diced
1 cucumber, peeled, cut in chunks
⅓ cup black olives, cut in half
¼ pound Feta or Gouda cheese, cut in chunks
¼ cup caper vinaigrette (see page 168)

• In a medium bowl, toss all ingredients.

Fruit Salad

Serves 4

2 large bananas, diced
1 large apple, diced
1 cup crushed pineapple
½ cup chopped pecans
½ cup miniature marshmallows
1 tablespoon mayonnaise

• Mix all ingredients well; serve on a bed of lettuce.

Pear & Kiwi Salad

Serves 4

1 tablespoon fresh lemon or lime juice
1 tablespoon sugar
2 kiwi fruits
2 ripe medium pears
3 tablespoons dried cranberries, dried cherries, or raisins

• Mix lemon juice and sugar in a small bowl.
• Peel kiwis, halve, and slice each half; add to sugar mixture.
• Core and slice pears; add to kiwis, with cranberries, cherries or raisins.

Kiwi Toby

Serves 4

2 kiwis, peeled, cut in chunks
1 large banana, peeled, sliced thin
1 medium papaya, peeled, seeded and sliced
1 cup vanilla yogurt

• Combine kiwis, banana, and papaya; toss gently with yogurt.

Carrot & Kiwi Salad

Serves 4

4 cups shredded carrots
4 teaspoons tarragon vinegar
2 teaspoons canola oil
dash of sea salt and ground black pepper
2 kiwis, peeled, cut into quarter slices

• In a medium mixing bowl, mix carrots with vinegar, oil and seasonings, toss well.
• Top with kiwi, serve.

Tomato Yogurt Dressing

Yields: 1½ cups

1 cup plain low-fat yogurt
½ cup low-sodium tomato juice
2 cloves garlic, minced
1 teaspoon red hot sauce

• Combine all ingredients into a small bowl, blend well.

➤ *Hint:* Mix a small amount of tomato-yogurt dressing; place on fish fillets. Coat with bread crumbs and sauté. (How to cook fish, page 245)

Butter Bean Salad

Yield: 6 servings

2 (15oz.) cans butter beans, rinsed and drained
2 tablespoons olive oil
⅓ cup fresh lemon juice
½ cup minced parsley
½ cup thinly sliced onions
2 large tomatoes, seeded, cored and diced
1 teaspoon ground black pepper
⅓ cup feta cheese

• Mix all ingredients, except feta cheese, in a large bowl; chill well.
• Crumble cheese onto salad just before serving.

Chicken and Pasta Salad

Yield: 10 servings

1 cup salad dressing or mayonnaise
2 tablespoons soy sauce
1 teaspoon ground ginger
¼ teaspoon red hot sauce
1 (8oz.) can sliced waterchestnuts, drained
2 cups chopped cooked chicken
1 cup snow peas, cut into chunks
1 cup chopped red bell pepper
¼ cup sliced green onions
8 ounces rotini, cooked, drained

• Combine dressing or mayonnaise, soy sauce, ginger and red hot sauce in large bowl; mix well.
• Add remaining ingredients; mix well. Chill until ready to serve.

Caper Vinaigrette

Yield: 1 ¼ cups

1 teaspoon dry mustard
½ cup white wine vinegar
3 tablespoons water
1 teaspoon capers, chopped
1 teaspoon fresh parsley, chopped
1 teaspoon pimento, chopped
1 teaspoon seasoned salt
dash of ground black pepper

• Combine all ingredients in bowl, whisk until well blended.

Honey Vinaigrette

Yield: 3½ cups

2 tablespoons plus 2 teaspoons Dijon mustard
2 tablespoons plus 2 teaspoons honey
⅓ cup balsamic vinegar
1 cup apple cider vinegar
2 cups olive oil
2 teaspoons dried oregano
1 teaspoon each: basil, thyme, black pepper, garlic powder, sea salt

• Combine mustard, honey and vinegars in a medium bowl; mix well.
• Add herbs, seasonings, and slowly add the oil in a stream while mixing.

➤ *Note:* To above recipe: substitute the 2 tablespoons mustard with 2 teaspoons curry powder for a honey curry vinaigrette dressing.

Fruit Salad Dressing

Yield: ½cup

½ cup mayonnaise
1 tablespoon peanut butter (crunchy or smooth)
1 tablespoon honey

• Combine all ingredients in a small bowl.

Yogurt Thousand Island Dressing

Yield: ¾ cup

½ cup plain nonfat yogurt
½ teaspoon Worcestershire sauce
3 tablespoons ketchup
2 tablespoons sweet pickle relish
1 teaspoon sugar
dash of hot red pepper sauce

• Combine all ingredients in bowl, blend well.

Easy Thousand Island Dressing

Yield: 1 ⅛ cups

½ cup mayonnaise
½ cup sour cream
2 tablespoons chili sauce
⅛ teaspoon salt
1 tablespoon sweet relish
ground black pepper to taste

• Blend all ingredients in medium bowl.

➢ *Note:* Pour above dressings over a mixture of greens, turkey breast strips, bean sprouts, diced tomatoes, slices of avocado.

Ranch Dressing

Yield: 1¾ cups

1 cup cottage cheese (1% fat)
⅔ cup buttermilk
2 tablespoons lemon juice
1 clove garlic
1 tablespoon onion flakes
½ teaspoon black pepper
1 teaspoon oregano
1 teaspoon thyme
4 tablespoons Parmesan cheese

• Place all ingredients in a hand food chopper with steel blade; blend until smooth.

➤ *Hint:* In a large salad bowl make a mixture of Romaine and Boston lettuce, broccoli florets, summer squash, chickpeas and black beans. Pour on your favorite dressing.

Mint Dressing

Yield: 1/4 cup

3 tablespoons olive oil
1 tablespoon lemon juice
1 tablespoon white wine vinegar
1 tablespoon chopped fresh mint
1 clove garlic, minced

• In a small bowl, whisk together all ingredients.

Tomato Soup French Dressing

Yield: 2 cups

1 can (10¾oz.) condensed tomato soup
½ cup canola oil

#1
¼ cup cider vinegar
½ teaspoon dry mustard
3 tablespoons crumbled bacon bits

#2
¼ cup fresh lemon juice
1 tablespoon onion, grated
¼ cup crumbled bleu cheese

#3
¼ cup red wine vinegar
1 tablespoon green onion, chopped
1 clove garlic, pressed

• Combine soup, oil and ingredients from one option into a large glass jar with cover. Secure lid; shake vigorously.

➢ *Note:* Make a mixture of Romaine and Boston lettuce; add broccoli florets, summer squash, chickpeas and black beans. Pour on one of the above dressing.

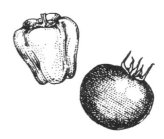

Apple Vinaigrette

Yield: 1 cup

⅔ cup apple juice
¼ cup canola oil
2 teaspoons cider vinegar
2 teaspoons fresh lemon juice
½ teaspoon dry mustard
dash of sea salt, black pepper and ground ginger

• Combine ingredients in glass jar with tight-fitting lid. Secure cover and shake vigorously.

➤ *Note:* On a mixture of mixed greens and slices of fresh fruit, pour on the above dressings.

Orange Vinaigrette

Yield: ½ cup

¼ cup fresh orange juice
2 tablespoons white wine vinegar
2 tablespoons safflower oil
1 tablespoon grated orange peel
2 teaspoons honey
2 teaspoons Dijon-style mustard
½ teaspoon ground black pepper.

• Whisk all ingredients in a small bowl until well blended. Pour on a bed of mixed salad greens.

Honey Poppyseed Dressing

Yield: 1 cup

⅓ cup rice vinegar
⅓ cup safflower oil
⅓ cup honey
1 tablespoon poppyseeds
¼ teaspoon ground black pepper

• Whisk all ingredients in small bowl until well blended.

Papaya Seed Curry Dressing

Yield: 1 ⅓ cups

½ cup peanut oil
¼ cup white wine vinegar
¼ cup fresh papaya, peel, cut in chunks (save seeds)
2 tablespoons whole papaya seeds
1 teaspoon sugar
¼ teaspoon ground ginger
¼ teaspoon whole green peppercorns
⅛ teaspoon sea salt
⅛ teaspoon curry powder

• Blend oil, vinegar in a hand food chopper.
• Add papaya and seeds; chop until seeds are flecks.
• Add remaining ingredients; twirl just 5 seconds.

Honey Poppyseed Dressing
Yield: 1 cup

⅓ cup rice vinegar
⅓ cup safflower oil
⅓ cup honey
1 tablespoon poppyseeds
¼ teaspoon ground black pepper

• Whisk all ingredients in small bowl until well blended.

Papaya Seed Curry Dressing
Yield: 1 ⅓ cups

½ cup peanut oil
¼ cup white wine vinegar
¼ cup fresh papaya, peel, cut in chunks (save seeds)
2 tablespoons whole papaya seeds
1 teaspoon sugar
¼ teaspoon ground ginger
¼ teaspoon whole green peppercorns
⅛ teaspoon sea salt
⅛ teaspoon curry powder

• Blend oil, vinegar in a hand food chopper.
• Add papaya and seeds; chop until seeds are flecks.
• Add remaining ingredients; twirl just 5 seconds.

Coleslaw Yogurt Dressing

Yield: 1¼

1 cup plain nonfat yogurt
2 hard-boiled eggs
1 teaspoon celery salt
2 tablespoons fresh lemon juice
1 teaspoon prepared mustard
¼ teaspoon sugar

• Combine all ingredients in a hand food chopper; blend until smooth.

➤*Note*: Make a mixture of grated red and green cabbage for slaw.

Bleu Cheese Dressing

Yield: 2 cups

1 cup cream-style cottage
½ cup sour cream
½ cup crumbled bleu cheese
2 tablespoons minced onion
2 tablespoons chopped pimento
2 tablespoons Worcestershire sauce
¼ teaspoon sea salt
dash of red hot pepper sauce

• Blend all ingredients in a small bowl.

Anchovy Dressing

Yield: 1½ cups

1 cup (½ pint) sour cream
4 tablespoons mayonnaise
1 can flat filets of anchovies, drained
2 tablespoons tarragon vinegar
1 tablespoon red wine vinegar
½ cup minced parsley
2 scallions with tops, chopped
⅛ teaspoon salt
dash white pepper

• Place all ingredients in a hand food chopper (see page 13)
blend until smooth.

➢ *Note*: Mixture of fresh spinach, watercress and slice red onions for
above recipe.

Banana-Nut Dressing

Yield: 1 cup

½ cup mayonnaise
1 medium banana, mashed
1 cup chopped nuts
1 tablespoon heavy cream
1 tablespoon lemon juice

• Blend all ingredients in a small bowl.

➢ *Hint:* Poppy seeds: sprinkle a generous handful over a green salad
with a vinaigrette dressing.

SPICES

SPICE IT UP! Spice foes are age, heat and humidity.

• *Shelf life strategies:* Ground spices begin to lose their aromatic strength in about 6 months. Whole dried herbs and spices can be stored for a year without losing their freshness. Whole seeds, barks and roots last even longer. Heat, light and air are the biggest enemies of dried herbs and spices. After purchasing, transfer them as soon as possible to small glass jars with airtight screw-top lids. Keep out of direct sunlight and away from heat sources. Hot spices are more prone to the effects of heat, such as cayenne, paprika, chili powder and red pepper. It is best to refrigerate them in hot weather. Some seasonings, such as poppy seeds and sesame seeds, contain oil and will become rancid if not stored properly; refrigerate them. To release the flavor of older herbs, rub them briefly in your hands or use twenty-five percent more than called for in the recipe.
To make up your own spice blends and seasoning mixes, look in starter section (see page 394-398).

• *ALLSPICE:* (spice) Nutmeg, cinnamon, and clove, with a hint of juniper berry. Whole or in powdered form. *Use:* fruit, spice cakes, pickling, cranberry sauce, applesauce, baked apples or pears, cabbage, curry dishes.

• *APPLE-PIE Spice:* (spice) *Use:* 1 to 1 ration of cinnamon and nutmeg and a pinch of allspice.

• *ANISE:* (spice) Sweet, licorice-flavored, both the seeds and leaves of the plant are used. Freshly ground anise seed is powerfully sweet, licorice-like, fruity. *Use:* breads, cakes, cookies, cordials.

• *BASIL:* (herb) Savory, best when fresh. *Use:* to make pesto sauce, on summer-ripe tomatoes, poultry, seafood, eggs, eggplant, salads.

• *BAY LEAVES:* (herb) Pungent and aromatic, complements thyme. *Use:* soups, stews, sauces, chicken, tomato juice, stuffing; add to boiling artichokes, potatoes, carrots and beets for unusual flavor.

• *BOUQUET GARNI:* Is a classic herb mixture used to flavor stews, casseroles and soups. *Make* your own by mixing equal amounts of crushed dried bay leaves, tarragon, parsley, thyme and rosemary in a glass jar for storage. *Use:* tie a tablespoon or two of the herbs in a piece of cheesecloth. Place in the pot when you begin cooking; remove before serving.

• *CARAWAY:* (spice) A spicy smell and aromatic flavor. *Use*: breads, sauerkraut, cabbage, stews, baked apples.

• *CARDAMON:* (spice) Sweet, powerful, almost peppery flavor. Both the pods and the seeds of the plant are used. Cardamom is a key ingredient in Danish pastries. *Use:* butter, cookies, cakes, curry, pickling spices.

• *CHERVIL:* (herb) Parsley-like with slight licorice and pepper flavors. *Use:* fish, butter, cream sauces, soups, salads, vege-tables, cream cheese, cottage cheese.

• *CHILI PEPPER:* (fruit) Their pungency is rated in heat units: zero to hot, to hotter, to hottest. Generally, the smaller the fruit, the hotter it is.

• *CHIVES:* (herb) Delicate onion-like flavor. *Use:* Snip them onto baked potatoes, cream and cottage cheese, dips, sauces, mix with butter to top grilled or sauté fish, roast chicken or turkey.

• *CILANTRO*; (herb) see Coriander.

• *CINNAMON:* (spice) Sweet, spicy, true stick cinnamon tastes mellow. *Use:* desserts, baked goods, puddings, savory dishes, beverages, fresh fruit.

Put 2 or 3 sticks of cinnamon in a jar, cover with sugar. Let stand for a few weeks, use this sugar in tea or coffee.

Mix 2 tablespoons of sugar and 1 teaspoon of powdered cinnamon for cinnamon sugar.

• *CLOVE:* (spice) Pungent, complements nutmeg and cinnamon. *Use:* pickling, fruit dishes, cakes, gingerbread.

• *CORIANDER/CILANTRO:* (herb) Known as Chinese parsley, pungent, distinctive flavor. *Use:* in Chinese, Mexican, Indian, Thai and South American dishes; in seviche, salsa; it also combines well with celery and avocado.

• *CUMIN:* (spice) Hot, bitter seeds essential in chili powder, along with hot peppers, garlic, paprika and oregano. *Use:* in Mexican dishes, curry, dried beans, chicken pot pie, stews, green beans, cauliflower.

• *CURRY POWDER:* (spice) A combination of ground seeds and herbs, cardamon, cayenne, chili pepper, coriander, cumin, fenugreek, ginger, and turmeric. *Use:* in meat, poultry, fish, veal, lamb, tomato dishes, vegetables, eggs.

• *DILL:* (herb) Lemony caraway flavor. *Use:* cauliflower, green beans, pea and lentil soups, eggs, poached fish, pickles, new potatoes, garnish, bread, fresh vegetables, vinegar. It's an excellent substitute for salt.

• *FENNE:* (herb) Mild licorice flavor, both leaves and seeds are used. *Use:* The same way as dill, on fish, salad dressing, spaghetti sauce, bread. Smells and tastes something like anise or licorice.

• *FINE HERB:* Combine equal parts tarragon, thyme, and parsley.

• *FIVE-SPICE POWDER:* (spice) A spice blend used in Asian cooking. *Make:* combine 4 teaspoons black peppercorns, 1 tablespoon cinnamon, 2 teaspoons fennel seeds, 2 teaspoons aniseed or 6 star anise, and ½ teaspoon cloves. Blend in blender or coffee grinder until powdery.

• *GARLIC:* (herb) Strongly scented, pungent bulb of a plant related to the onion. *Use:* GARLIC (see page 35)

• *GINGER:* (spice) Sharp aromatic. *Use:* in applesauce, baked goods, rhubarb, chutney, sweet root vegetables.

• *GARAM MASALA:* A spice blend used in Indian cooking, can substitute equal amount of curry powder.

• *MARJORAM:* (herb) Sweet, mild; similar to oregano. *Use:* in soups, stews, stuffing, sauces, green beans, root vegetables, lamb, pork, poultry, mushrooms, marinades, potatoes, and biscuits.

• *MINT:* (herb) Sweet flavor and cool aftertaste. The more peppery peppermint is the basis for an excellent herbal tea or as an accent in iced drinks or salads. Spearmint is generally preferred as a cooking mint. *Use:* on peas, carrots and potatoes. However, there are some mints with fruit flavors for use in fruit salads and desserts. Refreshing. *Use:* in yogurt, soups, cabbage, and roast lamb. Steep leaves in boiling water for tea.(or infusion)

• *MUSTARD:* (spice) Available as whole or powdered seeds or prepared mustard. Sharp. *Use:* Pickling, condiments, sauces, Chinese and Indian cookery.

• *NUTMEG:* (spice) Sweetened pungent whole or powdered. *Use:* in custards, pies, cheese dishes, quiches, hot beverages, eggnog.

• *OREGANO:* (herb) Sometimes called wild marjoram; similar, but more intense flavor, a staple of Italian cooks since the middle ages. *Use:* in all tomato dishes, zucchini, eggplant, beans, roast poultry, stuffing, veal, eggs, cheese dishes and pizza.

• *PAPRIKA:* (spice) Mild ground red pepper. *Use:* in Spanish, Moroccan and Hungarian cookery. Goulash, eggs, seafood, chicken, potato salad.

• *PARSLEY:* (herb) dried, *Use:* in stocks, soups, stews, salads. *Use:* fresh whenever possible. *Use:* as a garnish.

• *PEPPER:* (spice) Red, black, white or green, the stage of ripeness.
> **Black:** dried, immature pepper berries. Inside the dark pepper hull is a light-colored core; that's why ground black pepper is a mixture of dark and light particles. Black pepper has a penetrating, aromatic odor and a hot, pungent taste.
> **White:** The ripened pepper berry, uses only the creamy white inner core of the mature pepper berries. White pepper has a pungent flavor but lacks the bouquet of black. *Use;* on fish and in white sauces where black specks would mar the appearance.
> **Green:** Tender, immature pepper berries, are milder than black pepper and noticeably different from white. *Use:* freshly ground peppercorns are sharper and more flavorful. White pepper is mildest and used in white sauces.
> **Red:** The aroma is warm and pleasant; flavor is pungent and hot. Keep peppercorns in a dry, cool, dark place for up to a year. Ground pepper will keep about six months.

• *ROSEMARY:* (herb) Savory yet sweet, a member of the mint family. *Use:* in lamb, poultry, pork, potatoes, sauces, stews, stuffing, bland vegetables, orange sections, dumplings and biscuits. Taste is somewhat peppery, spicy.

• *SAFFRON:* (herb) Deep orange herb, made from the dried stamens of a crocus; colors food a rich yellow. Poor man's substitute is turmeric. *Use:* in rice, fish, bouillabaisse, risotto, paella.

• *SAGE:* (herb) Intense woodsy flavor, use with care. *Use:* stuffing, soups, stews, a pinch in cornbread, cheese and eggplant.

• *SAVORY:* (herb) Known as the "bean" herb. Pungent but very flavorful so use sparingly. *Use:* beans, stews, fish, poultry, pork, veal, tomatoes and salads.

• *TARRAGON:* (herb) Bittersweet, slight anise flavor and member of the sunflower family. *Use:* in Bérnaise sauce, fish, poultry, vinegar, omelets, tartar sauce.

• *THYME:* (herb) Pleasant but strong, popular in Creole dishes. *Use:* in stocks, bouquet garni, soups, stews, roast and braised dishes, stuffing, add to melted butter for shellfish, beets, carrots, mushrooms, clam chowder, creamed onions; often compared with bay leaf.

• *TURMERIC:* (Spice) Mild ginger-pepper member of ginger family *Use:* in dressings, fish, sauces and rice.

• *VANILLA:* (spice) Sweet, spicy, slightly woody with a hint of chocolate, mild, the indispensable baking spice. The fruit of a tropical Mexican orchid, vanilla is sold as a liquid extract; imitation vanilla flavoring also is available. Whole beans can be used to flavor brandy or sugar for baking. *Use:* Custard dishes, desserts, baking.

SPICE MIXTURES

These international toppings for use on your plain chicken breast, white fish, steamed vegetables, even an omelet. Use as a side dish accompaniment. Here is a list of a few favorites. Try them.

• *AIOLI:* mayonnaise. *Use:* fish, meats, vegetables, potatoes, toasted crusty bread.

• *BERBERE:* A blend of garlic, red pepper, cardamom, coriander, foenugee and much more. *Use:* in soups and stews.

• *BLATJANG:* South African preserve similar to chutney. *Use:* curry dishes.

• *CHIMICHURRI:* A parsley, garlic-based table sauce. *Use:* grilled meats.

• *CHOWCHOW:* A mustard flavored spicy vegetable relish. *Use:* side dish to poultry, pork and grilled meats.

• *CHUTNEY:* Fruit, vinegar, sugar and spices; ranging from chunky to smooth. Mild to very hot. *Use:* curry dishes, cream cheese and crackers.

• *GREMOLATA:* Grated lemon peel, garlic and parsley. *Use:* grilled poultry, veal, or pork.

• *HARISSA:* Hot red pepper sauce, garlic, cumin, coriander and caraway. *Use:* stews, sauces, couscous dishes

• *KIMCHI:* Pickled nappa cabbage. *Use:* as a side dish with poultry, fish, meat, pork.

• *MOJO CRIOLLO:* Garlic, sour orange juice with olive oil and spices. *Use:* yuca, pork marinade.

• *PEBRE:* Chilean hot pepper sauce. *Use:* grilled meat and poultry.

• *PESTO:* Thick green uncooked sauce of fresh basil, garlic, olive oil, Parmesan cheese and pine nuts. *Use:* Pasta.

• *PICALILLI:* Vegetable relish, tomatoes, peppers, onions, cucumber. *Use:* as a side dish with poultry, fish, meat and fish.

• *ROUILLE:* French garlic and red pepper sauce. *Use:* In bouillabaisse, and fish soups.

• *SAMBAL:* Extremely hot table sauce. *Use:* Side dish with rice and curry, soups, fried fish.

• *SKORDALI:* Garlic thick sauce. *Use:* Seafood and fried fish.

• *TZATZIKI:* Yogurt, cucumber and garlic. *Use:* gyros sandwiches or topping for salads

• *WASABI:* Japanese horseradish, pungent green paste. *Use:* Sushi.

Simple Corn Relish

Yield: 2 cups

1 (5½oz.) can whole kernel corn, drained
1 (2oz.) jar pimento, drained and chopped
2 green onions, sliced with tops
1 tablespoon canola oil
¼ cup sugar
⅛ teaspoon sea salt
¼ teaspoon celery seed
⅓ cup cider vinegar

• Combine corn, pimento, green onions and oil in small bowl
mix well.
• In a medium saucepan add sugar, salt, celery seed, and
vinegar. Bring to a boil, reduce heat, simmer 2 minutes.
Remove and add to corn mixture.
• Cool, place in glass jar with lid. Chill before serving.

Tomato Cucumber Indian Relish

Yield: 1 cup

1 large beef tomato, diced
1 cucumber, peeled and diced
2 tablespoons minced fresh cilantro
1½ tablespoons fresh lemon juice
1 teaspoon ground cumin
dash of cayenne pepper

• Combine all ingredients in a medium bowl, mix well.
• Cover and chill well before serving.

➢ *Hint:* Apply sauces with honey, brown sugar, molasses or tomato
during the last 10 minutes of grilling time to prevent burning and ensure
the best flavor.

Simple Mango Chutney

Yield: 2 cups

1 pound (firm) mangoes (how to cut see page 39)
⅓ cup brown sugar, packed
¼ teaspoon ground fennel
½ teaspoon ground cumin
¼ teaspoon crushed red pepper flakes
⅓ teaspoon sea salt
⅔ cup water
¼ cup black currants or golden raisins
2 teaspoons cornstarch (dissolved in 2 tbsp. water)
2 teaspoons canola oil
1 teaspoon celery seed

• Peel mangoes and cut in half. Remove pit and discard. Cut flesh into ¼-inch thick slices.
• Combine mango, sugar, fennel, cumin, pepper flakes, salt, water and currants in a large saucepan, bring to a boil. Reduce to a medium heat cook for 5 minutes. Stir in cornstarch mixture and continue cooking until chutney thickens. Add oil and celery seeds, stir until blended. Remove from heat, Cool.
• In a sterilized glass jar with lid, fill mango chutney, secure lid, refrigerate and use as needed. (If using ripe mangoes, add 1 tbsp. of lemon juice to cut the sweetness).

➤ *Hint:* Avoid the burn of chili peppers. Hold the chili in place with a grapefruit spoon, slice the chili lengthwise with a chef's knife. Holding the knife at the stem end of the chili, use the grapefruit spoon to scrape out the seeds and ribs. Otherwise use a pair of sandwich baggies as gloves to prepare the chilies.

Mango Salsa

Yield: 2 cups

2 ripe mangoes, peeled, seeded, diced (see page 40)
1 cucumber, peeled, seeded, diced
1 tablespoon chopped green chiles
2 slices minced fresh ginger-root
2 green onions, chopped, use tops
2 tablespoons of lime juice
¼ teaspoon ground black pepper
1 teaspoon brown sugar

• Combine all ingredients in a medium bowl, chill.

➤ *Hint:* Choose firm mangoes without any blemishes. Allow about 5 to
7 days for a green mango to ripen. Mangoes ripen from the seed outward
and ripen at room temperature. To prevent further ripening place in
refrigerator.

Cranberry Chutney

Yield: 1 cup

1 cup fresh cranberries, rinsed and cleaned
⅔ cup diced apple, peeled
¼ cup maple syrup
2 teaspoons chopped fresh cilantro
juice and grated zest from 1 orange

• Cook all ingredients except cilantro over moderate heat in
covered medium saucepan, until cranberries pop, about 5
minutes. Remove from heat, cool slightly, add cilantro, stir in.

➤ *Hint:* A few suggestions for *MANGOES:* top your poached fish with a
mixture of fresh mango slices and chunky salsa; slices of fresh ripe
mango with vanilla yogurt; mango milk shake.

Tomato Chutney

Yield: 1¼ cups

½ teaspoon unsalted butter
2 tablespoons minced onion
2 tablespoons minced ginger-root
¼ teaspoon chopped green chilies
1 cup chopped tomatoes
2 tablespoons honey
2 tablespoons fresh lemon juice

• Melt butter in a small nonstick skillet. Add onions, cook until soft. Add remaining ingredients, simmer for 5 minutes.
• Cool, store in airtight container, chill.

Fruity Chutney

Yield: 2 cups

8 dried apricot halves, chopped
1 small apple, peeled, diced
¼ cup dark raisins
3 tablespoons water
3 tablespoons rice vinegar
juice and zest of one medium lemon
2 tablespoons brown sugar
½ teaspoon ground cinnamon
dash of ground black pepper
2 pears, peeled, cored, diced

• Place all ingredients except pears into a medium saucepan. Cover and cook over medium heat for 10 minutes. Add pears, cover cook for 5 minutes more.
• Cool, store in airtight container, chill.

➢ *Note:* Substitute peaches for pears if you like.

Cranberry-Apple Relish

Yield: 4 cups

1 (12oz.) bag cranberries, rinsed, drained
½ cup brown sugar, packed
½ cup raisins
2 medium Granny Smith apples, peeled, cored and diced
1 cup chopped onion
¼ cup apple cider vinegar
2 teaspoons freshly grated lemon zest
⅛ teaspoon ground cinnamon
1 teaspoon celery seed
⅛ teaspoon ground cloves
½ teaspoon sea salt

• Combine all ingredients in a large saucepan, cover and cook on medium heat for 5 minutes. Reduce heat , simmer for 20 minutes or until cranberries have completely popped. Stir occasionally. Remove from heat.
• Store in air-tight container, place in the refrigerator.

➤ *Variation:* Recipe #2: 1 cup water, 1 cup sugar, 2 cups fresh cranberries, rinsed and drained, 2 tablespoons orange zest,
1 orange, seeded, finely chopped. Combine water, sugar in saucepan, bring to a boil, stirring to dissolve sugar. Add cranberries and zest, lower heat and cook on medium low, covered until berries pop, about 4-6 minutes. Stir occasionally. Remove from heat, cool, add chopped orange, chill before serving. The above versatile relish can be used for one of the following choices: serve as a side dish with poultry, meat or pork. A topping on ice cream, stuffed baked squash, assorted chunks of mixed fresh fruits.

Star Fruit Salsa

Yield: 2 cups

2 cups thinly sliced star fruit, rinsed
½ cup sliced green olives
½ cup diced sweet red pepper
2 tablespoons extra virgin olive oil
½ cup tarragon vinegar
1 cup diced red onion
1 tablespoon minced ginger-root
1 teaspoon ground black pepper
¾ teaspoon minced jalapeño chili pepper
2 tablespoon minced cilantro

• Combine all ingredients in a large bowl, cover. Chill before serving.

➤ *Hint:* Jalepeño peppers: Hot peppers may be green or red. Can be found fresh in the produce department or pickled in the specialty canned goods aisle. When handling fresh Jalepeño peppers most of the heat is in seeds and inner stems. Use care when handling jalapeños and other hot chillies. Wear plastic gloves as you prepare them, avoid touching nose and eyes.

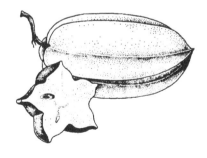

Fruit Salsa

Yield: 5 cups

½ cup finely diced jícama
½ cup diced red onion
1½ cups finely diced watermelon
½ cup diced honeydew melon
½ cup diced cantaloupe
½ cup fresh chopped cilantro
½ cup lime juice

- Combine all ingredients in a medium bowl, mix well.
- Chill before serving.

Red Beet Relish

Yield: 2 cups

2 cups cooked beets, finely diced
5 tablespoons horseradish
2 teaspoons honey
1½ teaspoons sea salt
3-4 teaspoons apple cider vinegar

- Combine beets, horseradish, honey, salt and vinegar.
- Place mixture in a airtight container, chill until ready to serve.

Garden Salsa

Yield: 2 cups

1 large ripe beef tomato, chopped
1 cup shredded zucchini
¼ cup chopped fresh cilantro
1 tablespoon vinaigrette dressing
⅛ teaspoon hot red pepper sauce

- Place all ingredients in a medium bowl, toss gently but thoroughly to mix.

➢ *Hint:* Cilantro: Chinese parsley or fresh coriander, it's a flat-leafed herb, with a distinctive taste.

Spicy Fish Sauce

Yield: ⅔ cup

½ cup quick salsa (see page 199)
2 tablespoons water
1 tablespoon prepared mustard
1½ teaspoons frozen apple-juice concentrate
1 teaspoon soy sauce
1 teaspoon chili powder
½ teaspoon cornstarch
dash of hot red sauce

• Combine all ingredients in a large saucepan, mixing well.
• Bring to a boil, stirring constantly, reduce heat, simmer until the mixture thickens. Serve hot or cold with fish.

Ham Mustard Sauce

Yield: ¾ cup

¼ cup Dijon mustard
1 (8oz.) can crushed pineapple, drained
½ cup light brown sugar, packed

• Combine all ingredients in a medium saucepan.
• Bring to a quick boil, simmer 2 minutes.
• Pour ½ cup onto ham during the last 30 minutes of baking.
• Heat remaining sauce to serve with sliced ham.

Spicy Fish Marinade

Yield: ½ cup

½ cup olive oil
1 teaspoon sea salt
⅛ teaspoon ground black pepper
2 cloves garlic, minced
1 tablespoon paprika
⅛ cup dry sherry
⅛ teaspoon thyme
2 tablespoons, onion chopped
1 teaspoon Old Bay seasoning
1⅛ teaspoons dried dillweed
2 tablespoons fresh lemon juice

• Combine all ingredients in a medium bowl. Place fish in a zip-lock bag, marinate half hour in refrigerator, turn often.

Spicy Yogurt Fish Marinade

Yield: 1 cup

2 teaspoons ground coriander seeds
1 teaspoon cumin
½ teaspoon cayenne
½ teaspoon turmeric
¼ teaspoon ground ginger
¼ teaspoon ground white pepper
1 cup plain non-fat yogurt

• Place spices in a nonstick skillet; heat for 30 seconds.
• Add heated spices to yogurt and mix well.

➤ *Hint:* ½ cup marinade for every pound of fish to be marinated. Always marinate in the refrigerator for no more than half hour. If marinating a whole fish to bake or grill, score two medium cuts about ½-inch deep on each side. Turn fish once in the marinade.

Tangy Beef Marinade
Yield: 1 cup

¾ cup safflower oil
¼ cup red wine vinegar
2 teaspoons dry minced onion
2 teaspoons celery salt
1 teaspoon red horseradish
1 teaspoon dry mustard
1 teaspoon ground black pepper
2 cloves garlic, minced

• Combine all ingredients in a glass jar with lid. Shake well.
• Place beef in a shallow dish, pour marinade over beef. Cover and marinate 2 hours.
• Baste meat with marinade during grilling.

➤ *Hint:* Marinades: Vinegar, wine or citrus juice which tenderizes; an oil to moisturize; flavorings such as garlic, mustard, herbs; and often a sweetener sugar or honey to take the edge off the acid. The length of marinating time depends on the delicacy of the food: shorter for fish, medium time for poultry, longer for beef. For maximum flavor, baste with the marinade as well.

Beef or Pork Rip Marinade
Yield: 1¾ cups

1 bottle (12oz.) dark beer
½ cup fresh lime juice
1 tablespoon lime zest
¼ cup dark brown sugar
¼ teaspoon cayenne
2 tablespoons Worcestershire sauce
2 cloves garlic, minced

• Combine all ingredients in medium shallow glass dish. This mixture will be enough marinade for 2 pounds of beef or ribs.
• Place all in a zip-lock bag, refrigerate, let marinate 2-3 hours.

Teriyaki Marinade

Yield: ¾ cup

½ cup soy sauce
¼ cup brown sugar, packed
2 tablespoons lemon juice
1 tablespoon canola oil
½ teaspoon ground ginger
2 cloves garlic, pressed

• Combine all ingredients, mix well.
• This marinade can be used on chicken, pork or beef.

Ginger Marinade for Fish

Yield: ¼ cup

4 teaspoons fresh lime juice
2 teaspoons soy sauce
2 teaspoons grated gingerroot
1 teaspoon sesame oil
¼ teaspoon sea salt
⅛ teaspoon freshly ground black pepper

• Combine the ingredients in a small bowl. Pour mixture over fish in a shallow pan, marinate in refrigerator, 1 hour.
• This amount of sauce is enough for one pound of fish.

➤ *Hint:* To remove tomato paste without any waste, cut open both ends of a full can. Remove one end's lid, carefully push the other end down through the can, forcing all the tomato paste out. This also makes it easier to dispose of the empty can.

Pasta Onion Sauce

Yield: ¾ cup

2 tablespoons olive oil
2 cups thinly sliced red onions
2 cloves garlic, pressed
2 tablespoons Dijon mustard
½ cup skim milk
sea salt and ground black pepper taste

• Combine olive oil and onions in non-stick skillet. Cook on low heat until onions are translucent.
• Add garlic, mustard and cook for 1 minute.
• Add milk and mix thoroughly, cook for 2 minutes.

➢ *Note:* For above recipe, use ½ lb. of fettuccine, cook according to package directions. Toss sauce lightly on fettuccine, sprinkle with fresh cilantro and Parmesan cheese.

Mandarin Orange Lemon Sauce

Yield: 1½ cups

2 tablespoons cornstarch
1 cup cold water
¼ cup sugar
¼ cup fresh lemon juice
⅛ teaspoon sea salt
2 teaspoons grated lemon peel
1 (6½oz.) can Mandarin oranges, drained

• Dissolve cornstarch, water and sugar in small saucepan. Stir constantly over medium-low heat until thickened. Remove from heat and blend in remaining ingredients, then oranges.
• Serve warm or refrigerate in covered glass jar.
• Can be served as a side dish with roast turkey or grilled chicken.

Crème Fraîche Nice N Easy

Yield: 1 cup

1 cup heavy cream
2-3 tablespoons buttermilk or sour cream

• Heat 1 cup heavy cream to lukewarm, pour it into a clean glass jar with tight fitting lid. Add buttermilk or sour cream, close with lid and shake well.
• Stand at room temperature until thickened, about 6 hours; refrigerate once the cream has thickened.

Basic Mayonnaise

Yield: 1¾ cups

2 tablespoons cider vinegar
2 tablespoons fresh lemon juice
1 large whole egg
¼ teaspoon dry mustard
¼ teaspoon sea salt
1¼ cups safflower, corn or vegetable oil
pinch of cayenne pepper

• Combine vinegar, lemon juice, egg and salt in hand food chopper fitted with the steel blade. Blend with two or three turns.
• Slowly add the oil in through the feed tube of the hand food chopper. Blend, until thick.

Picante Fish Sauce

Yield: 1½ cups

1 (14oz.) can stewed tomatoes, chopped
1 cup picante sauce
¼ cup olive oil
3 cloves garlic, minced
2 tablespoons red wine
1 teaspoon rosemary

• Place all ingredients in large saucepan, simmer for 15 min.

➢ *Note:* To the above recipe, add 1½ lbs. swordfish, tuna, or any firm lean fish. Cut into bite-size pieces. Cook until firm but flakes easily.

Tangy Tomato Sauce

Yield: 1¼ cups

1 cup tomato catsup
2 tablespoons red horseradish
1 teaspoon Worcestershire sauce
1 tablespoon lemon juice
⅛ teaspoon red hot sauce

• Whisk all ingredients until thoroughly blended. Serve with cold or fried shrimp.

Mango Mint Butter

Yield: 1¼ cups

½ cup plus 2 tablespoons unsalted butter, softened
8 ounces fresh mango purée
2 tablespoons fresh lime juice
2 tablespoons finely chopped fresh mint
dash of sea salt.

• In a hand food chopper, blend all ingredients. Chill.

➢ *Note*: Put a pat of mango-mint butter on grilled fish.

Marinara Sauce

Yield: 2 cups

1 tablespoon olive oil
1 small onion, chopped
3 cloves garlic, minced
1 rib celery, chopped
¼ cup chopped green bell pepper
1 (6oz.) can tomato paste, plus 2 cans water
1 (8oz.) can tomato sauce
2 tablespoons chopped fresh parsley
1 teaspoon oregano
½ teaspoon thyme
½ teaspoon basil
¼ teaspoon ground black pepper
dash of crushed red pepper flakes

• Heat olive oil slightly; stir in onion, garlic, celery and green pepper. Sauté until softened.
• Stir in remaining ingredients. Cover, simmer for 20 minutes.

White Yogurt Clam Sauce

Yield: 1½ cups

1 (10½oz.) can white clam spaghetti sauce
1 cup plain low-fat yogurt
½ cup low calorie mayonnaise
2 teaspoons prepared mustard
1 tablespoon pimento, diced
1 clove garlic, minced (more to suit taste)

• Place clam sauce in a medium saucepan. Whisk briskly remaining ingredients in a medium bowl. add to clam sauce, simmer for 10 minutes. Pour onto prepared pasta.

➢ *Note:* Prepare 1 lb. package of thin spaghetti according to package directions. Top with above sauce.

Pesto Butter

Yield: ¾ cup

½ cup fresh basil leaves
3 cloves garlic, peeled
1 tablespoon toasted pine nuts
½ cup unsalted butter, cut into small pieces
⅛ teaspoon black pepper

• Place basil leaves, garlic and pine nuts in a hand food chopper, with the steel blade. Chop fine, add butter and pepper, blend until smooth.
• Pack into a sterilized clean glass jar with lid, refrigerate. Use as needed.

Dill Sour Cream Caper Sauce

Yield: 1 cup

1 cup sour cream
¼ cup mayonnaise
3 tablespoons chopped fresh dill or 1 tablespoon dried dillweed
1 tablespoon capers, mashed

• Combine all ingredients well in a medium bowl.
• Spoon on top of steamed asparagus, broccoli or cauliflower.

➢ *Hint:* Oils: extra virgin olive oil, for salads and some sautéing; peanut, safflower, canola oil for wok (stir-fry); vegetable oil for deep-frying; Chinese sesame oil for seasoning.

Quick Salsa

Yield: ½ cup

1 large ripe beef tomato, diced
1 small onion, finely diced
2 teaspoons chopped fresh cilantro
1 tablespoon chopped jalapeño pepper

• Mix all ingredients in a small bowl.

No Sugar Barbecue Sauce

Yield: 2¼ cups

1 cup tomato purée
1 cup water
¼ cup fresh lemon juice
1 tablespoon prepared mustard
1 teaspoon celery salt
sugar substitute equal to 3 tablespoons sugar

• Place all ingredients, except sweetener, in a medium saucepan.
• Simmer for 10 minutes, remove from heat, stir in sweetener.

Chunky Tomato Sauce

Yield: 1¾ cups

2 teaspoons olive oil
1 medium onion, chopped
2 cloves garlic, minced
1 can (16oz.) crushed tomatoes, do not drain
2 tablespoons chopped fresh basil
2 tablespoons chopped fresh parsley
1 teaspoon dried oregano
½ teaspoon sea salt
¼ teaspoon ground black pepper
¼ teaspoon crushed red pepper flakes
⅛ teaspoon sugar

• Heat olive oil over medium heat, add onion, garlic and cook until onion is soft.
• Add remaining ingredients, stir, reduce heat to a simmer, cook partially covered for 30 minutes.

Thai Salad Dressing

Yield: ⅔ cup

3 tablespoons fresh lime juice
3 tablespoons water
2 tablespoons Asian fish sauce
2 tablespoons chopped fresh mint
1 tablespoon sugar
1 tablespoon light soy sauce
1 tablespoon crushed red pepper flakes

• Combine all ingredients, whisk well.

➤ *Hint:* To store fresh garlic for months. Peel cloves, place them in a small glass jar, cover with olive or safflower oil, secure cover and place in refrigerator. Use as needed. Use the flavorful oil for sautéing or in salad dressing.

Spicy Fish Marinade

Yield: ½ cup

½ cup olive oil
1 teaspoon sea salt
⅛ teaspoon ground black pepper
2 cloves garlic, minced
1 tablespoon paprika
⅛ cup dry sherry
⅛ teaspoon thyme
2 tablespoons onion, chopped
1 teaspoon Old Bay seasoning (see page 43)
1⅛ dried dillweed
2 tablespoons fresh lemon juice

• Combine all ingredients in a medium bowl. Marinate fish for 30 minutes in refrigerator, turn once.

Pimento Pepper Sauce

Yield: ½ cup

1 (7oz.) can of red pimentos, drained
2 cloves garlic, minced
1 tablespoon olive oil
dash of sea salt and ground black pepper

• Combine all ingredients in a glass jar with lid. Shake well.
• Top on grilled chicken or hamburgers.

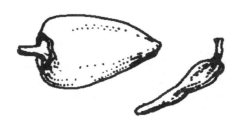

Tartar Sauce

Yield: 1 ½ cups

1 cup mayonnaise (see page 196)
1½ tablespoons tarragon vinegar
½ tablespoon fresh lemon juice
½ cup chopped gherkins
3½ tablespoons minced onion
2 tablespoons minced fresh parsley
1 teaspoon powdered mustard
dash of sea salt and ground black pepper
⅛ teaspoon cayenne pepper

• Combine all ingredients in a bowl, blend well. Chill.

Vegetable Saucery

Basic White Sauce

Ingredients	Thin	Medium	Thick
Butter	2 tablespoons	¼ cup	6 tablespoons
Flour	2 tablespoons	¼ cup	6 tablespoons
Milk	2 cups	2 cups	2 cups
Salt	1 teaspoon	1 teaspoon	1 teaspoon

Melt butter in saucepan over low heat. Stir in flour until smooth. Add milk gradually, stirring constantly. Cook over medium heat until bubbly, stirring constantly. Season with salt and pepper to taste.

• *Substitute 1 cup chicken broth for 1 cup milk if preferred.*

• *Substitute evaporated skim milk for whole milk to make low-calorie Basic White Sauce.*

Variations

Sauce	Add to basic sauce	Use with
Cheese	½ cup sharp Cheddar cheese 2 drops of Worcestershire sauce	broccoli, Brussels sprouts, cabbage, cauliflower
Curry	2 or 3 teaspoons curry powder, ⅛ tsp. ginger	asparagus, carrots, mushrooms, squash
Dill	1 to 2 teaspoons dillweed	cauliflower, green beans
Mushroom	½ cup sautéed mushrooms	broccoli, peas, spinach
Mustard	1 to 2 tbls. prepared mustard or Dijon mustard	bok choy, green beans, onions, tomatoes
Parsley	2 tbsp. chopped parsley	peas, potatoes
Tomato	¼ cup chili sauce dash of Tabasco sauce	eggplant, onions, peppers, zucchini

Corn Pudding

Serves 4-6

1 (16oz.) can white cream style corn
1 (12oz.) can evaporated milk
1 cup sugar
3 tablespoons corn starch
2 eggs
butter

• Place sugar and corn starch in 1½ quart casserole dish, mix.
• Combine eggs, corn and milk in medium bowl; pour into casserole dish. Dot with butter.
• Bake at 350 degrees for 50-60 minutes.

Potato Latkes

Yield: 24 latkes

4 medium pared potatoes or 3 cups grated/finely shredded
1 medium onion, grated
2 tablespoons matzoh meal (can use all-purpose flour)
2 eggs, beaten
1 teaspoon sea salt
¼ teaspoon ground black pepper
2 tablespoons all-purpose flour
¼ cup canola oil

• As you peel each potato place in a large bowl of cold water. Then drain, pat dry. Grate potatoes, onion in a mixing bowl. Add remaining ingredients to the potato mixture, stir well.
• Heat oil over medium-high heat in a large nonstick skillet; drop 2 tablespoons potato mixture into pan at a time; flatten with a spatula. Fry for 5 minutes, turn, repeat.
• Once browned; remove to a warm serving platter, cover with aluminum foil to keep warm, or place in a 300 degree oven while you make the rest. If more oil is needed during cooking, add a little at a time.

Sweet Potato Salad

Yield: 2 cups

½ pound uncooked sweet potatoes, peeled and grated
⅓ cup raisins
½ small apple, peeled, cored and diced
¼ cup apple juice
2 or 3 teaspoons mayonnaise
dash of sea salt and ground black pepper to taste

• In a small bowl, combine all ingredients and blend.
• Place in a airtight container, chill until serving time.

Skillet Apples & Yams

Serves 4

6 medium yams, cooked, peeled and quartered
3 Granny Smith apples, peeled, cored and quartered
⅓ cup butter
½ cup sugar
1 cup apple juice
½ teaspoon ground cinnamon
½ teaspoon ground nutmeg
½ teaspoon ground cloves

• Mix yams and apples in a large bowl.
• In a large nonstick skillet or Dutch oven, melt butter over medium heat. Stir in sugar, juice, spices and simmer for 5 minutes. Add the yam-apple mixture, cover and simmer. Stir occasionally, until apples are fork tender to touch.

➤ *Hint:* Bell sweet peppers roasted: line a rack of broiling pan with foil and place the peppers on it. Broil them close to the heat for 3-5 minutes turning on all side until charred and blistered or use the smokeless top grill, (see page 11), and turn often. Remove and place charred peppers in a brown paper bag; set in sink and let cool down. The skin will remove easily; brush away seeds, cut off ribs. Slice peppers over a bowl, stir in a small amount of olive oil, toss gently.

Yellow Squash

Serves 2-4

1 medium onion, chopped
1 medium green pepper, chopped
2 tablespoons butter, melted
1½ pounds yellow squash, cut into thin slices
1 teaspoon sea salt
⅛ teaspoon ground black pepper
1 teaspoon lemon juice

• In a nonstick skillet sauté onion, green pepper in butter until onions are translucent. Stir in remaining ingredients.
• Cover and cook over low heat 6-8 minutes or until squash is fork tender.

Glazed Orange Beets

Serves 4

¼ cup butter
½ cup orange marmalade
¼ cup orange juice
1 (16oz.) can sliced beets, drained

• Melt butter in a medium saucepan, add marmalade and orange juice. Gently stir in beets, cook 5 minutes or until thoroughly heated.

➤ *Hint:* Save the liquid from pickle jars after all the pickles are gone. Add a can of drained sliced beets to the juice along with thinly sliced onions, let sit for a day in the refrigerator for easy pickled beets. If you are not a pickled beet fan, use raw cucumber and carrot strips, green beans and cauliflower in the liquid. Refrigerate for several days for easy appetizer snack or side dish. Use liquid only once.

Apple Latkes

Yield: 24 latkes

2 eggs, well beaten
1½ cups orange juice, yogurt or milk
2 cups all-purpose flour
1 teaspoon baking powder
dash of sea salt
¼ cup sugar
3 medium apples, peeled and coarsely grated
canola oil for frying
*optional: confectioners' sugar

• In a large bowl, mix eggs, orange juice, yogurt or milk.
• In a separate bowl, combine the flour, baking powder, salt and sugar. Add dry ingredients to the egg mixture along with the grated apples.
• Heat a small amount of oil in a nonstick skillet, place 1 large tablespoon of mixture into hot oil. Cook about 3 minutes on each side or until slightly golden. Drain on paper towels, sprinkle with confectioners' sugar.

Skillet Cabbage

Serves 4

2 tablespoons butter
⅔ cup chopped onion
2 cloves garlic, minced
4 cups shredded cabbage
½ cup shredded carrots
⅛ teaspoon paprika
dash sea salt and ground black pepper
2 teaspoons soy sauce

• Heat butter in nonstick skillet, add onions, garlic, sauté briefly. Add cabbage and carrots, stir-fry for 5 minutes over medium heat. Add remaining ingredients, toss and serve.

Hot Slaw
1 sm. head cabbage, chop.
1 med onion, diced
1 Tbsp salt
3 Tbsp sugar
2 tsp mustard
3 Tbsp oil
1 egg
½ c vinegar
¼ c H2O.
Cook 1st 5 ing. in pan.
Add beaten egg, vinegar
H2O — cook 20", stir
ocas.
serve.

Bean Sprout Patties
Yield: 4 dozen

1 cup bean sprouts, chopped
¼ cup wheat germ
½ cup plain non-fat yogurt
½ cup grated Swiss cheese
1 egg, slightly beaten
2 cloves garlic, minced
½ teaspoon dried oregano
¼ teaspoon onion powder
⅛ teaspoon ground black pepper

• Combine sprouts, wheat germ, yogurt, cheese and egg in large bowl, mix well. Add remaining ingredients, mix well.
• Place by tablespoons an inch apart on a baking sheet. Bake 350 degrees for15 minutes or until lightly browned and firm.

Zucchini Fry
Serves 4

2 tablespoons olive oil
2 large zucchini, sliced into ¼-inch rounds (3 cups)
3 green onions, sliced use green portion as well
1 teaspoon dillweed
1 teaspoon sea salt
¼ teaspoon ground black pepper

• Heat oil in large nonstick skillet over medium heat.
• Add remaining ingredients, stir-fry until zucchini is fork tender, about 4-6 minutes.

➤ *Hint*: Rehydrating dried foods? Dehydrated foods such as mushrooms or chili peppers, cranberries and tomatoes. Place the dried food in a glass cup, cover with warm water. Place a size smaller cup over the dried ingredients. Fill the upper cup with water using it as a weight. This keeps the ingredients completely submerged so they rehydrate properly.

Brown Orange Carrots

Serves 2

1 ½ cups sliced carrots
½ cup water
2 tablespoons orange juice
1 teaspoon brown sugar

• Combine carrots and water in a medium saucepan. Cover and bring to a boil, cook for 8-10 minutes.
• While carrots are cooking, mix orange juice and sugar together. Drain carrots, place in bowl. Heat orange mixture until sugar melts; pour over cooked carrots, toss well.

Skillet Vidalia Onions

Serves 6

5 medium Vidalia onions, sliced
½ teaspoon sea salt
½ teaspoon ground black pepper
½ teaspoon sugar
⅓ cup unsalted butter
½ cup dry sherry
2 tablespoons grated Parmesan cheese

• In a large bowl, coat onions with salt, pepper and sugar.
• Melt butter in a nonstick skillet, add onion mixture and cook 5-7 minutes stirring occasionally. Add sherry, cook for 2 minutes.
• Sprinkle with cheese, remove from heat. Serve hot.

➢ *Hint:* Garlic oil on hand: Save a small narrow neck glass bottle with screw top. Place 4 peeled whole garlic cloves in a clean sterilized bottle. Top it off with canola oil, place top on. Next time you need some garlic oil for that salad, or stir-fry, use a little bit from the bottle. When you get down to the end, take those soaked cloves and mince fine, blend with butter and dash of paprika, to make garlic spread. Repeat beginning for a new batch.

Nut Burger

Yield: 2 burgers

½ cup ground walnuts (or walnuts and Brazil nuts)
1 cup uncooked oatmeal
2 eggs, beaten
1 tablespoon powdered milk
3 tablespoons water
1 tablespoon instant minced onions
1 teaspoon sage
½ teaspoon sea salt
2 tablespoons canola oil

• Combine all ingredients except oil, form into four patties.
• In a nonstick skillet, heat oil on medium-high, cook 5 minutes, turn over and cook for 5 minutes more.

Toby's Summer Squash Casserole

Serves 8-10

2 pounds yellow squash, sliced (6 cups)
¼ cup chopped onion
1 can condensed cream of chicken soup
1 cup sour cream
1 cup shredded carrots
1 (8oz.) package herb-seasoned stuffing mix
½ cup melted unsalted butter

• Cook squash and onion in boiling salted water 5 minutes, rinse under cold water, then drain well.
• In a large bowl, combine soup, sour cream, carrot. Fold in squash and onion mixture. Preheat oven to 350 degrees.
• Combine stuffing and butter in separate bowl. Spread ½ of stuffing mixture in bottom of 11x7x1½ baking dish. Spoon vegetable mixture next, top with stuffing. Bake for 25-30 minutes.

Chayote & Tomatoes
Serves 4-6

2 tablespoons canola oil
2 tablespoons unsalted butter
2 medium chayotes, pared and cut in ½-inch slices
1 small onion, minced
½ medium bell pepper, chopped
4 large tomatoes, each cut in 8 wedges
1 teaspoon sugar
dash of sea salt and ground black pepper to taste

• In a large nonstick skillet heat oil and butter over medium-high heat. Sauté chayote, onion, bell pepper, stir often until vegetables are fork tender.
• Add tomatoes, sugar, salt and pepper, sauté just until tomatoes are hot.

Cauliflower with Almonds
Serves 4

1 medium cauliflower, divided in florets
4 tablespoons butter
½ cup sliced almonds
2 cloves garlic, minced
¼ cup grated Parmesan cheese

• Steam cauliflower for 15 minutes, drain.
• Melt butter in nonstick skillet, sauté almonds and garlic until almonds are golden.
• Add cauliflower to almond mixture, toss, sprinkle with Parmesan cheese. Serve immediately.

➢ *Hint:* Add 1 tablespoon vinegar to water when cooking cauliflower to help it retain its white color.

Green Tomatoes

Serves 4

2 pounds green tomatoes, sliced in quarters
1 teaspoon red hot sauce
1 teaspoon soy sauce
1 teaspoon Worcestershire sauce
1 cup all-purpose flour
1 teaspoon cayenne pepper
½ teaspoon chili powder
¼ teaspoon dry mustard
¼ teaspoon ground cumin
dash each: sea salt and ground black pepper
peanut oil for frying

• In a large bowl place tomatoes and the next three ingredients, marinate for ½ hour.
• Place remaining ingredients except oil in a plastic zip lock bag. Add tomato mixture into flour mixture, zip and coat well.
• Heat a small amount of oil in nonstick skillet and fry the tomatoes on both sides until well brown and crisp.

Squash, Broccoli with Ginger Butter

Serves 2-4

4 cups broccoli florets
1 pound yellow crookneck squash, cut into 1-inch cubes
¼ cup unsalted butter
3 tablespoons chopped crystallized ginger
1 teaspoon ground ginger
dash of sea salt and ground black pepper

• Steam broccoli, squash until just tender, about 5 minutes.
• Melt butter in nonstick skillet over medium heat. Mix in chopped ginger, ground ginger. Add broccoli, squash and seasonings, coat well, heat thoroughly and serve.

Baked Turnips & Apples

Serves 6

4 cups sliced turnips, cooked
2 cups sliced raw apples
¼ cup brown sugar, packed
1 teaspoon sea salt
¼ cup unsalted butter
¼ cup bread crumbs

• Lightly grease 1½ quart casserole dish. Layer 2 cups turnips
and 1 cup sliced apples. Sprinkle with 2 tablespoons brown
sugar, ½ teaspoon sea salt, dot with 2 tablespoons butter.
Repeat layers. Preheat oven to 350 degrees.
• Cover, bake 20 minutes; uncover, sprinkle with bread
crumbs. Bake additional 10 minutes or until apples are fork
tender and crumbs lightly browned.

Quick Corn Casserole

Serves 4-6

2 (15oz.) cans yellow cream-style corn
1 (4oz.) can chopped green chilies, drained
1 cup milk
1 cup yellow cornmeal
½ teaspoon baking soda
2 cups shredded Cheddar cheese
½ onion, finely chopped
2 eggs, lightly beaten
1½ teaspoons garlic salt

• Combine corn, chilies and milk in bowl; mix well.
Stir in mixture of remaining ingredients.
• Spoon into lightly greased 11x7x1½ baking pan.
• Bake at 350 degrees for 50 minutes or until set.

➢ *Hint:* Add a sprig of fresh rosemary when you steam carrots.

Broccoli & Cheese Casserole
Serves 6

6 cups fresh broccoli divided in florets
1 (10oz.) can cream of mushroom soup
1 cup shredded Cheddar cheese
¼ cup milk
¼ cup mayonnaise
2 eggs, beaten
1 teaspoon lemon juice
dash of sea salt and ground black pepper
¾ cup cracker crumbs

• Preheat oven to 350 degrees.
• Steam broccoli until fork tender. Spread broccoli over bottom of 2-quart casserole dish.
• Mix soup, ½ cup cheese, milk, mayonnaise, eggs, lemon juice, salt and pepper in a large bowl. Pour mixture over broccoli. Top with remaining cheese, then cracker crumbs. Bake uncovered for 35-40 minutes.

Zucchini Stir-Fry

Serves 4

2 tablespoons of olive oil
2 large zucchini, sliced into ¼-inch rounds (3 cups)
3 green onions, sliced (⅓ cup)
1 tablespoon fresh dill or 1 teaspoon dried dillweed
1 teaspoon sea salt
¼ teaspoon ground black pepper

• Heat olive oil in large nonstick skillet over medium-high heat.
• Add remaining ingredients. Stir-fry until zucchini is fork tender, about 4 minutes.

➤ *Hint:* Grate raw beets into cooked couscous or quinoa.

Broccoli-Cheddar Cups

Yield: 10 cups

1 (10-count) can buttermilk biscuits
2 cups chopped broccoli, cooked, drained
5 ounces Cheddar cheese, shredded
1 large plum tomato, chopped
¼ cup chopped green onions
1½ tablespoons melted unsalted butter

• Roll each biscuit into a 4-inch circle between sheets of waxed paper. Press evenly over bottom and sides of non-stick muffin cups. Preheat oven to 400 degrees.
• Combine remaining ingredients in a bowl; mix well. Spoon into muffin cups. Fill unused muffin cups with water to keep pan from warping. Bake for 10 minutes or until golden brown.

Vegetarian Chili

Serves 4

1 pound zucchini, sliced in chunks
1 large onion, chopped
1 medium bell pepper, chopped
4 cloves garlic, minced
1 (16oz.) can garbanzo beans, do not drain
2 (16oz.) cans Mexican chili beans
1 (16oz.) kernel corn, drained
1 (4oz.) can green chilies
2 cups tomato sauce, or stewed or whole tomatoes
1 tablespoon chili powder
½ teaspoon cumin
⅛ teaspoon oregano
⅛ teaspoon allspice
dash sea salt and ground black pepper

• Place all ingredients in a large deep saucepan. Bring to a boil, then reduce heat, simmer until zucchini chunks are fork tender.

Zucchini Bake

Serves 8-10

3 cups thinly sliced zucchini
½ cup chopped onion
2 cloves garlic, minced
2 tablespoons chopped parsley
½ teaspoon sea salt
4 eggs, slightly beaten
1½ cups biscuit mix (see page 407)
½ cup grated Parmesan cheese
½ teaspoon oregano or basil
dash of ground black pepper
½ cup peanut oil

• Preheat oven to 350 degrees; grease 9x13 baking pan.
• Mix all ingredients in large bowl, pour in prepared pan.
• Bake 25 minutes or until golden brown. Cool slightly, cut
into squares.

Mixed Vegetables

Serves 4-6

1¼ cups plain yogurt
½ cucumber, chopped
1 small onion, finely diced
2 medium tomatoes, chopped
2 ribs celery, finely diced
1 small apple, cored, diced
2 boiled Irish potatoes, peeled, cut in small chunks
¼ teaspoon sea salt
¼ teaspoon ground black pepper
1 teaspoon coriander, chopped

• Beat the yogurt in a medium bowl.
• Add remaining ingredients, coat well. Chill before serving.

Plantain Patties
Yield: 2 dozen

2 ripe plantains (about 2 cups when grated)
2 cups grated, Granny Smith apples
½ cup chopped onion
2 teaspoons ground cinnamon
2 cloves garlic, minced
1 egg white
dash sea salt and ground black pepper
canola oil for frying

• Peel the plantains by making slits along the ridges of the skin, peel it off in strips. Grate the plantain and apple together into a large bowl. Add the onion, cinnamon, garlic, egg white, salt and pepper; combine well.
• Heat a small amount of oil in a nonstick skillet. Drop by tablespoon into skillet, over medium-high heat, brown one side until golden, turn and brown second side. Drain on paper towels. Use additional oil as needed for frying.

Cucumber & Papaya
Serves 2

½ cucumber, thinly sliced
½ ripe papaya, cubed
juice of 1 orange
dash of sea salt and ground black pepper to taste

• Arrange cucumber slices on individual plates. Spoon the papaya cubes on top. Sprinkle with orange juice, season with salt and pepper.

➤ *Hint:* Crisp topping substitute when you have no lettuce: bean sprouts, diced water chestnuts, chopped radishes will do.

Turnip au Gratin

Serves 4

3 tablespoon unsalted butter
2 garlic cloves, minced
1½ pounds turnips, scrubbed and thinly sliced
⅓ cup chopped fresh dill
¼ cup grated Gruyere cheese
½ cup heavy cream
½ cup bread crumbs
dash of sea salt and ground black pepper

• Preheat oven to 400 degrees; grease 12x8 shallow baking
dish with 1 tablespoon of butter. Spread garlic on bottom of
pan.
• Make a layer of turnip slices, season with salt and pepper,
sprinkle with a third of the dill. Make two more layers, top
with cheese, pour cream over all, sprinkle with bread crumbs.
Dot with remaining butter.
• Bake 30-45 minutes or until turnips are fork tender and top is
golden.

Carrots & Leeks

Serves 4-6

10-12 carrots, peeled, thinly sliced
4 leeks, wash well, thinly sliced
¼ cup unsalted butter, melted
2 tablespoons cold water
2 teaspoons sugar
1 teaspoon sea salt
½ teaspoon ground black pepper

• In a medium saucepan, melt butter, add water, sugar, salt,
pepper, carrots, and leek.
• Cover and cook over medium heat; stir occasionally for about
20 minutes. Remove from heat and serve immediately.

Jamie Jícama

Serves 4

1 lb. boneless, skinless chicken breasts, cut into 1-inch cubes
2 tablespoons olive oil
juice 1 lime
1 teaspoon cayenne pepper
dash of sea salt and ground black pepper
1 medium onion, diced fine
2 ribs celery, diced fine
1 jícama (about ¼lb.), peeled, diced fine
4 large dates, pitted and chopped
¼ cup pecans or walnuts, chopped
¼ cup chopped fresh cilantro
½ cup mayonnaise

• Place the cubed chicken in a large bowl, toss with the next four ingredients. Spoon mixture into a 9x13 baking pan
• Preheat oven to 375 degrees; bake for 20-25 minutes. Remove from oven and place chicken in refrigerator to cool, then add remaining ingredients, toss well and serve.
• (You can prepare half of the recipe in the morning, toss and serve for lunch or dinner later in the day).

Carrot Orang-ee

Serves 4

2½ cups cut-up cooked carrots
2 tablespoons unsalted butter
2 tablespoons sugar
¼ teaspoon grated orange rind
½ a medium orange, peeled and thinly sliced

• Place all ingredients except slices of oranges into a nonstick skillet. Simmer, stir often until thoroughly heated.
• Remove, add slices of oranges, mix gently. Pour into a medium bowl and serve.

Mushroom-Wheat Pilaf

Yield: 4 servings

½ cup unsalted butter
1 small onion, diced
½ pound fresh mushrooms, sliced
1 cup bulgur
1¼ cups chicken broth
sea salt to taste
* optional:1 cup chopped cooked chicken or turkey

• Melt butter in a medium saucepan, add onion and
mushrooms, simmer until golden brown.
• Add bulgur and broth, cover and simmer until bulgur is
tender and broth is absorbed. Stir often. Add salt and choice of
poultry. Mix well, serve hot.

Baked Onions with Cheese

Serves 4-6

1½ pounds onions, thinly sliced
3 tablespoons unsalted butter
½ cup milk
4 ounces sharp cheese, shredded
Paprika to taste
½ cup bread crumbs

• Preheat oven to 375 degrees; lightly grease 2-quart casserole
dish.
• Sauté onions with butter in a nonstick skillet until translucent.
Add milk, cheese and paprika, stir until cheese is melted.
Pour into casserole dish. Sprinkle with bread crumbs.
• Bake, uncovered for 30 minutes.

BEYOND BASIC BURGERS, BE BOLD!

Add one of the International choice ingredients below to 1½ lbs. of ground beef and combine ingredients, shape six ¼-inch thick patties or as indicated at the recipe itself; pan-fry, grill or broil. One of these lip-smaking versions will be a favorite soon.

• *Cajun:* see Cajun seasoning mix, (see page 395)

• *Oriental:* ¼ tsp. onion powder, ¼ tsp. ground ginger, ¼ cup chopped water chestnuts for a crunchy burger.

• *French:* 1½ tsp. onion powder, 1 tsp. dried crushed thyme, ½ tsp. garlic powder, ¼ tsp. salt, ¼ tsp. pepper, 2oz. of Brie or Camembert cheese cut into cubes.

• *Greek:* 1½ tsp. of onion powder, 1 tsp. of dried crushed oregano, ½ tsp. garlic powder, ¼ tsp. garlic powder, ¼ tsp. pepper, 2oz. crumbled Feta cheese, 1 tbsp. lemon juice.

• *Greek:* use **1lb ground Lamb:** 1tbsp. Dijon mustard, 1 tbsp. lemon juice, 1 tbsp. minced onion, 1 garlic clove, minced, ½ tsp. dried rosemary, crushed, ½ tsp. sea salt, ¼ tspn. ground black pepper. Combine the first eight ingredients, mix well. Shape and cook, top with diced cucumber, tomatoes and ranch dressing. *Yield: 4 hamburgers*

• *Italian:* 1¼ tsp. Italian seasoning, ¾ tsp. garlic powder, ½ tsp. onion powder, ¼ tsp. salt, 2oz. of mozzarella cheese cut into small chunks.

• *Italian saucy pizza:* use **1lb. ground beef,** ½ tsp. garlic salt, 1 cup shredded mozzarella cheese, 1 (8oz.) can pizza sauce, 1 (4oz.) can mushroom stems and pieces, drained, ½ tsp. dried oregano, 1 medium onion, chopped. Combine beef and garlic salt. Shape into eight patties; top four of the patties with cheese. Cover with remaining patties; press edges to seal, refrigerate. In a medium saucepan, combine pizza sauce, mushrooms and oregano, cover and simmer for 10 minutes, stir occasionally. In a nonstick skillet, sauté onion in butter until translucent, remove and set aside. Cook hamburgers, spread firm bun with a little of the sauce, top with burgers, onion and remaining sauce. *Yield: 4 hamburgers*

• *Hefty:* **2 lbs. ground beef,** ¼ cup finely chopped onion, 2 eggs, slightly beaten, 2 tsp. Worcestershire sauce, 1 tsp. sea salt, ¼ tsp. black pepper, 1½ cups (6oz.) shredded Cheddar cheese, 3 tbsp. mayonnaise, 4 tsp. prepared mustard, 4 tsp. dill pickle relish, shredded lettuce, red onion slices, tomato slices. Combine the first six ingredients, mix well. Shape into 12 thin patties. Broil or grill ¾ of the way. In a small bowl, combine cheese, mayonnaise, mustard and relish, mix well. Spoon 2 tbsp. on each cooked burger, return to the grill or broiler and cook just until cheese softens. Remove and top with lettuce and onion on bottom of buns; top each with two burgers, tomato and top with bun. *Yield: 6 hamburgers*

• *Mexican:* 1 tbsp. of chili powder, ½ tsp. ground cumin, ½ tsp. onion powder, ¼ tsp. salt, 2oz. Monterey Jack cheese cut into cubes.
  OR
• *Mexican:* **2lbs. ground beef,** 2 eggs, beaten, 2 (4oz.) cans chopped green chilies, ¼ cup finely minced onion, ⅓ cup salsa, 1 tsp. sea salt, ½ tsp. black pepper, 1 clove garlic, minced, ¾ cup finely crushed corn chips. Combine all ingredients except chips and beef, then add chips and beef; mix well. Shape and cook, wrap burgers in tortillas, with your choice of toppings, and munch away. *Yield: 8 hamburgers*
OR
• *Mexican:* 1 (4oz.) can green chilies, chopped and 2 tbsp. taco seasoning, 1 clove garlic, minced, ¼ cup finely minced onion.

• *No-salt seasoning mix:* (see page 394 or 395)

• *Zippy:* **1lb. ground beef or turkey,** 4 tsp. prepared horseradish, 2 tsp. Dijon mustard, 1 tsp. Hungarian paprika, ¼ tsp. black pepper, ⅛ tsp. sea salt. Combine the first six ingredients; mix well. Shape and cook. *Yield: 4 hamburgers*

• *Toppings* for any burger: shredded lettuce, thinly sliced red onion, chopped jalapeños, chutney, sauté mushrooms, salsa, slices of red onion and cucumber.

• *Breads:* whole wheat buns, hard Kaiser roll or your favorite firm bun.

Frankfurter Casserole
2 1lb cans baked beans
1 envelope onion soup
⅓ C. ketchup
¼ C. water
2 Tbsp brown sugar
1 Tbsp prepared mustard
2 tsp sweet relish
6 franks, sliced

Mix all in casserole.
Bake 350° 20-30 min.

Indian Meatloaf

Serves 6-8

1½ pounds ground beef
1 egg, slightly beaten
½ cup corn meal
2 teaspoons sea salt
¼ teaspoon ground black pepper
½ teaspoon sage
¼ cup chopped onions
¼ cup chopped green pepper
½ cup cream style corn
1½ cups chopped tomatoes

• Combine all ingredients in a large bowl, blend well.
• Pack in a 5x9 loaf pan. Bake at 350 degrees, for 1½ hrs.

Corned Beef Casserole
6 oz macaroni (or) 8 oz noodle
¼ lb American or cheddar (1C)
1 C milk
½ C onion, chopped
12 oz can corned beef, cut up
1 can cream chicken soup
buttered crumbs (3/4 - 1C)
parsley; sliced olives.
Cook macaroni. Drain.
Combine rest ingred - except
crumbs. Alternate macaroni
& meat layers in 2 qt.
casserole. Top c crumbs.
Bake 375° 1 hour.

Beefy Stew

Serves 2-4

1 can corned beef, break up
2 large onions, thinly sliced
4 slices bacon, diced
3 cups shredded cabbage
1 cup Irish potatoes, diced
1 cup thinly sliced carrots
dash of sea salt, black pepper, cayenne pepper
1 bay leaf
1 cup beef bouillon

Quick Corned Beef Cass.
1 can corned beef
½ C bread crumbs or wheat germ
1 pkg. dry onion soup
2 C cooked white rice
1 sm. can tomato sauce
1 C cheddar, shredded.
Combine all x cheese in
lg. bowl. Pour in greased
baking dish. Bake
350° 15-20". Add
cheese. Bake til melts.

• Sauté onions and bacon in a deep Dutch oven. Add remaining ingredients and cook on low heat for 25-35 minutes.

➤ *Hint:* Marinate meats in a re-sealable plastic bag. Eliminates splashes when turning the meat.

Island Pork

Serves 2

1 (12oz.) pork tenderloin
¼ cup white rum
3 cloves garlic, minced
2 green onions, chopped
¼ cup chopped green pepper
½ teaspoon oregano
½ teaspoon sea salt
⅛ teaspoon ground black pepper
½ cup chopped fresh cilantro
3 tablespoons olive oil

Corned Beef Stir Fry

1 tin corned beef
1 tin corn (med.)
1 tin sliced potatos (med)
1 red onion, sliced
1 green pepper, sliced
dash salt, pepper.
In slightly oiled pan, fry
onion & green pepper. Add
rest — break up beef.
Stir fry.

• Preheat oven to 400 degrees. Remove as much fat as possible from pork. With a paring knife make a few slits all over the pork, place in a small roasting pan.
• Mix all remaining ingredients in a medium bowl, place pork in bowl and marinate for 10 minutes. Remove pork from marinade, place in small roasting pan. Bake 20-25 minutes, basting often.

Stormy Beef Casserole

Serves 2

2 large onions, sliced
2 tablespoons peanut oil
1 (160z.) can roast beef, with gravy
2 cups prepared instant mashed potatoes
1 cup shredded Cheddar cheese

• Sauté onions with oil in a nonstick skillet until translucent. Place in 1½ quart casserole dish. Add roast beef with gravy.
• Spoon mashed potatoes over roast beef. Bake at 350 degrees for 30 minutes; remove from oven, sprinkle cheese over top. Return to oven and bake for 5 minutes longer or until cheese melts.

➤ *Hint:* Stretch leftover stew further: place in a casserole dish, top with refrigerator biscuits, bake until the biscuits are golden brown.

Pork Peachy Fajitas

Yield: 12 Fajitas

1½ lbs. boneless pork loin, cut into thin strips
1 teaspoon sea salt
¼ teaspoon ground black pepper
6 teaspoons peanut oil, divided
2 large green peppers, cut into thin strips
2 cups sliced yellow onions
1 cup chunky, mild salsa
¼ cup peach preserve
¼ cup sliced green onions
¼ cup chopped cilantro
12 flour tortillas (7-inch)
⅔ cup sour cream or plain yogurt

• Toss pork with salt and pepper in a medium bowl. Heat 2 teaspoons oil in nonstick skillet over high heat. Add half of pork, cook stirring often until brown. Remove with slotted spoon, repeat with 2 more teaspoons oil and remaining pork. Remove pork from skillet.
• Over medium heat add remaining oil; cook peppers and yellow onions, until translucent. Return pork to skillet, stir in salsa and preserve, heat thoroughly. Stir in green onions and cilantro, mix well, remove from heat.
• Fill each tortilla with ½ cup pork mixture. Top with a spoonful of sour cream or yogurt.

➤ *Hint:* Bake meat-loaf in greased muffin cups for a quick way to serve a crowd. The meat will cook more quickly and will be in handy single serving portions.

Hamburger Casserole
1 lb. hamburger
1 onion, diced
1 gr. pepper, chopped
1 clove garlic, minced
with thyme, oregano, basil
Boz can tomato sauce

1 (50z) can white beans
1 lb. kielbasa, sliced thin.
Brown hamburger, onion, gr pepper, spices.
Add rest. Simmer 20." Serve z hard rolls.

Dijon Pork Chops

Yield: 2 chops

3 tablespoons dry bread crumbs
1 tablespoon grated Parmesan cheese
1 tablespoon chopped fresh parsley
⅛ teaspoon ground black pepper
1 teaspoon vegetable oil
2 (5-ounce) pork chops
2 teaspoons Dijon mustard

• Combine the first five ingredients in a medium bowl. Spread pork chops on both side with mustard.
• Press crumb mixture over chops to coat.
• Place chops on a smokeless grill, (see page 16).
• Grill for 5-6 minutes on each side.

Easy Stuffed Peppers

Serves 2

3 green peppers
½ pound ground beef
1 cup instant rice
1 can tomato sauce or soup

• Core peppers, place in Dutch oven pot; fill pot half full with water, heat to boiling to soften peppers. Remove, drain, set aside.
• Brown ground beef in a nonstick skillet; prepare rice. Mix rice and meat well, stuff peppers. In Dutch oven place stuffed pepper, tomato sauce or soup, simmer for 10 minutes or until heated thoroughly.

➢ *Hint:* Top casseroles with corn bread, mashed potatoes, toasted wheat germ, potato chips or pretzel crumbs, dry stuffing mix, pastry cutout, French-fried onions, chow mein noodles, sesame seeds, toasted nuts, crumbled bacon, bacon bits, pepperoni slices.

How to cut up a whole chicken!
Use a sharp chef's knife, work on a cutting board.

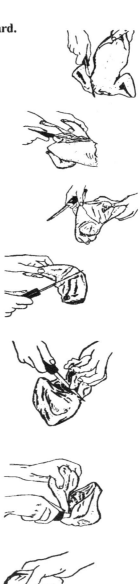

1. With breast side down, grasp chicken by legs. Using a chef's knife, remove wing by cutting close to body of chicken through joint attaching wing to breast. Remove second wing.

2. With legs toward you, place chicken on back, grasping one leg, cut skin between thigh and body to thigh joint.

3. Lifting chicken, bend leg back until thigh joint "pops". Cut around thigh joint to remove leg. Repeat second side.

4. Separate thigh from drumstick by cutting through joint, following the yellow line of fat.

5. To separate breast and back, set bird on neck end. Holding tail section, cut diagonally along rib cage to back bone.

6. Keeping knife very close to bone, cut along backbone through neck end. (Apply extra pressure as you cut through bones.) Repeat on opposite side to completely loosen back section.

7. Whole breast is ready to use as is or may be split. To split, place breast skin side down. Make a cut through "V" of wishbone. Bend breast back until keel bone "pops." Run thumb between meat and keel bone to loosen tissue. Pull bone from breast.

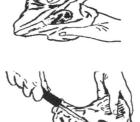

8. Split breast down the center. Halves may be boned if desired.

Broiler	1½ - 2½ lbs.	All-purpose, with emphasis on broiling
Fryer	2-3 lbs.	All-purpose with emphasis on frying
Roaster	3-5 lbs.	Roast, bake, fry
Capon	4-7 lbs.	Sauté, fricassée
Stewing	Over 3 lbs.	Stew, fricassée

½ breast = 1 serving

Thigh with attached leg = 1 serving

3 lb. chicken = 4 servings or approximately 2½ cups diced cooked meat

Boning A Chicken Breast

1. Holding breast half in both hands, bend and break keel bone.

2. Run thumb between meat and keel bone, removing the bone and strip of cartilage.

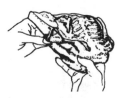

3. Using both thumbs, loosen meat from rib cage.

4. Sliding your thumb between breast meat and bone will enable the meat to pull off.

International Chicken Your Choice!

Basic Basted Chicken

2-2½ lbs. frying chicken, cut up
1 medium onion, chopped
1 cup fat-skimmed chicken broth
¼ teaspoon ground black pepper
½ teaspoon sea salt

• Preheat oven to 450 degrees. Wash and pat dry chicken, trim fat. Arrange the pieces, skin side up, in a shallow oven-proof roasting pan or heavy iron skillet.
• Bake for 20-25 minutes or until skin is crisp and well rendered of fat. Drain, discard fat, add remaining ingredients to pan. Lower oven to 350 degrees; continue baking, basting occasionally until fork can be inserted in chicken with ease, or when juices run clear, 25-30 minutes. Spoon pan juice over chicken. Serves 4

• **Try** *one of the* **International Chickens** *below to modify the above basic recipe.*

• *African Chicken:* Replace part of the chicken broth with 2 tbsp. lemon juice. Add ⅛ tsp. turmeric, a bay leaf, 2 cloves garlic, minced.

• *Chinese Chicken:* Replace part of the broth with ¼ cup sherry and 2 tbsp. light soy sauce. Add ⅛ tsp. garlic powder and powdered ginger.

• *Cuban Chicken:* Replace part of the broth with ¼ cup rum. Sprinkle lightly with garlic powder, paprika, bay leaf and a pinch of saffron.

• *Czechoslovakian Chicken:* Replace part of the broth with ½ cup V-8 juice and 2 tbsp. red or white wine. Season chicken lightly with garlic salt, paprika and a pinch of coriander seeds.

(International Chickens continued next page)

hicken: Replace part of the broth with ¼ cup dry white ⌐ chicken with a pinch of nutmeg, a dash of mixed ⌐ning. After browning the chicken, place two carrots ⌐ in chunks and ½ cup sliced mushrooms under the chicken in the pan.

• *German Chicken:* Replace part of the broth with ½ cup light beer. Season chicken with garlic powder, a bay leaf and ½ tsp. caraway seeds.

• *Greek Chicken:* Replace the broth with ¾ cup tomato juice and 2 tbsp. lemon juice. Season with bay leaf, a sprinkle of oregano, garlic powder, cinnamon and nutmeg.

• *Hungarian Chicken:* Reduce broth to ½ cup. Season chicken liberally with Hungarian paprika, garlic salt, dill weed. Just before serving, combine ½ cup plain low-fat yogurt with 1 tbsp. flour, add to pan juices and heat until bubbling. Serve over roasted chicken.

• *Indian Chicken:* Replace half of the broth with ½ cup orange or pineapple juice. Sprinkle chicken lightly with curry powder, cinnamon and garlic salt, add 2 tbsp. golden raisins.

• *Italian Chicken:* Replace broth with 1 cup tomato or V-8 juice, 2 tbsp. red wine. Add one green bell pepper, diced. Season with oregano, basil, garlic salt. Sprinkle with 2 tbsp. shredded extra-sharp Romano cheese just before serving.

• *Mexican Chicken:* Follow Italian directions, in addition add a pinch of chili powder, a few cumin seeds. *Use:* shredded Cheddar cheese instead of Romano.

• *Spanish Chicken:* Follow Italian directions, substitute ¼ cup orange juice for wine, add bay leaf instead of basil, add 4 stuffed green Spanish olives slices. Omit cheese.

• *South Seas Chicken:* Substitute ½ cup pineapple juice and 2 tbsp. soy sauce for part of the liquid. Season chicken with garlic salt and ground ginger. After browning the chicken, add one green bell pepper diced, ½ cup diced pineapple, ½ cup thinly sliced carrots.

Cranberry Stuffing
Yield: Enough for 1, 6 pound bird

1½ cups whole fresh cranberries
¼ cup granulated sugar
¼ cup melted butter
4 cups toasted bread cubes
¾ cup golden raisins
¾ teaspoon sea salt
⅛ teaspoon ground cinnamon
2 teaspoons lemon juice
¼ cup chicken stock

• In a hand food chopper, chop the cranberries. Add berries and remaining ingredients to a large bowl, mix lightly. Stuff bird.

Pickle-Fruit Stuffing
Yield: Enough for 1, 4 pound bird

2½ cups soft bread crumbs
1 egg, lightly beaten
¼ cup melted butter
¼ cup sweet pickle juice
¼ cup chopped sweet mixed pickles
½ cup chopped dried apricots
¼ cup raisins
¼ cup chopped walnuts

• Combine all ingredients lightly in a large bowl. Stuff bird.

Oyster Stuffing
Yield: Enough for 1, 6 pound bird

7 cups white bread crumbs, packed loosely
¼ teaspoon ground black pepper
½ teaspoon sea salt
½ teaswpoon poultry seasoning
¼ cup butter
½ cup finely chopped celery
1 small onion, finely chopped
¾ cup drained, chopped oysters

• Combine bread crumbs and seasonings in a large bowl, set aside.
• Melt butter in a nonstick skillet, sauté celery and onion lightly, stir in oysters.
• Remove from heat, pour mixture over bread crumbs. Toss lightly, stuff bird.

Chestnut-Sausage Stuffing
Yield: Enough for 1, 6 pound bird

1 cup soft bread cubes
1 pound chestnuts
1 pound bulk pork sausage, cooked, drained.
1 teaspoon ground black pepper
½ teaspoon sea salt
1 small onion, finely chopped
1 tablespoon chopped fresh parsley
1 egg, lightly beaten

• Score each chestnut with an X and drop into a saucepan of boiling water for 10 minutes. Drain, peel, cut in small chunks, combine chestnuts with remaining ingredients, stuff bird.

Chicken Chutney

Serves 2

2 cups diced cooked chicken
1 (13oz.) can pineapple tidbits, drained
1 cup thinly sliced celery
½ cup sliced green onions
¼ cup salted peanuts
⅔ cup mayonnaise
2 tablespoons chopped chutney
½ teaspoon grated lemon rind
2 tablespoons lemon juice
½ teaspoon curry powder
¼ teaspoon sea salt
*Garnish with one or more of the following: deviled eggs, artichoke hearts, tomato-avocado slices, black-green olives.

• In a large bowl toss together chicken, pineapple, celery, green onions, and peanuts, set aside.
• In a small bowl combine mayonnaise with remaining ingredients, stir lightly into chicken mixture. Chill. At serving time, place on bed of lettuce. *Garnish, as above.

Chicken Mexican Casserole

Yield: 12 servings

6 large chicken breasts, cooked, cut into cubes
1 large green bell pepper, chopped
1 large onion, chopped
2 (10oz.) cans chopped green chilies
2 cups milk
1 (10oz.) can cream of mushroom soup
1½ pounds sharp Cheddar cheese, shredded
1 (10oz.) can cream of chicken soup
1 (16oz.) package nacho-flavored tortilla chips, crushed

• Sauté green pepper, onion, butter, in a nonstick skillet.
• Heat tomatoes, milk, and soups in a large saucepan, stirring to mix well. Layer chips, chicken, soup mixture, sautéed mixture and cheese, half at a time into a 9x13 baking dish. Bake at 400 degrees for 20-25 minutes or until bubbly and light brown.

Cold Overnight Chicken Cabbage
Serves 4

1½ cups cooked chicken or turkey, diced
1 medium cabbage, chopped
4-5 green onions, sliced
1 package Ramen chicken soup and packet, uncooked
¾ cup canola oil
⅓ cup rice vinegar
2 tablespoon sesame seed
few dashes of Italian blend seasoning, (see page 398)
dash of ground black pepper
*optional: 1 teaspoon sugar

• In a large bowl mix oil, vinegar, seasoning packet from soup, sugar if desired, add remaining seasoning till dissolved.
• Break up uncooked noodles, add to oil mixture, add all other ingredients, toss lightly. Must sit overnight in refrigerator.

Apricot Chicken
Serves 2-4

1 (16oz.) can apricots, drained
1 package dry onion soup mix
½ cup slivered almonds
2-2 ½ pound fryer cut-up in large pieces
* garnish: with pineapple slices

• Mix soup mix, drained apricots and almonds in a bowl.
• Place chicken in roasting pan, pour apricot mixture on top.
• Bake at 375 degrees for 40-45 minutes, or until juices run clear when chicken is pierced with a fork.
• Garnish with slices of pineapple. Serve with cooked rice, couscous, or kasha.

➤ *Note:* No whole apricots; use 1 baby jar food of strained apricots.

Chicken Anchovy Wave

Serves 6

1 tablespoon olive oil
6 boneless, skinless, chicken breast halves
½ teaspoon sea salt
dash ground black pepper
1 cup chopped onion
4 cloves garlic, minced
6 flat anchovy fillets, chopped
1 (14oz.) can plum tomatoes, cut in chunks
½ cup Niçoise olives (see note below)
2 tablespoons chopped parsley
3 teaspoons capers

• Rinse, pat chicken dry, sprinkle with salt and pepper. Heat oil
in a nonstick skillet over medium-high heat. Place chicken in
skillet, cook until golden brown and firm to the touch. Transfer
chicken to covered deep casserole dish.
• Add onion to skillet, cook over low heat for 5 minutes. Stir in
garlic, anchovies and cook for1 minute. Next, add tomatoes
cook on medium to high heat for 5 minutes
• Stir in olives, parsley and capers, heat thoroughly. Spoon
mixture over chicken.

➤*Hint:* Capers are the buds of the caper bush; Niçoise olives are small
black olives from Nice, France. They have a small pit inside so be careful
when eating them. You could substitute pitted black olives.

Chicken Normandy
2 apples, peeled & sliced
4 tbsp raisins
4 tbsp honey
5 Tbsp cider or wine
1 chicken, cut in pieces
dash salt & pepper.

Place apples in pie dish. Place chicken
on top followed by remaining ingred.
Cover. Bake at
375° 45"
basting once.

Papaya Chicken

Serves 2

¾lb. boneless, skinless chicken breasts, cut 1-inch cubes
1 medium papaya, peel, deseeded, cut 1-inch cubes
¼ cup orange marmalade
¼ cup lemon juice
½ teaspoon chopped fresh ginger
½ teaspoon ground nutmeg
pinch cayenne pepper
1 tablespoon canola oil
¼ cup chopped cilantro

• Place marmalade, lemon juice, ginger, nutmeg and cayenne in a large sauce pan, heat until marmalade is melted.
• Heat oil in nonstick skillet and brown chicken cubes. Add papaya, toss several minutes. Add sauce and cook until chicken is cooked through, about 4-5 minutes. Place on serving platter, sprinkle with cilantro.

Chicken Livers Sauté

Serves 4

1 pound chicken livers, halved
½ pound mushrooms, cleaned, sliced
¼ cup unsalted butter
¾ teaspoon dried rosemary, crushed
dash of sea salt and ground black pepper
¼ cup dry red wine

• In a nonstick skillet sauté mushrooms and chicken livers in melted butter, until lightly browned.
• Add remaining ingredients, simmer uncovered until the wine is almost absorbed. Serve on cooked rice or coucous.

Oven-Fried Chicken

Serves 4

3 pound chicken, cut up
1 cup breading mix, (see page 402)
¼ cup milk

• In a medium bowl pour milk and moisten chicken.
• Place breading mix in a plastic bag, evenly coat a few pieces
of chicken at a time. Place coated chicken in a single layer on a
lightly greased baking pan.
• Bake at 350 degrees for 45-55 minutes or until fork can be
inserted in chicken with ease, or when juices run clear.

Quick à la King

Serves 2-4

2 ounces canned mushrooms
¼ cup chopped green pepper
¼ cup unsalted butter
1 (10oz.) can cream of chicken or cream of celery soup
½ cup cream or evaporated milk
1 cup diced cooked chicken or turkey
¼ cup chopped pimiento
* optional: dash of sea salt and ground black pepper
2 tablespoons sherry or sweet vermouth

• Sauté mushrooms in a nonstick skillet with green pepper in
butter.
• Add soup, cream or evaporated milk, and simmer for 1-2
minutes. Add remaining ingredients and cook for 2-4 minutes
more. Serve with cooked kasha, couscous or rice.

Leuder's Curry

Serves 2

2 cups cooked diced chicken
1 can each, cream of chicken and cream of celery
2 tablespoons curry powder
ginger powder and cayenne pepper to taste
1 large white potato, cooked and diced
2 cups cooked rice

* Condiments: Place of the following on a large serving platter:
chopped green onions, cucumbers and nuts, crushed pineapple,
jam, chutney, jellied cranberry sauce, tomatoes diced, hard-
boiled eggs chopped.

• Heat soups in a large saucepan, toss in remaining ingredients,
simmer for 5-8 minutes or until thoroughly heated. Serve over
cooked rice. Pass around the condiment platter.

Turkey Chili

Yield: 4 servings

1 cup chopped onions
4 teaspoons peanut oil
1 pound ground turkey
1 cup chopped green bell peppers
1 cup chopped celery
1 cup tomato sauce
½ teaspoon red hot sauce
2 teaspoons chili powder or more to taste
¼ teaspoon each, garlic powder and black pepper
1 (16oz.) can red kidney beans

• Sauté onion in oil, in large saucepan or Dutch-oven pot.
• Add remaining ingredients except beans, mix well, bring to a
boil, reduce heat. Simmer for 25 minutes. Stir in beans, until
heated through.

Breaded Curry Chicken

Serves 4

3-3½ pound chicken, cut into 8 pieces
3 tablespoons curry powder
1 cup seasoned dry breadcrumbs

• Preheat oven to 375 degrees, lightly oil large baking sheet.
• Mix breadcrumbs and curry powder in deep bowl. Season chicken lightly with salt and pepper. Press chicken pieces in breadcrumb mixture and coat completly. Arrange on prepared baking sheet.
• Bake chicken for 45 minutes or until juices run clear when pierced with fork.

Chicken Salsa Kasha

Serves 4

3 cups cooked kasha, (see page 272)
2 cups cooked chicken, cut into bite-size pieces
½ cup diced onion
1 (7oz.) can green chilis, diced
1½ cups shredded Cheddar cheese
1 cup salsa
½ cup crushed nacho chips

• Prepare kasha; preheat oven to 350 degrees.
• In a large bowl, combine chicken, kasha, onion, chilis, ¾ cup cheese and salsa. Pour into well geased 9x13 baking pan.
• Sprinkle with remaining cheese and nacho chips. Bake for 25-35 minutes or until cheese is bubbly.

Chicken Legs & Thighs

Serves 4

2½ lbs. (8 chicken thighs or drumsticks, skin pulled off)
2 tablespoons all-purpose flour
½ teaspoon sea salt
⅛ teaspoon ground black pepper
1 tablespoon peanut oil

• Mix flour, salt, pepper well. Coat chicken with mixture.
• Heat oil in a deep 12-inch nonstick skillet with cover or a
Dutch oven; add chicken, cook for 5 minutes, brown all over.
• Stir in ingredients from one of the following choices listed in
the recipes below:

• *Creamy Thai:* 1 (14oz.) can coconut milk, 1½ tsp. curry
powder, 3 cups quartered small red potatoes, ½ tsp. sea salt.
Bring to a boil, reduce heat, cover and simmer for 15 minutes.
Add 1 cup broccoli and cauliflower florets. Bring back to a boil,
cover and simmer for 12-14 minutes, stirring occasionally.

• *Italian:* 1 (28oz.) can whole tomatoes in purée, 3 cups chunk
potatoes, 2 green bell peppers, cut in strips; 12oz. muchrooms,
halved; 2 tsp. minced garlic. Bring to a boil; reduce heat, cover;
simmer for 25 minutes, stirring occasionally.

• *French:* 1 cup dry white wine, boil for 1½ minutes. Stir in 1
cup water, 1 (9oz.) dry vegetable soup mix, 4 carrots cut in thin
slices, 8 halved small red potatoes, 2 whole parsnips, ½ tsp.
dried thyme. Return to a boil; cover, simmer for 25 minutes,
stirring occasionally.

• *Southern, USA:* 2 cups chicken broth, 1 (10oz.) frozen collard
greens or kale, 1 cup thinly sliced onions. Cover, simmer for 5
minutes to thaw greens. Stir in 1 cup each long-grain white rice
and sliced kielbasa. Bring to a boil, reduce heat, cover and
simmer for 15 minutes or until rice in tender.

(Chicken Legs and Thighs continued next page)

• *Middle Eastern:* 1 cup chopped onions, ¼ tsp. each ground cinnamon and cumin. Cook for 2 minutes. Add 4 cups sliced zucchini, 1(14½oz.) can whole tomatoes, drained and cut up, 1 (13½oz.) can chicken broth. Cover, simmer for 30 minutes. Stir in 1 cup couscous. Remove from heat, let stand for 5 minutes before serving.

• *Midwestern,USA:* 1 (10¾oz.) can cream of celery soup, 1 (10oz.) box each frozen lima beans and corn, 1 tsp. Old Bay seasoning. Bring to a boil, reduce heat, cover and simmer for 15 minutes.
Using canned vegetables, add last 3 minutes of cooking time.

• *Southeastern, USA:* 1¾ cups water, 1 pack dry onion-mushroom soup mix, 3 cups sweet potatoes, peeled and cut into chunks. Cover and simmer for 20 minutes, add 4 cups shredded cabbage, ½ tsp. dried thyme. Cover, simmer 15 minutes, stirring occasionally.

• *Spanish:* Add 1¾ cups water, bring to a boil. Stir in 1 (8oz.) box yellow rice mix. Reduce heat, cover, simmer for 20 minutes. Add 1 cup frozen green peas, 1 (4oz.) jar sliced pimientos. Cover, cook additional 5 minutes.

• *California:* Add 1 (29oz.) can tomato sauce, 1 cup finely chopped onions, 2 tsp. grated orange rind, 1 tsp. oregano, 2 tbsp. chili powder, ½ tsp. ground ginger, 1 tsp. sea salt, cover and simmer for 20minutes, add 1 (16oz.) can red kidney beans, cover and heat thoroughly.

Chicken Pineapple
6 breasts & 6 thighs
1/4 c butter
1/2 c flour
1 tsp salt
1/2 tsp pepper
1 can sliced pineapple, save juice
1/4 c soy sauce
1/4 tsp ginger | 1 tsp dry mustard
1 tbsp curry | 2 clove garlic, minced

In Dutch oven or lg. skillet, melt butter. Add flour & stir. Gradually add pineapple juice. Add rest, x pineapple – stir well. Put chix in. Simmer 40". Add chunks pineapple the last 5" & serve c white rice.

Walnut & Herb Crusted Chicken

Serves 4

¾ cup finely chopped walnuts or pecans
¼ cup plain bread crumbs
1½ teaspoons dried basil leaves
¾ teaspoon dried rosemary leaves
2 tablespoons all-purpose flour
½ teaspoon sea salt
1 egg or egg white
2½ lbs. chicken pieces, skin removed, rinse and pat dry

• Preheat oven to 350 degrees; lightly grease a 9x13 baking dish.
• Combine nuts, bread crumbs, basil, rosemary, flour and salt in a medium bowl. In another medium bowl, lightly beat egg. Coat chicken in egg, then in nut mixture.
• Place chicken in prepared baking dish, bake 40-45 minutes or until crust is browned.

Chicken Casserole 1, 2, 3.

Serves 4

4 chicken breasts rinse and pat dry
1 (10oz.) can cream of chicken soup
1 (10oz.) can cream of celery soup
1 (10oz.) soup can, milk
1 (8oz.) package stuffing mix
5⅓ tablespoons melted butter
1½ cups chicken broth

• Cook chicken in water to cover until tender; drain saving some of this water as cooking broth, chop chicken. Cut chicken in chunks spread in oblong baking dish. Mix soups and milk in bowl, spoon over chicken.
• Mix stuffing mix, butter and chicken broth in bowl; mix until moistened. Spread over chicken, bake at 350 degrees, 40 min.

Turkey-Sausage Puffy

Yield: 6-8 servings

1 pound bulk sausage
½ cup minced onion
1 cup diced celery
2 eggs, beaten
1 cup milk
2 cups soft bread crumbs
1 teaspoon poultry seasoning
1 cups leftover turkey gravy
2 cups diced, cooked turkey (or chicken)
sea salt and ground black pepper to taste

[handwritten note:]
Cornish Hens
2 hens, split in half
3 Tbsp butter
½ C honey
1 Tbsp lemon juice
dash cayenne
½ C rose wine.
Combine & simmer.
Sprinkle hens ē salt,
grill, basting ē sauce.
(Can make in skillet)

• Cook sausage over medium heat in a nonstick skillet until nearly done, drain leaving about 2 tablespoons of fat in pan; add onion and celery and continue cooking for about 5 minutes.
• Preheat oven to 350 degrees; lightly grease a 10x7 baking pan.
• In a large bowl add the next 4 ingredients and 1 cup of gravy, combine well, stir in turkey. Add salt and pepper as needed. Stir in sausage mixture and turn into prepared pan.
• Bake for 45 minutes or until set and browned.

➢ *Note:* If you have additional gravy leftover from turkey roast, use this gravy at serving time for above dish.

[handwritten note:]
Chicken Loaf
1 Tbsp butter
(sm. can mushrooms
1.5 C soft bread crumbs
1 C milk
1 C chix broth
2 egg
½ tsp salt
¼ tsp paprika
¼ C cut pimiento
3 C sliced cooked chix

Mix all & pour into greased
loaf pan. Bake 350°
40-50 min

Chicken South

Serves 4-6

3 pound chicken, cut up
½ cup unsalted butter, melted
1 envelope onion soup mix
6 ounces barbecue sauce

• Rinse chicken and pat dry. Place melted butter in a 9x13 casserole dish; stir in soup mix and barbecue sauce. Place chicken in dish, turn and coat both sides.
• Bake covered, at 350 degrees for 1 hour or until chicken juices run clear when pierced with a fork.

Yogurt-Herbed Chicken

Yield: 6 servings

6 chicken breast fillets
1 cup non-fat plain yogurt
1 cup wheat germ cereal
2 tablespoons dried rosemary, minced
2 tablespoons lemon pepper
1 (10oz.) can tomato soup

• Rinse chicken and pat dry. Spread both sides with yogurt.
• In a medium bowl combine cereal, rosemary, lemon-pepper; dip chicken into mixture and coat well. Place in greased baking pan. Bake at 325 degrees for 25 minutes or until brown.
• Remove from oven; spread tomato soup on top and around chicken, bake 10 minutes more.

Easy Turkey Quiche
6 oz pkg stuffing mix
1 C chopped cooked turkey
1 C Swiss, shredded
4 eggs, beaten
5⅓ oz can evaporated milk
⅛ tsp pepper.

• Prepare stuffing & press into pie pan.
Bake 400° x 10". Mix meat & cheese. Sprinkle into crust.
Beat eggs, milk, pepper.
Pour into shell, Bake 350°
30-35" or until center set.
Let stand 10".

FISH; splash, swim or swish, it's fish.

Fish can be steamed, grilled, fried, sautéed, pan fried, baked, stewed and made into soup. Cold cooked fish is great in salads, while leftover cooked fish can be added to the sauce just before pouring on top of your cooked pasta or rice.

• *Purchasing:* The first test of freshness is made with your nose, **SMELL IT**. Fish should have a mild, briny scent, not a strong odor. Any hint of ammonia is a bad sign. The eyes of whole fish should be clear and bright, the gills should be a light, reddish color (the darker the gills, the older the fish), the scales should be shiny and tight against the body, and the flesh should be firm to the touch.

• *Fillets* and *Steaks* should look moist and freshly cut, and there should be no dryness at the edges. Fresh fish is extremely perishable so keep it cold; cook and eat it promptly. If it is not to be cooked immediately, clean and wrap it with transparent plastic wrap, or put it in a tightly covered dish. Store in the refrigerator.

• *Cooking:* Keep it moist and tender, it should be cooked no longer than 10 minutes per inch of thickness. This applies to baked, broiled, grilled, poached and sautéed. For instance, a piece of fish 1½-inches thick? Cook 7½ minutes per side.

• *The Canadian rule of thumb* for cooking fish is to cook *ten* minutes for every *inch* of thickness (measured at the thickest part). Add five minutes more for fish cooking in foil or sauce.

• *Broiling* fish that's 1-inch thick or less should cook 2-4-inches from the heat; thicker pieces should go 5-6-inches away. Place fish on a lightly buttered, foil-lined broiling pan. Place your favorite herbs, lemon and a dash of paprika. Broil or cook according to *Canadian rule* above.

• *Butterflied:* A pan-dressed fish cut in half lengthwise with the backbone removed. Nice for stuffing.

• *Deep fry it:* Have oil at 350 degrees, cook until golden brown, drain on paper towels or plates. Let oil return to 350 degrees before starting second batch.

• *Fillet:* Boneless pieces of fish cut off either side of the skeleton and skinless.

• *Grill:* Steaks, thick fillets or whole fish. Brush the fish and the grill with oil. Fish 1-inch thick or less should go 2-4-inches above heat; place thicker fish 5-6-inches away. Baste, fre quently, turn once. Marinades help a lot with grilled fish. *Use* a fish grilling basket which enables you to grill delicate fish or shrimp without worrying that they'll fall into the fire. Swordfish and tuna are excellent grilled.

• *Head or pan-dressed:* Same as whole, but with head removed, or head, fins and tail removed.

• *Steaked:* Slices of fish cut across the backbone, with skin and bone on. Usually 1-inch or more thick, swordfish, shark, salmon and tuna are cut this way.

• *Steam:* Steam fish in a shallow dish, or on a platter set on top of a rack over boiling water and covered. Use your wok, or deep skillet with cover to steam. This way all of the wonderful juices are saved and can be treated as a sauce.

• *Is it done?* Fish should be firm but juicy and opaque in color, not translucent. It should pull easily away from the bone, too. The juices should run clear when the flesh is pierced with a fork at the thickest part.

• *Ciguatera* is a toxin sometimes found in large reef fish, such as barracuda, grouper and snappers. Experts recommend choos- ing fish smaller than 5 pounds to lessen the risk.

• *Categories:* Fish fall into two categories: the darker, oilier firm fish and the whiter, more delicate, leaner fish.

• *Darker* fish include such varieties as swordfish, tuna, shark, mackerel, kingfish, salmon. and bluefish. Best to grill, broil or bake them.

• *White* fish include varieties such as halibut, cod, snapper, trout and grouper. Best to sauté, steam or poach them.

• *Whole fish:* A fish in the round, gutted, scaled, with head, tail and fins left on. When purchasing get ¾ to 1lb. per person. A 2lb. fish will yield 2-8ounce portions.

Readying whole fish: remove scales, fins, check the fish's cavity. Be sure the gills have been closely trimmed and rinse out any blood or membrane with running cold water. Do not remove the tail and head. The cheeks, in fact, are the sweetest meat.

Readying to cook: Beginning about 1-inch from the base of the head, cut diagonal slashes crosswise along the body of the fish, spacing them about 1-inch apart and stopping about 2-inches short of the tail. The slashes should go no deeper than within ½-inch of the backbone. Flip the fish over and repeat slashing pattern on the second side. The fish may also be steamed without scoring.

• *Microwave:* (see page 323)

I personally try not to over season my seafood or drown them with sauces. Let your palate taste the marvelous flavor of the great gift of the sea. It's easy to prepare; cooks in minutes.

• *When* your catch has finished cooking, squeeze on lemon juice or flavor vinegar for a topping. Sprinkle on citrus juices with fresh chopped herbs, or top it off with fresh salsa. Take care not to overcook, it will be dry. Properly cooked fish will be moist, tender and flaky. If you are using frozen fish, be sure to cook it before it completely thaws.

• *Leftover* cooked fish can be flaked and used in chowders, casseroles, salads and pasta dishes.

A quick *side dish:* serve couscous (page 265,276-278) which will soak up the juices from the cooked seafood.

Quick and easy for *pasta dishes* and *stir-fry:* use the new imitation crab product. It's really *surimi* and comes from the white fish Alaskan pollock.

• *Washing Seafood:* While it is important to clean shellfish properly, it is also important not to remove the flavor of the sea.

Shrimp: to wash shrimp, rinse with cold water before peeling to remove any sand or foreign particles. Peel and remove the vein but do no wash again as the water will leave the shrimp tasting bland.

Squid: rinse squid briefly to remove sand or foreign particles. All cartilage should be removed by pulling it loose with your fingers.

Clams/Mussels: scrub shells thoroughly with a brush and water to remove foreign bodies. If they appear very sandy, soak them, uncooked in cold water for 30 minutes.

Appearances:

• *Fresh shrimp* will have a mild odor, the meat is firm in texture. The colors of the shell may vary from grey to dark grey. Shellfish require little cooking time, and over boiling makes them tough.

• *Fresh scallops* should have a sweet odor, a firm white flesh, and should be almost free of liquid when bought in packages.

• *A live lobster* should curl under its body when he is picked up; if it is limp and hangs down, the lobster is probably dead. Frozen rock or spiny lobster tails should have a clear white meat and no odor.

• *Live clams, mussels, oysters* in the shell should be tightly closed, or if slightly open, they should close immediately when tapped gently. Discard all that don't, this shellfish is dead and should not be eaten. Shucked oysters should be plump, naturally creamy in color, and in clear liquid. Avoid any oysters in containers that have an excessive amount of liquid. Too much liquid indicates poor quality and careless handling.

• *CRABS: Blue, Dungeness, King, and Stone* what a great variety! They can be served as appetizers, soups, salads, crab cakes, soft shell, deviled and imperial. Dungeness crabs are two to three times larger than the Blue crab. Fresh cooked meat is picked from both body and claws. King crab is sold as legs or claws in the shell. Stone crab, only the claws are eaten. They are cooked immediately on landing and are sold cooked. Eat them cold or steam only long enough to heat. *Use* a heavy-duty nut cracker or hammer to crack the claws.

Steamed crabs: after steaming, break off the claws, lay the crab on its back and lift the apron. It will come up like the hinge on a door. *Using* your thumbs, one on the edge of the back on one on the edge of the bottom where you removed the apron, pry up top shell. Flip the crab back onto the bottom and scrape off the feathery gills. Break apart at the center and pick out the meat. In a mature crab, there will be a golden "mustard" and the beginnings of a new crab in the shell wing tips. This is a true delicacy.

Soft shell crab: preparation they can be baked, sauteed, deep fat fried or pan fried. You can purchase them live, fresh dressed or frozen. To prepare for cooking, cut crab across the face, lift the top body gently to remove feathery gills. Cut off the apron and pat dry. Lightly dust with flour, melt butter in a nonstick skillet and sauté. (Place on rye bread toast, mayonnaise, lettuce and tomato).

Seafood cooking equipment:

nonstick skillet or large iron frying pan
top stove smokeless grill (see page 16)
1 medium size steaming kettle for cooking crabs, clams,
lobsters (or use your pressure cooker)
oyster knife, filet knife, poultry shears, wooden mallet
tongs (to pick up live crabs and lobsters)

Bake, Grill, Poach or Sauté Fish Steak or Fish Fillet!

Basic recipe:

• Nonstick skillet with cover, baking pan or smokeless grill.

Use the following sauces such as Star Fruit Salsa toppings for
grilled fish, Spicy Fish Sauce to poach in, Chunky Tomato
Sauce to poach or bake with, Spicy Yogurt Fish Marinade to
grill with(see page 192). Here are some basic easy recipes
based upon 2 pounds of fillet or fish steaks

• *Fillets for sautéing:* flounder, grouper, yellowtail, snapper,
dolphin (mahi-mahi) or any white flesh fish fillets.

½ cup unsalted butter
1 tablespoon Seafood seasoning blend (see page 394)
2 scallions, thinly sliced
2 tablespoons lemon juice
lemon slices for garnish

• In a nonstick skillet, melt butter, stir in remaining ingredients.
Add fish fillets, turn once. Cook Canadian rule, or until fish
flakes easily. Remove from heat, place on platter, pour butter
sauce over fish. Garnish with lemon slices, serves 4.

• *Fish steaks:* broil or grill such as kingfish, tuna, bluefish or shark (darker oily fish)

3 tablespoons lemon juice
3 tablespoons soy sauce
1 teaspoon sea salt
1 teaspoon ground ginger
2 cloves garlic, minced

• Combine all ingredients in shallow dish, place fish in mixture, cover and marinate half hour in refrigerator. Remove and place on hot grill or under broiler. Cook Canadian rule, or until fish flakes easily, serves 4-6
OR
½ cup mayonnaise
½ cup Dijon mustard
2 tablespoons butter, soft

• Combine all ingredients and lightly coat fish. Grill following Canadian rule on time, or until fish flakes easily.

• *Fish fillets for poaching:* such as grouper, yellowtail, red snapper or other white flesh fish.

1 recipe thin white sauce as basic liquid (see page 203)
1 large onion, thinly sliced
2 teaspoons curry powder
½ teaspoon ground pepper
⅛ teaspoon ground ginger

• Combine all ingredients in skillet, except fish. Bring up to boil, add fish to mixture, reduce heat to medium high, cover, cook (Canadian rule), or until fish flakes easily, turn once. Serves 4-6.

• ***Poach or Bake:*** use white fleshed fish fillets

3 ripe tomatoes, peeled, seeded and cut into chunks or
substitute with 1 medium can of stewed tomatoes
1 medium onion, chopped
2 tablespoons parsley
2 tablespoons dill
¼ cup white wine
¼ teaspoon sea salt
¼ teaspoon ground black pepper
2 tablespoons oil (canola, peanut, etc., see page 42)

• Heat oil in skillet, add onion and sauté until translucent. Add
tomatoes and remaining ingredients, add fish last. Cover and
cook or bake at 375 degrees, Canadian rule or until fish flakes
easily. Serves 4-6.

• ***Mushroom bake for fillets:*** such as salmon, red snapper,
yellow tail.

¼ teaspoon sea salt
¼ teaspoon ground black pepper
1 can cream of mushroom soup, plus ⅓ soup can water
2 tablespoons lemon juice
2 tablespoons chopped basil
1 tablespoon oregano

• Arrange fish in shallow baking dish, sprinkle salt, pepper,
basil and oregano. Combine soup with lemon juice and water,
pour over fish. Bake at 350 degrees, Canadian rule or until fish
flakes easily. Serves 4-6.

Tuna & Zucchini Cakes

Serves 2

½ cup chopped onion
1 tablespoon butter
1 (6½oz.) can tuna, drained and flaked
1 cup shredded zucchini
⅛ teaspoon ground black pepper
2 tablespoons canola oil

• In a small saucepan, cook onion in butter until translucent. Remove from heat. Add tuna, zucchini, eggs, ½ cup of bread crumbs, parsley, and pepper, stir till combined. Shape into six ½-inch patties, coat with remaining bread crumbs.
• In a nonstick skillet heat oil; cook the patties over medium heat, 3 minutes per side or until golden brown.

➤ *Hint*: Spread sour cream or mayonnaise on fish to be baked, broiled or grilled before breading, helps keep it moist and flavorful as it cooks.

PJ Grouper

Serves 2

¾ pound grouper fillet
1 teaspoon dried rosemary, crushed
1 teaspoon olive oil
sea salt and ground black pepper to taste

• Rinse fish and pat dry. Sprinkle with rosemary. Heat oil very hot in a small nonstick skillet, add fish and brown for 1 minute. Turn, sprinkle with salt and pepper, lower heat and cook 5 minutes more.

➤ *Hint:* Cantaloupe, papaya, or a large peach or nectarine make a delicious bowl for any seafood salad. Cut a thick slice off its bottom to stabilize it. Make a fish salad from leftover cooked fish.

Clam Stew

Serves 4

6 slices bacon, chopped
3 medium onions, chopped
1 green pepper, chopped
2 ribs of celery, chopped
2 large potatoes cut into ½-inch cubes
2 cups clam juice (use juice from canned clams)
2¾ cups water
2 teaspoons red hot sauce
1 bay leaf
dash of sea salt and ground black pepper
instant mashed potatoes to thicken
2 cups minced canned clams (use this liquid)
3 cups milk

• Fry bacon in a 6-quart Dutch oven, drain excess fat leaving enough to sauté vegetables. Pour in clam juice and water, add potatoes and seasonings. Cook till potatoes are fork tender.
• Add milk and enough instant potatoes to thicken. Add clams and cook for 2 minutes then let set a few minutes before serving. Remove bay leaf.

Grilled Salmon Steaks

Serves 2

2 salmon steaks
Cajun seasoning (see page 395)
dash of sea salt, ground black pepper
¼ cup melted butter
¼ cup lemon juice

• Sprinkle salmon with seasoning. Mix butter and lemon juice in a small bowl, brush salmon steaks with butter mixture. Grill salmon steaks basting with butter sauce often. Cook Canadian rule.(see page 245)

DJ Bake

Serves 4

1½ pounds fresh fish fillets
1 tablespoon lemon juice
½ cup grated Parmesan cheese
3 tablespoons unsalted butter, softened
2 tablespoons mayonnaise
2 tablespoons chopped chives
¼ teaspoon sea salt
¼ teaspoon garlic powder
⅛ teaspoon red hot pepper sauce
paprika

• Rinse fish, pat dry, place in a lightly oiled shallow 2-quart casserole dish. Brush with lemon juice and let sit for a 2-3 minutes.
• Combine remaining ingredients, except paprika. Spread mixture over the fish, sprinkle paprika on top. Bake for 15 minutes at 350 degrees.

➤ *Hint*: When selecting clams, mussels or oysters, be sure the shells are tightly closed. Do not overcook them or they will toughen. When the shells open, they are cooked. Discard any that do not open.

SM Patties

Serves 4

1 (14¾oz.) can pink salmon (use liquid, remove bones)
1 (10¾oz.) can condensed cream of celery soup, reserve ¼ cup
for the sauce
1½ cups crushed herb-seasoned stuffing mix
⅓ cup finely chopped onion
Dill Sauce:
        3 tablespoons milk
        Reserved ¼ cup soup
        ½ teaspoon dried dillweed

• Mix first four ingredients in a medium bowl. Form into eight
patties or pack into a lightly greased 1½-quart loaf pan.
• Fry patties in a lightly greased nonstick skillet over medium
heat for 2 to 3 minutes on each side until lightly browned, or
bake loaf in 350 degrees oven, for 35 minutes or until firm to
touch.
• Mix dill sauce ingredients in a small bowl, spoon on patties or
loaf.

Baked Shad & Roe

Serves 2

1 medium to large shad, split
1 set shad roe
1 cup sour cream
paprika to taste
4 lemon slices

• Preheat oven to 400 degrees. Place shad skin side down in
shallow baking dish. Place a piece of roe on each piece of shad.
Cover with a thick layer of sour cream. Sprinkle with paprika.
• Top each piece of shad with 2 thin lemon slices, bake for 30
minutes.

NR Shrimp Oriental

Serves 4

½ cup chicken broth
2 teaspoons sesame seeds
2 teaspoons shredded fresh ginger
1 tablespoon soy sauce
¼ teaspoon red hot pepper sauce
1 teaspoon cornstarch
1 cup julienne jícama (cut in match stick slices)
1 cup julienne carrots
1 cup julienne red bell pepper
1 pound large shrimp, shelled, deveined
2 cloves garlic, minced
3 cups rice, cooked

• Blend together in a large bowl, broth, sesame seeds, ginger, soy sauce, hot pepper sauce and cornstarch. Set aside.
• In a large nonstick skillet or wok, heat 2 tablespoons of oil. Stir-fry jícama and carrots for 3 minutes, remove from pan, set aside. Add more oil if needed and stir-fry peppers, shrimp, and garlic for 3 minutes or until shrimp turns pink and opaque.
• Stir sauce again; pour into center of wok or skillet and cook until mixture bubbles. Return jícama and carrots to the pan, cover and cook for 2 minutes or until heated through. Serve over hot cooked rice.

➤ *Hint:* Prepare steamed shrimp to go further by peeling and de-veining the shrimp, then halve them lengthwise and steam or stir-fry. The cooked shrimp will curl into spirals and stretch the portions of shrimp.

Tuna Chop Suey

Serves 2

2 tablespoons peanut oil
1 large clove garlic, minced
1½ cups celery, chopped
1 large onion, cut in 8 wedges
1 medium green pepper, cut into strips
2 tablespoons cornstarch
1 cup water
1 tablespoon soy sauce
1 (9oz.) can tuna, drained and flaked
2 cups cooked rice
* Garnish: ⅓ cup sautéed almonds, optional

• In nonstick skillet, sauté garlic, celery, onion and green pepper in oil until fork tender but still crisp.
• Blend cornstarch with 2 tablespoons water, add remaining water and soy sauce to vegetables in skillet; gradually stir in cornstarch mixture. Add tuna.
• Cook and stir until liquid thickens and vegetables are glazed. Serve over rice, garnish with almonds.

Critter Fritters

Serves 2

½ pound shredded crab meat or bite-size lobster pieces
1 teaspoon garlic salt
½ lemon squeezed over the seafood
1 teaspoon coarse ground black pepper
1 egg
1 cup biscuit mix, (see page 407)
¼ cup milk
canola oil for frying

• Combine all ingredients, allow mixture to sit for 10 minutes. Drop about 1 teaspoon at a time in nonstick skillet, fry both sides until golden brown.

Marinated Swordfish

Serves 4

4 swordfish steaks
2 tablespoons soy sauce
2 tablespoons orange juice
1 tablespoon olive oil
1 tablespoon catsup
1 tablespoon chopped parsley
1 clove garlic, minced
½ teaspoon lemon juice
¼ teaspoon ground black pepper
¼ teaspoon oregano

• Combine all ingredients except swordfish in a small bowl to make a marinade. Place fish in a shallow dish, cover with marinade, marinate for 1-2 hours, basting frequently in refrigerator.
• Preheat oven to 350 degrees, take fish out of refrigerator 10 minutes before baking. Bake for 30 minutes, or until fish flakes easily.

Poached Bluefish

Yield: 6 servings

2 pounds Bluefish (or other fish), fillets
1 medium onion, thinly sliced
2 ribs celery, including tops, cut in strips
2 carrots, thinly sliced
¼ teaspoon ground black pepper
2 teaspoon sea salt
water, just barely to cover

• Place bluefish in a single layer in a nonstick skillet with cover. Add vegetables, seasonings and water to just barely cover. Bring to a boil, cover and simmer slowly just until fish flakes easily, 5 to 10 minutes.

Beer Shrimp

Yield: 8 servings

3 pounds shrimps in the shell
4 cloves garlic, minced
1 hot, dried red pepper or 1 tespoon red pepper flakes
dash sea salt and ground black pepper
1 bay leaf
6 sprigs fresh parsley
2 sprigs fresh dill
1 (12oz.) can beer

• Combine all ingredients in a heavy skillet, cover and bring to a
boil. Let the shrimps simmer for 2 minutes and remove from
skillet. Serve in the shell, along with melted lemon butter.

Steamed Whole Fish

Serves 2

1 pound whole fish (yellowtail, snapper)
1 cup thinly sliced mushrooms
4 scallions, thinly slice
1 carrot, cut into thin strips
2 teaspoons chopped fresh ginger
3 tablespoons dry sherry
1 teaspoon soy sauce
½ teaspoon sesame oil
½ teaspoon sugar

• Rinse the fish and pat dry, slash both sides diagonally to the
bone at about 1-inch intervals. Place fish on a plate that will fit
in a steamer.
• Place vegetables and ginger on top of fish. Mix together
sherry, soy sauce, sesame oil and sugar. Pour over fish. Bring
the water in the steamer to a boil, place the plate on a steaming
rack and cover. Steam for 15 minutes.

Coconut Milk Seafood

Yield: 6 servings

18 to 24 medium shrimp, shelled, deveined
¾ to 1 pound scallops
¾ to 1 pound red snapper, cod, or orange roughy fillets
1 medium lemon
2 (14oz.) cans coconut milk
½ small yellow onion, thinly sliced
1 teaspoon curry powder
dash of red hot pepper sauce
dash of ground black pepper
6 cups cooked basmati rice

• Clean shrimp, rinse scallops and fish, cut fish into small chunks, pat dry. Place seafood in a large bowl, squeeze lemon juice on top, gently mix and set aside.
• Place coconut milk in large nonstick skillet or wok. Add sliced onion, curry powder, hot pepper and ground pepper. Bring to a boil, and cook for 5-7 minutes. Lower heat, add seafood with juices from bowl, cook until shrimp are pink and scallops and fish are done for 8 to 10 minutes.

AM Crusty Country Fried Oysters

Serves 4

2 eggs, beaten
3 tablespoons cold water
1 pint fresh select oysters, drained
1½ cups saltine cracker crumbs
canola oil

• Combine eggs and water in a small bowl. Dip oysters in egg mixture and roll each in cracker crumbs.
• In a nonstick skillet heat oil; fry oysters for 2 minutes or until golden brown, browning both sides. Drain on paper plate.

Fillets de Sole

Serves 4

1¼ pounds sole fillets
¼ cup milk
dash of sea salt and ground black pepper
½ cup all-purpose flour
½ cup canola oil
¼ cup unsalted butter
1 small lemon, peeled and chopped
1 tablespoon drained capers, mashed
1 tablespoon finely chopped parsley

• Arrange fish in single layer in a shallow dish. Add milk, salt and pepper; turn fish to coat both side. Let stand for several minutes; drain. Coat with mixture of flour, salt and pepper. In a large skillet, heat oil and 1 tbsp. butter, cook for 4-5 minutes or until fish flakes easily. Remove to warm platter. Add remaining 3 tbsp. butter, cook until butter foams, remove from heat. Stir in lemon and capers. Spoon evenly over cooked fish; sprinkle with parsley.

➤ Hint: Sour cream or mayonnaise spread on fish to be baked, broiled or grilled before breading, helps keep it moist and flavorful as it cooks.

Grilled Fillets Salsa
Serves 2

4 fish fillets (grouper, snapper, tuna or swordfish)
1 cup seeded tomato, diced
½ cup red pepper, diced
½ cup yellow or green pepper, diced
½ crushed pineapple
2 tablespoons green chilies, chopped
2 tablespoons cilantro, chopped
2 tablespoons onion, minced
1 tablespoon balsamic vinegar
4 tablespoons lime juice
2 cups cooked rice

• Combine tomato, peppers, pineapple, chilies, cilantro, onion, vinegar and two tablespoons of the lime juice. Let stand one hour or more.
• Place fish in remaining lime juice for 30 minutes, then grill. Place grilled fish on plate and top with salsa. Serve with rice.

Buttered Steamed Fish
Serves 4

1 pound fish fillets (red snapper, sole scrod or turbot)
1 tablespoon white wine
sea salt and ground black pepper to taste
¾ to 1 teaspoon dillwee
1 lemon, thinly sliced
2 tablespoons unsalted butter
Paprika

• Place fish in a 8-inch round baking dish. Pour on wine.
• Sprinkle with salt, pepper, and dillweed.
• Cover each fillet with 3 slices of lemon, sprikle with paprika and dot with butter. Cover dish lightly with foil, place on steamer rack in wok and add 2-inches hot water. Bring to boil.Place fish on rack.
• Steam 5 min. ½-inch thick fillet, 10 min.1-inch thick fillets.

Jambalaya

Serves 4

1 pound raw shrimp, shelled, deveined
3 tablespoons vegetable shortening
2 tablespoons all-purpose flour
1 cup chopped onion
½ cup chopped celery
1 clove garlic, minced
1 (28oz.) can tomatoes, chopped
1 tablespoon dried basil
1 bay leaf
dash of sea salt
1 cup uncooked rice
1 ½ cups water
dash of cayenne pepper

• Heat shortening in a Dutch oven; stir in flour and cook over low heat, stirring frequently, until golden brown to make roux.
• Add tomatoes, basil, bay leaf, salt and cook, covered over low heat for 25 minutes. Add rice, shrimp, water and pepper; cook, covered over low heat for 30 minutes or until rice is tender, adding more water if mixture appears dry. Discard bay leaf.

➤ *Note*: For above recipe, you can use up to 1 pound diced, cooked chicken and kielbasa sausage may be added, if desired.

Let's get *acquainted* with a few out of the ordinary grains!

Aside from your familiar cereal grains, these can be served as side dishes to main courses, added into soups and baked goods and used as stuffing for vegetables, poultry or fish.

• *Bulgur:* is a processed form of cracked wheat. The plant is related to rhubarb and garden sorrel and has little white or pink-tinted flowers. The part of the plant we eat isn't even a seed, as it is in cereal grains; it's a tiny fruit.

• *Kasha:* are often labeled buckwheat groats. They come in whole, coarse or fine, hulled buckwheat grains. Generally served with some type of gravy, usually pot-roast. Kasha varnishkas is an East European staple. It is chewy, dry with a strong flavor of its own.

• *Couscous:* is a coarsely ground form of hard wheat. Also available in a quick instant form.

Rice is nice, so let's explain the grain!

• *Short grain rice:* has a soft texture when cooked and is commonly used in puddings. It is considered "sticky" but that very characteristic makes it valuable for rice balls or sushi.
• *Medium grain rice:* is similar to short grain but longer and used in dishes with yogurt or vegetables sauces.
• *Long grain rice:* is slender in shape; when cooked, it is light and fluffy. I recommend this for general usage as it is the most versatile. 1 cup of uncooked white rice yields about 3 cups of cooked rice.
• *Precooked or "instant" rice:* is cooked first then dehydrated. It has a taste and texture of its own. It usually is not sticky.
• *Arborio:* is the variety used for creamy Italian risotto. Like other medium-grain rice, it's best cooked until still slightly firm in the center; broth instead of water for richer flavor.
(rice continued on next page)

• *Brown rice:* is the whole unpolished grain. It has a nutty flavor and higher vitamin content. 1 cup of uncooked brown rice yields about 2½ cups cooked.

• *Wild rice:* is not a cultivated rice. It has many of the characteristics of brown rice and has large dark grains. It should be rinsed several times, then soaked for 15 minutes before cooking. It requires longer cooking time than white or brown rice. Wild rice triples in bulk when it is cooked.

• *Basmati rice:* is an aromatic white rice similar to long grain with a sweet nutty taste; also sold by the name of Texmati.

• *Sweet brown rice:* is sweet and moist when cooked and is ideal for desserts.

• *Pecan rice:* has a nutty taste.

• *Jasmine rice:* is sweet smelling, sweet tasting and has a fluffy texture.

• *Wehani rice:* turns a rust color when cooked; the flavor is similar to oatmeal and nuts.

• *Glutinous rice:* is also known as sticky, waxy or sweet rice. Used in Asian cuisines for its soft, sticky texture.

• *Rizcous:* is tiny chunks of brown rice that look and taste like the semolina product call couscous.

Rice Taste Tips

For some interesting tastes: for every 1 cup of raw white rice and its correct amount of water add one of the following: ½ tsp. curry powder and a pat of butter or 2 tbsp. chopped parsley and a pat of butter or 2-3 bay leaves (remove after cooking) or a pinch of saffron and a pat of butter or a few sprigs of tarragon, dash of white wine vinegar and a pat of butter.

After your rice has cooked you could add one of the following: shredded Cheddar cheese or a few snips of chives or a handful of toasted pine nuts.

Rice Storage Tips

Keep plenty of cooked rice on hand for quick and easy recipes. Cooked rice stays fresh refrigerated, tightly covered, up to one week. Uncooked brown rice will keep on the shelf up to six months. Refrigerate for longer shelf life
To reheat cooked rice, add 2 tbsp. of liquid per cup of rice. Cover and heat about 5 minutes on top of the stove or in the oven. Microwave oven, cook on HIGH 1½ minutes per cup.

Pasta

A wonderful choice for the health-conscious cook. Easy to prepare for unexpected company. It can be anything from a first course, main dish, or a salad or soup. You can make it home-made, buy it fresh, or commercial dried type. Pasta comes in infinite varieties of shapes and sizes.

European and American style noodles are made from durum flour and contain egg solids. Medium and wide egg noodles, bow ties and so on are used as accompaniments for stews and cooked meat. Fine egg noodles and small various shapes are often added to soup. Asian style noodles are usually made without egg, Chinese lo mein and Japanese udon are made of wheat. These varieties of noodles are found in your Asian markets.

How To Figure The Servings

• *Long pasta:* (spaghetti, linguine, fettuccine) for 1-cup serving: use 2oz. uncooked or a batch measuring ½-inch in diameter.
• *Short pasta:* (penne, shells, rigatoni) for 1-cup serving: use 2oz. uncooked or just over ½ cup.
• *Thin* and *delicate pasta:* such as angel hair (cappelini), vermicelli, spaghettini: top with a light tomato sauce, cream sauce or soupy shellfish sauces. Just about anything that will not overwhelm the pasta. Remove pasta from cooking while still stiff, for it continues to cook in the heat of the sauce.
• *Long pasta:* such as spaghetti, fusilli, bucatini should be paired with meat, cream and cheese, or pesto.

• *Flat noodles:* such as fettucine, bucatini, linguine call for rich sauces based on meat, butter, cheese or cream.

• *Thick pasta:* with holes and grooves, such as garden rotini, penne rigate, rigatoni, elbow macaroni, cut ziti are served with sauces containing chunks of meat, vegetables sauces, baked pasta and cold dishes.

• *Catchers:* such as lasagna, manicotti, cannelloni are best for stuffing and baking casseroles.

• *Petite pastas:* as small shells, tubetti, bow ties, conchiglette, orzo, orecchiette, pennette, acini di pepe, hold small chunks of beans, grains, or chopped vegetables. Also used in some soups.

• *Soba:* is a dark buckwheat noodle which can be found in the oriental markets and is usually tossed with stir-fry vegetables and seafood.

Preparation Tips

To speed up the process of preparing a cold pasta dish, rinse pasta in a colander under cold water. If cooked pasta has to stand a short time before serving, drain it and drizzle a small amount of oil on top. Mix gently, this will prevent it from sticking together. Put the drained pasta back in the colander over a pot of simmering water. Cover the pot and the pasta will keep for a short while. Just before serving, place colander in sink, pour hot boiling water on pasta and drain well; pour sauce over pasta and toss lightly and serve. "Al dente" means firm to the bite, just tender. To testing the pasta periodically so it does not overcook, take out a piece of pasta or strand and chew it, it should be firm but tender.

For some simple but delicious additions to cooked pasta, try canned or marinated artichoke hearts, pesto sauce, cannelloni beans, capers (drain and mix with some olive oil), garlic and onions, black and green olives, roasted red peppers, sun-dried tomatoes, extra virgin olive oil.

Beans (legumes)

Look for bright uniform color and size. Once purchased store in zip-lock bags or sturdy containers with an air-tight lid.

Preparation

• *Beans:* are easy to prepare from scratch. Your choice of cooking the beans are slow cooker, regular cooking method, and pressure cooker method.
• *Prepare:* dry beans for cooking: rinse first, removing dirt and any discolored beans.
• *Cover:* beans with three to four times their volume in warm water and let them soak at least four hours or overnight, depending upon size. Small beans need only about four hours.
• *Quick soak:* place beans and cover with water in a large sauce pan, bring to a boil and simmer for six minutes, then soak for 1 hour and drain liquid.
• *Pressure-cooker soak:* three cups of water per one cup of dried beans, bring up to pressure for one minute, let pressure drop of own accord, drain, rinse, continue with recipe
• *No soaking:* is required for lentils, black-eyed peas, split peas, garbanzos and pigeon peas.
• *When:* beans are soaked and cooked, they double or triple in volume.
• *Salting beans:* during soaking and cooking tends to toughen them; instead season beans toward the end of cooking or as they are added cooked to the recipes.
• *Proper:* soaking and rinsing is vital to prevent the flatulence often associated with beans.

Cooking Methods

• *Slow cooker:* a patented crock-pot device, really not applicable to cruising boaters. (There are exceptions) Cooking time will vary from 6-10 hrs. depending on the bean you are cooking. Manufacturers have a cooking chart for their specialty pots.
• *Regular method:* follow chart on following page.
• *Pressure cooker method:* most fuel and time efficient method.

Regular Cooking Method

1 cup dry beans	Water	Cooking
Baby limas	2 cups	1½ hrs.
Black beans	4 cups	1½ hrs.
Black-eyed peas	3 cups	1 hr.
Garbanzos (chick-peas)	4 cups	3 hrs.
Great northern beans	3½ cups	2 hrs.
Kidney beans	3 cups	1½ hrs.
Lentils	3 cups	1 hr.
Limas	2 cups	1½ hrs.
Navy beans	3 cups	1½ hrs.
Split peas	3 cups	1 hr.

Pressure Cooker Method

➤ *Note: Bring up to pressure, reduce heat so that pressure knob jiggles lightly. After cooking time, remove from heat and let pressure drop of own accord.*

1 cup dry beans*	Water	Cooking Time
Baby limas	2 cups	20 min.
Black beans	2 cups	22 min.
Black-eyed peas	1½ cups	6 min.
Garbanzos (chick-peas)	2 cups	25 min.
Great northern beans	2 cups	15 min.
Kidney beans	2 cups	25 min.
Lentils	2 cups	15 min.
Limas	2 cups	25 min.
Navy beans	2 cups	25 min.
Pinto beans	2 cups	6 min.
Red beans	2 cups	25 min.
Split peas	2 cups	5 min.

* dry beans have a tendency to foam, froth and sputter and may sometimes clog the vent pipe. Add ½ tbsp. oil to prevent foaming

• *Azuki beans:* dark red beans, small, extremely tasty. Can be cooked right in the same pot with rice or barley.

• *Black beans:* use in soups or casseroles.

• *Dried peas:* yellow, green and split. Green peas have a more dominant taste than yellow. Split peas are dried green or yellow peas that have been cracked in half and had their skins removed. Any of the three can be used for a thick pea soup. Puréed, they can be added to casseroles or mixed with a grain as a stuffing.

• *Garbanzo beans:* can be mashed with sesame oil into humus. Cold garbanzos are great in salads. Hot, they're excellent in soups and stews.

• *Great northern beans:* these beans are often boiled, then baked. They're large and are better in casseroles and stews.

• *Kidney beans:* red kidney made chili famous. Kidney beans are one of the tastiest varieties of bean and can be added to salads, soups, beans mixtures.

• *Lentils:* should be combined with vegetables in a casserole, hearty soup, stew or combined with rice or barley as a stuffing.

• *Lima beans:* come either large or small and are excellent in casseroles or alone with butter and herbs.

• *Mung beans:* are the smallest beans, usually eaten sprouted rather than cooked. (see sprouts page 399)

• *Navy beans:* various sizes of small and firm white bean. Good in casseroles, soups, and home-baked beans.

• *Pinto beans:* These speckled beige beans are somewhat smaller than kidney beans. Good in salads and for chili.

• *Red and Pink beans:* Reds taste stronger than pinks. Both are used in Mexican dishes, refried beans, salads and for chili.

• *Soybeans:* used in casseroles or loaves, but because they're the toughest bean of all to digest, soybeans are more often eaten in another form such as tofu or miso.

Basic Kasha

Yields: 3 cups (6, 4oz. servings)

2 cups liquid (water is o.k., but broth, consommé or bouillon adds more flavor)
1 egg, slightly beaten
¼ teaspoon ground black pepper
½ teaspoon sea salt
1 cup medium-grain kasha (buckwheat groats)
2 tablespoons peanut oil

• Combine liquid, salt and pepper in a small saucepan, bring to a boil, cover, shut off heat and set aside.
• In a small bowl, combine the beaten egg into the kasha and mix well, making sure all the kernels are coated. Heat peanut oil in a nonstick skillet (need cover later), add coated Kasha and, on medium high heat, constantly stir and chop the egg-coated kasha with a wooden spoon for 2 to 4 minutes or until egg has dried on kasha and kasha kernels are very hot and separate. For just a second remove skillet from heat and add liquid measure slowly, watch out for spattering. Return skillet with kasha mixture on heat reduced to low, cover, steam kasha for 18 minutes. Remove cover, stir and quickly check to see if kernels are tender and liquid has been absorbed. If not, cover and continue steaming for 3-5 minutes. Remove cover, fluff the grains with a fork.

• *Variations:* Follow directions and quantities for above recipe, but before adding liquid to saucepan, briefly sauté in 1 tbsp. butter, ½ cup chopped onions and/or ½ cup sliced mushrooms. Then proceed with directions. (*This wonderful grain can be tossed in cooked egg bowties or served with pot roast, and the gravy can be used as the topping to cooked kasha*).

➤ *Note:* Leftover plain kasha can be refrigerated up to 3 days; use as a filler in soup or salad.

Cheese Grits

Serves 4-6

1 cup grits
1 teaspoon sea salt
4 cups boiling water
1½ cups (6oz.) grated Cheddar cheese
½ cup butter
½ cup milk
2 eggs, slightly beaten
1 clove garlic, minced

• Preheat oven to 350 degrees, lightly grease a 2-quart casserole dish.
• In a medium saucepan, stir grits into boiling salted water. Return to a boil, reduce heat and cook for 3-5 minutes. Add cheese, butter milk, eggs and garlic, stirring till cheese melts.
• Pour hot grit mixture into prepared casserole dish, bake for 1 hour, uncovered.

Tuna & Kasha

Yield: 4 servings

¾ cup cooked kasha (see page 272)
1 (7oz.) can chunk or solid tuna, drained
2 hard-boiled eggs, chopped
¼ cup chopped celery
¼ cup chopped onion
2 tablespoons chopped green pepper
½ cup mayonnaise
1 tablespoon prepared mustard
2 teaspoons lemon juice
dash of sea salt and ground black pepper

• Prepare kasha according to package directions or (see page 272).
• Combine all ingredients in large bowl, toss gently.

Lentil Kasha Chili

Serves 4-6

2 tablespoons olive oil
1 cup diced onions
½ cup diced green pepper
2 cloves garlic, minced
1½ tablespoons chili powder
1 teaspoon paprika
1 teaspoon ground cumin
½ teaspoon ground oregano
3½ cups beef broth
2 cups canned crushed tomatoes
½ cup dry lentils
½ cup kasha (medium)
¼ teaspoon ground black pepper
½ teaspoon celery salt
tortilla chips
shredded Cheddar cheese
picante sauce

• In a heavy saucepan, heat oil on medium heat. Add onions, green pepper, garlic, chili powder, paprika, cumin, and oregano. Cook, for 8-10 minutes stirring often.
• Add broth, tomatoes and lentil; bring to boil. Reduce heat, cover and simmer for 30 minutes. Stir in kasha, cover and simmer for 15 minutes, stirring occasionally. Season with celery salt and pepper.
• Serve hot, topped with tortilla chips, cheese and/or picante sauce as desired. (For thinner chili, use an entire (28oz.) can of crushed tomatoes.)

➤ *Hint*: Filling stuffed MANICOTTI: getting the filling into stuffed shells or manicotti can be a frustrating chore. Use an infant spoon with a long handle. This spoon enables you to fill the pasta and withdraw the spoon, depositing the filling along the way.

Chickpeas & Kasha

Serves 4

1½ cups cooked kasha, (coarse or whole)
1 (16oz.) can chickpeas, rinsed and drained
6 ounces of feta cheese, crumbled
2 medium tomatoes, seeded and diced
1 medium cucumber, seeded and diced
2 green onions, thinly sliced
dash of ground black pepper

• Prepare kasha according to package directions
or (see page 272).
• Combine all ingredients in a large bowl, toss gently, serve.

Tabbouleh

Serves 4-6

2 cups bulgur
½ cup chopped fresh parsley
¼ cup chopped fresh mint
4 green onions, thinly sliced
2 medium tomatoes, seeded, diced
1 cucumber, peeled, diced
3 tablespoons olive oil
3 tablespoons fresh lemon juice
1 teaspoon sea salt
½ teaspoon cumin
¼ teaspoon pepper

• In a large bowl, soak the bulgur in 4 cups boiling water for 30
minutes. Drain in a fine-mesh strainer, pressing out as much
water as possible. Place bulgur in a large salad bowl.
• Add parsley, mint, scallions, tomatoes and cucumber. Mix
well.
• In a small bowl, combine remaining ingredients. Pour over the
bulgur mixture and toss gently, serve immediately.

Couscous & Fresh Parsley

Serves 4

1 tablespoon olive oil
1 tablespoon unsalted butter
½ cup onion, minced
1⅓ cups water
¼ teaspoon red hot sauce
dash of sea salt and ground black pepper
1 cup couscous
2 tablespoons fresh lemon juice
4 tablespoons fresh parsley, chopped

• Heat olive oil and butter in a small saucepan. Add onion and cook, stirring until translucent. Add water, hot sauce, salt and pepper, bring to a boil.
• Add couscous, stir and cover. Remove from heat and let stand 5 minutes. Stir in lemon juice and parsley, fluff with fork and serve.

Basmati Rice

Serves 4

1½ cups basmati rice
1 teaspoon unsalted butter
½ teaspoon sea salt
3 cups water

• Rinse rice thoroughly and place in a large saucepan. Add 1 teaspoon butter, salt and water. Bring to a boil, reduce heat, cover the rice and cook for 20 minutes.
• Remove from heat, uncover, fluff with a fork, cover again and let sit for 5 minutes before serving.

Couscous & Raisins
Serves 2-4

⅓ cup golden raisins
1 tablespoon olive oil
¼ cup chopped onion
1 clove garlic, minced
1½ cups boiling water
⅛ teaspoon ground cinnamon
⅛ teaspoon ground cumin
dash of sea salt and ground black pepper
1 cup quick-cooking couscous
1 teaspoon lemon juice
1 teaspoon balsamic vinegar

• Place raisins, in a small bowl, cover with lukewarm water, set
aside and soak about 12 minutes then drain.
• Heat oil in a medium saucepan over low heat, add onion,
garlic and cook until onions are translucent. Do not brown. Add
the water, raisins, cinnamon, cumin, salt and pepper. Bring to a
boil, remove from heat.
• Add couscous, mint, lemon juice and vinegar. Cover and let
stand 5 minutes. Uncover and fluff with a fork, serve.

Cheese Tetrazzini
Yield: 8 servings

1 (16oz.) package spaghettini, broken, cooked
16 ounces extra-sharp Cheddar cheese, shredded
1 to 1½ cups milk
dash sea salt, ground black pepper and paprika to taste
1½ tablespoons unsalted butter

• Preheat oven to 350 degrees; grease 9x13 baking dish.
• Alternate layers of cooked pasta and cheese.
• Mix milk, salt and pepper; pour over layers. Sprinkle with
paprika; dot with butter. Bake for 1 hour.

Tomato Couscous

Serves 2

⅓ cup tomato juice or V-8 juice
⅓ cup chicken broth
½ cup pre-cooked couscous
½ cup diced ripe tomato
¼ cup chopped fresh cilantro
1 teaspoon olive oil
dash of sea salt and ground black pepper

• Combine tomato juice and broth in a medium saucepan. Bring to a boil, remove from heat and add couscous. Cover and let stand for 6 minutes.
• Place remaining ingredients into a medium bowl, add couscous, toss well and serve.

➤ *Note:* For variety, add to a bowl of cooked couscous one or more of the following: chickpeas, raw sunflower seeds and other vegetables such as shredded carrots, diced yellow squash or zucchini, toasted pine nuts or slivered almonds or sweet red pepper strips.

Egg Noodles

Serves 2

½ pound egg noodles, cooked
¼ cup sour cream
½ pound cottage cheese
dash of sea salt and ground black pepper

• In a large bowl add sour cream, cottage cheese and seasonings, let sit at room temperature as noodles cook.
• Cook noodles according to package directions; drain well and add to prepared cheese mixture while hot, toss well. Serve immediately.

JL Pepper Lentils

Serves 2

1 cup chicken broth
1 cup water
1 small onion, diced
⅛ teaspoon crushed red pepper flakes
½ cup lentils
2 tablespoons chopped fresh or 2 teaspoons dried oregano
dash of sea salt and ground black pepper

• Rinse lentils and drain well.
• In a medium saucepan, bring chicken broth and water to a
 boil. Add onion, pepper flakes, lentils and cook for 1 minute.
Reduce heat and simmer covered for 20 minutes. Check after 10
minutes, if lentils are dry, add ½ cup water. If there is liquid left
in pan after 20 minutes, remove the lid and let boil several
minutes until it evaporates. Remove from heat, add salt and
pepper pour into a medium bowl and toss gently.

Spicy DJ Lentils

Yield: 6 cups

1½ cups lentils
1 medium onion, chopped
4 cloves garlic, minced
½ cup chopped fresh cilantro
1 teaspoon chili powder
1½ teaspoons ground cumin
1 teaspoon ground coriander
1 (7oz.) can green chile salsa
2 cups tomato sauce, (see page 197, 200)
2 cups water

• Place all ingredients in a large saucepan, bring to a boil; then
reduce heat to moderate, cover and cook until lentils are tender,
about 30 minutes, stir frequently.

Gazpacho Pasta

Serves 2-4

8 ounces macaroni
2 tablespoons olive oil
2 cups diced cucumber, peeled and seeded
1 cup thinly sliced green bell pepper
½ cup slice green onions
½ cup sliced celery
1 cup cherry tomatoes, cut in half
1 tablespoon chopped fresh parsley
1 clove garlic, minced

• Cook pasta according to package directions; drain well.
• Place macaroni and remaining ingredients in a large bowl, toss well and serve.

Manicotti

Yield: 12 shells

12 cooked shells, cook half-done, about 12 minutes
Cheese filling;
1 pound ricotta cheese
¼ pound mozzarella cheese, sliced thin strips
¼ cup grated Parmesan cheese
1½ teaspoons sugar
2 eggs, beaten
dash of sea salt and ground black pepper
 3-4 cups chunky tomato sauce (see page 200) or
marinara sauce (see page 198)
additional Parmesan for topping

• Mix filling ingredients together, then stuff the half-cooked shells. Pour a little sauce in the bottom of the baking pan. Place filled manicotti side by side. Pour remaining sauce on top, sprinkle with Parmesan cheese.
• Preheat oven to 350 degrees; bake for 20-25 minutes.

➢ *Note:* To above dish, you can add large pieces of half-cooked sausage and place in between stuffed shells before baking.

Chicken Tetrazzini
Yield: 6 servings

16 ounces spinach fettucini
¼ cup unsalted butter
4 ounces fresh mushrooms, sliced
6 tablespoons all-purpose flour
1 cup chicken broth
2 cups light cream
3 cups diced cooked chicken
dash ground black pepper
grated Parmesan cheese to taste

• Preheat oven to 350 degrees; cook fettucini according to package directions, drain. Spread fettucini in a lightly greased 9 x 13 casserole dish.
• Heat butter in a large saucepan, sauté mushrooms for 5 minutes. Stir in flour; add broth and cream to mushroom mixture gradually. Cook over medium heat stirring constantly until sauce bubbles and thickens.
• Add chicken to saucepan and season with pepper. Spoon sauce over cooked fettucini and sprinkle with Parmesan cheese.
• Bake, uncovered, for 20-25 minutes.

Spaghetti Scampi
Serves 4

2 pounds shrimp, shelled, deveined
3 cloves garlic, minced
¼ cup canola oil
2 tablespoons butter
2 tablespoons cream sherry
1 pound spaghetti, cooked

• Sauté garlic and oil in a nonstick skillet, add sherry and shrimp. Cook for 2 minutes or until shrimp are pink.
• Serve over cooked spaghetti; sprinkle with parsley.

Cream Pasta with Scallops
Serves 4-6

2 cloves garlic, minced
2 cups heavy cream
1 pound scallops
2 tablespoons chopped smoked salmon
4 tablespoons unsalted butter
nutmeg to taste
1 pound linguine, cooked

• In a nonstick skillet, sauté garlic in 2 tablespoons butter; add cream and nutmeg. Simmer until reduced by ⅓; add scallops and salmon. Heat through.
• Toss pasta with remaining butter in large bowl. Pour cooked scallops over pasta, toss and serve.

Pasta Primavera
Serves 2-4

8 ounces uncooked rotini pasta
3 tablespoons olive oil
3 cups thinly sliced zucchini
1 cup sweet red pepper strips
3 cloves garlic, minced
¼ teaspoon dried oregano
¼ teaspoon sea salt
¼ teaspoon dried basil
⅛ teaspoon ground black pepper
Parmesan cheese

• Cook pasta to package directions, drain. Place in large bowl, drizzle with 1 tablespoon of olive oil, cover.
• In a non-stick skillet, heat remaining oil, add remaining ingredients and sauté vegetables until they are fork tender. Remove from heat and toss well with cooked pasta. Serve with grated Parmesan cheese.

Turkey-Ziti Casserole

Serves 4-6

8 ounces ziti
1 (30oz.) jar spaghetti sauce
1½ cups cubed turkey or 3 (5oz.) cans turkey (or) chicken
8 ounces shredded mozzarella cheese, divided
1 tablespoon grated Parmesan cheese

• Cook ziti according to package direction, drain.
• Preheat oven to 350 degrees.
• Stir together spaghetti sauce, ziti, turkey and ½ cup mozzarella cheese in 2-quart casserole dish. Sprinkle with remaining mozzarella and Parmesan cheese.
• Bake for 30 minutes uncovered.

Penne, Black Beans & Mangoes

Serves 2

1 (14oz.) can crushed tomatoes
1 small onion, sliced
3 cloves garlic, minced
1 (15oz.) can black beans, rinsed, drained
2 tablespoons olive oil
¼ pound penne pasta
1 ripe medium mango, cubed, (see page 40)
½ cup fresh basil leaves
dash of sea salt and ground black pepper

• Cook pasta according to package directions, drain. Place in a serving bowl, drizzle 1 tablespoon olive oil, cover with clean dish towel.
• In a large nonstick skillet, add tomatoes, onion, garlic, beans and oil. Simmer for 10 minutes. Remove, pour onto cooked pasta, add mangoes, basil and salt and pepper. Toss and serve.

Rice or Spaghetti Crust Pepperoni Pizza
Serves 4-6

Crust:
4 cups cooked rice or spaghetti
2 eggs, slightly beaten
1 teaspoon sea salt
1 cup shredded mozzarella cheese

Topping:
2 cups chunky tomato sauce, (see page 200)
1 medium green pepper, chopped
⅓ cup chopped onion
2 teaspoons Italian seasoning
1 cup shredded mozzarella cheese
16 slices pepperoni
ground black pepper to taste

• Preheat oven to 375 degrees, coat lightly two 9-inch pie plates with cooking spray..
• Combine all crust ingredients, mixing well (if using spaghetti, cut them into small pieces.) Divide mixture into half and spread each half into pie plates. Gently push mixture up sides of pie plates to form crust. Make sure the pie plate is evenly covered with mixture.
• Bake for 10 minutes, remove crusts from oven, divide toppings in half, place on each crust in order listed. Return to oven for 10 more minutes. Remove from oven, let stand 5 minutes before slicing.

➤ *Hint:* Use cooked vermicelli or spaghetti as a substitute for a regular pie shell when making a meat or vegetable pie.

Tuna Linguine

Serves 2

4 tablespoons olive oil
4 slices red onion
4 slices yellow onion
¼ cup pitted black olives, thinly sliced
2 tablespoons dried basil
2 cloves garlic, minced
1 (14oz.) can crushed tomatoes
1 (6oz.) can tuna in oil
dash of sea salt and ground black pepper
¼ pound linguine
grated Parmesan cheese

• Cook linguine according to package directions, drain, set in large bowl, drizzle with 1 tablespoon of olive oil.
• Heat remaining oil in a large nonstick skillet, over medium-low heat. Add onions, cook until translucent, stirring occasionally, about five minutes.
• Add remaining ingredients and cook until heated through. Serve over cooked linguine, toss, then sprinkle with Parmesan cheese.

Tomato-Cheese Pasta

Serves 4

2 pounds ripe tomatoes, sliced ⅓-inch thick
½ teaspoon sea salt
1 cup chopped basil, packed
¾ cup low-fat ricotta cheese
3 ounces mozzarella cheese, shredded
8 ounces pasta, cooked

• Combine tomatoes, salt, basil, ricotta and mozzarella cheese in a large bowl; mix well.
• Pour over pasta, toss to coat.

Baked Macaroni & Cottage Cheese
Serves 4-6

1 (8oz.) box elbow macaroni
4 tablespoons unsalted butter
3 tablespoons all-purpose flour
1 (16oz.) can tomatoes, diced
1 small onion, minced
1 egg, slightly beaten
2 cups cottage cheese
dash of sea salt and ground black pepper
½ cup fine dry bread crumbs

• Preheat oven to 350 degrees.
• In a medium saucepan, melt butter, stir in the flour and cook over medium heat for about 5 minutes or until roux is lightly browned. Remove from heat, stir in tomatoes, onion, egg, cheese and salt and pepper.
• Pour over macaroni, stir and turn into casserole dish. Top with bread crumbs, bake for 30 minutes.

Cherry Cheese Noodle Pudding
Serves 4

½ pound broad noodles, cooked, drained
1 pound creamed cottage cheese
½ cup sugar
2 cups sour cream
5 eggs, beaten
1 teaspoon vanilla
1 (16oz.) can cherry pie filling

• Mix all ingredients except pie filling in a large bowl. Preheat oven at 350 degrees.
• Place mixture into a lightly buttered 8x12 baking dish; bake for 35-45 minutes. Remove from oven, spread pie filling, return to oven and bake 20 minutes. Serve warm.

Coconut Orange Rice

Serves 6-8

2 tablespoons unsalted butter
1 cup finely chopped onion
2 cups long-grain rice
4 cups chicken broth
1 tablespoon lime juice
2 teaspoons freshly grated orange rind
dash of sea salt
toasted coconut

• In a Dutch oven, melt butter, add onions and sauté until translucent. Add rice and sauté until well-coated with the butter and onions.
• Add remaining ingredients, bring to a boil, cover tightly, reduce heat and simmer for 18-20 minutes or until all liquid is absorbed and rice is dry and fluffy. Remove from heat, fluff with a fork, cover and let sit for 5 minutes.
• Place cooked rice in bowl, garnish with toasted coconut.

Beef & Macaroni Mix

Serves 4

1½ pounds ground beef
1 medium onion, chopped
¼ medium bell pepper, chopped
3 (8oz.) cans tomato sauce
3 cups water
1 (16oz.) can tomatoes with juice, chopped
2 cups elbow macaroni
2 bay leaves
1 tablespoon oregano
2 cloves garlic, minced
sea salt and ground black pepper to taste

• In a nonstick skillet, brown beef, onion and bell pepper, drain. Add remaining ingredients, bring to a boil, then simmer and cook until macaroni is tender.

Apple Kugel

Serves 4-6

1 (12oz.) package broad egg noodles
¾ teaspoon sea salt
¼ cup unsalted butter
⅔ cup sugar
2 cups applesauce
½ teaspoon cinnamon
3 eggs, beaten
4-5 apples, peeled, cut in thick slices
½ cup golden raisins
2 tablespoons lemon juice

• Cook noodles according to package directions, drain well.
• Mix all ingredients in large bowl, pour into a lightly greased
9 x 13 casserole dish. Bake at 400 degrees for 35-40 minutes.

Cold Pasta

Yield: 4-6 servings

8 ounces shell or wheel pasta
1 tablespoon olive oil
3 eggs, hard-boiled, sliced
2 large tomatoes, diced
⅓ cup capers, mashed
⅔ cup black olives, chopped
2 large onions, chopped
1 (7oz.) jar pimentos, chopped
½ cup parsley, chopped
½ cup celery, finely chopped
Dressing:
 ¼ cup white wine vinegar
 ½ cup olive oil
 2 cloves garlic, minced
 sea salt and black pepper to taste

• Cook pasta until al dente; drain. Toss with olive oil, set aside.
• Mix dressing ingredients in a large bowl. Add cooked pasta,
remaining ingredients and dressing mix, toss well.

Let's eat light, substitute your way to lower-fat eating.

Read labels carefully and moderate use of foods that contain large amounts of hydrogenated vegetable oils, cocoa butter, coconut and palm oils. *Read* the ingredients list on the package carefully. I like to avoid those products listing sugar, salt or msg as one of the first ingredients. The following are hints about oil and light eating choices.

• Use safflower oil, sunflower, corn, canola, peanut or olive oil.
• Make your own salad dressings.
• Remove the skin from poultry, trim the fat around meat and use lean beef, pork or veal.
• Increase you number of meatless meals per week.
• Snack on pretzels, air-popped popcorn, rice cakes, and fruit.
• Drink skim or low-fat milk and use low-fat condensed milk and eat low-fat cheese.
• Boil potatoes in their own skin.
• Poach fillets of fish in a small amount of wine or apple juice concentrate.
• Vegetables to be used for dipping: green pepper strips, radishes, cauliflower, broccoli florets, celery and carrot sticks.
• Toppings for baked potatoes: as chives, yogurt, salsa, mustard and low-fat cheese.
• For extra-juicy hamburgers, add some evaporated skim milk to your mixture.
• Use a small amount of brown sugar, honey, molasses or pure maple syrup. A little bit of the real thing is A-ok. Remember moderation.
• Cut calories in baked goods by cutting down added fat in them. Try substituting applesauce measure for measure for some or all the butter, oil or shortening in your cake, cookie or muffin recipe.
• For a quick friendly snack with a low-cal option: a child-size box of animal crackers (about130 calories). A cup of non-fat yogurt (130 calories) fat-free granola bar (140 calories) a cup of 1% fat cottage cheese (160 calories) and 1oz. package of pretzels (110 calories).
• Make baked tostadas instead of fried ones by putting corn or flour tortillas on a cookie sheet at 375 degrees oven for about

ten minutes. They'll be crisp and ready to take on that salsa, plus shredded lettuce, sliced tomatoes and peppers and grated low-fat cheese.

• For enhanced flavor and low-fat alternatives, use lemon juice, flavored vinegars, hot sauces and reduced sodium soy sauce.

• Instead of 1 cup sour cream, use 1 cup low-fat cottage cheese, give it a whirl in the hand food chopper, nice and creamy.

• Make Italian style cheeseburgers, add crushed oregano, black ground pepper and top off with a slice of part-skim mozzarella cheese.

•Toast chickpeas and eat them like roasted peanuts. Rinse and drain a can chickpeas (garbanzo beans), place in a nonstick skillet and on medium heat, tossing often. Season with salt or chili pepper. Remove, cool slightly and munch away..

• Layer that baked potato with spicy red beans or hickory baked beans, top with non-fat yogurt or non-fat sour cream.

• Toss some tofu or bean curd in your stir-fried dishes at the last minute of cooking.

•Make rice at least twice a week, try hearty brown rice or nutty basmati. Make a little extra, next morning at breakfast, top it with some yogurt and honey.

• Instead of 1 cup granulated sugar, use 4tsp. Sweet'nLow, 24 packets equal 1 cup Sugar Twin or 12 packets Sweet One.

•Orange baste for chicken bake or broil. Mix together equal parts dry white wine and low-calorie orange marmalade. Add a dash of soy sauce.

• Take regular soy sauce, dilute with equal parts of water before using.

• Oil dressings: use half water half oil.

• Use water packed foods instead of oil packed foods.

• Make one slice bread open sandwich; eat with fork and knife.

• A low-cal crouton substitute can be made by mixing two cups of whole wheat bread crumbs with a tbsp. of soy sauce and a tsp. of garlic powder. Bake at 350 degrees, place on cookie sheet bake until brown, stir occasionally.

• To make hot cereal a complete breakfast in a bowl, add sliced banana, chopped apple or pear instead of butter or milk.

• Use nonstick pans for sautéing; use wine, vermouth, apple, orange or lemon juice concentrate (once these small containers defrost, they'll keep in refrigerator for about one week.)

Use flavored vinegars and chicken, beef or vegetable broth with no MSG.

• Steam vegetables, top with salsa or lemon pepper dressings.

• Instead of 1oz. baking chocolate, *use* 3 tbsp. cocoa powder and 1tbsp. oil.

• Instead of whole milk use non-fat milk.

• Thicken soups with puréed vegetables instead of cream.

• Make cream sauces with low-fat yogurt, add 1tbsp. of cornstarch or flour when heating.

• Broil, steam, microwave or bake meat and vegetables. If you must sauté or fry, limit the amount of cooking oil. Use a non-stick vegetable cooking spray.

• Instead of 1 egg, use 2 egg whites or ¼ cup egg substitute.

• Look for turkey breakfast sausage, turkey bologna, salami, and pastrami.

• Instead of 1 cup cream, *use* 1 cup evaporated skim milk.

• Prepare meat by cutting off all visible fat and removing the skin before cooking.

• Broil, steam, microwave or bake meat and vegetables. Limit the amount of cooking oil you *use* to 1 tbsp.

•Evaporated skimmed milk will whip after it has been thoroughly chilled.

• Prepare soups and stews a day ahead and refrigerate. The fat will rise to the top, congeal and can be removed easily.

• Flavor food with wine, herbs, garlic, pepper and fruit juices, instead of butter and oil.

• Worcestershire sauce is low in sodium.

• Use fresh season fruit whenever possible. The taste is great and the price is generally lower.

Season With The Following

Fresh lemons
Fresh limes
Vinegars: cider, red wine, rice, black, balsamic
Fresh herbs: cilantro, basil, thyme, chives, parsley
Fresh ground black pepper
Worcestershire sauce
Reduced-sodium soy sauce
Horseradish, Dijon mustard, dry mustard for salad dressings
Fresh garlic
Shallots, scallions or green onions, Bermuda or red onion
Fresh ginger

Stock In the Refrigerator

Low-fat cottage, part-skim mozzarella or other low-fat cheeses
Salsa
Unsalted butter
Corn or flour tortillas
Variety of raw vegetables and fresh fruits, look for in season
abundance, lower prices as well. This will give you a chance to
try a small size of a first time fruit or vegetable; you might just
like it and buy a larger amount second time around.

Keep On the Shelf

Nonfat and low-fat shelf milk, evaporated skimmed milk
Tuna packed in water
Herbal tea
Buttermilk powder
Chicken, beef and vegetable broth (read ingredient label carefully); or make your own broth, (see page 427-429).
Canned tomatoes, crushed, purée, stewed
No-salt tomato paste makes for an easy sauce, add water for juice consistency and a few herbs for a tasty drink.
Can green chilies, salsa, water chestnuts
Dry vermouth for steaming fish, vegetables
Dry sherry for stir-frying
Whole-wheat, all-purpose flour
Regular oatmeal, Wheatena cereals
Corn, safflower, peanut, canola and extra-virgin olive oil
Honey
Active dry yeast
Buckwheat noodles (soba)
Variety of noodles from Oriental grocery
Variety of pastas
Brown, white and basmati rice
Bulgur (cracked wheat)
Lentils
Sun-dried tomatoes
Dried mushrooms
Pine nuts
Molasses
Brown sugar
Raisins
Vegetable cooking spray
Pure maple syrup
Pure vanilla extract
No-sugar jams sweetened with juices
Unsweetened apple juice

Packaging Terms

• *Diet:* contains no more than 40 calories per serving. Also may have a least ⅓ fewer calories than the product it replaces or resembles.

• *Extra lean:* denotes meat and poultry products that have no more than 5% fat by weight.

• *Lean:* on meat and poultry products, indicates no more than 10% fat by weight. *"Lean"* may also be used as part of a brand name with no restriction other than it must have a nutritional label.

• *Leaner:* used on meat and poultry products with 25% less fat than the standard product. Does not necessarily mean that the product is low in fat.

• *Low calorie:* denotes products with no more than 40 calories per serving or 0.4 calories per gram of food.

• *Reduced calorie:* must contain at least ⅓ fewer calories than the product it replaces or resembles. Label must show a comparison between the two.

• *Sugar free:* does not contain sucrose (table sugar) but may contain additional sweeteners such as honey, molasses or fructose, all of which increase the total calories.

• *Naturally sweetened:* food sweetened with a fruit or juice rather than sugar. There is no regulation on this term, however, so a naturally sweetened product can contain sugar or other refined sweeteners such as high-fructose corn sweetener.

• *No salt added/unsalted/without added salt:* these terms mean no salt was added during processing, but the product may still have high sodium levels due to the use of other sodium-containing ingredients such as sodium phosphate, monosodium glutamate or baking powder.

• *Sodium free:* contains fewer than 5 milligrams of sodium per serving.

• *Reduced sodium:* reduced by at least 75% from usual level of sodium per serving.

• *Low sodium:* no more than 140mg of sodium per serving.

• *Very low sodium:* 35 or fewer mg per serving.

• *Natural:* regarding meat and poultry, indicates the product contains no artificial flavors, colors, preservatives or synthetic ingredients. No legal definition exists for the *"natural"* in processed foods; e.g. natural potato chips, can have artificial colors or flavors added.

• *Naturally flavored:* flavoring must be from an extract, oil or derivative of a spice, herb, root, leaf or other natural source. Naturally flavored products can have artificial ingredients, however.

• *Organic:* no legal definition exists. Use of the term is prohibited on meat and poultry.

• *No cholesterol:* may not contain cholesterol but may contain large amounts of saturated fat such as coconut or palm oil, which tend to raise the level of cholesterol in the blood.

• *Saturated fats:* usually harden at room temperature. Found in animal and some vegetable products. Tend to raise cholesterol levels in the blood. Primarily in beef, veal, lamb, pork, ham, butter, cream, whole milk and regular cheeses. Saturated vegetable fats are found in solid and hydrogenated shortenings, coconut oil, cocoa butter, palm oil and palm kernel oil.

• *Hydrogenated fats:* fats and oils changed from their natural liquid form to become more solid, such as most margarines and shortenings. May be partially or almost completely hydrogenated. Nutritionists generally advise us to avoid these since they resemble saturated fats.

Mustard Dill Dressing

Yield: ⅔ cup

¼ cup Dijon mustard
⅓ packet artificial sweetener
⅛ cup white wine vinegar
¼ cup plain low-fat yogurt
¼ cup dill, chopped
dash of sea salt, ground black pepper

• Combine all ingredients in a small covered jar and shake vigorously to blend.

➤ *Note:* Serve with cold poached salmon, fresh steamed vegetables.

V-8 Dressing

Yield: 1 cup

½ cup V-8 vegetable juice
3 tablespoons non-fat or 1% buttermilk
2 tablespoons fat-free mayonnaise
1 clove garlic, minced
1 teaspoon fresh lemon juice
¼ teaspoon lemon-pepper seasoning
1 teaspoon canola oil
3 drops Worcestershire sauce

• In a hand food chopper, blend all ingredients. Pour mixture into a small covered jar and chill until ready to use.

Dijon Vinaigrette

Yield: ⅓ cup

3 tablespoons tarragon vinegar
1 tablespoon water
1 tablespoon olive oil
1½ tablespoons Dijon mustard
1 clove garlic, minced
1 teaspoon sugar
⅛ teaspoon ground black pepper
1 teaspoon fresh lemon juice
1 tablespoon low-fat sour cream substitute
2 to 3 drops white wine Worcestershire

• Combine ingredients in a small covered jar and shake vigorously to blend.

Mustard Slaw

Yield: 8 servings

8 cups coarsely chopped green cabbage
¼ cup chopped dill pickle
⅓ cup plain low-fat yogurt
⅓ cup low-fat sour cream
1½ tablespoons prepared mustard
1 tablespoon white wine vinegar
1 teaspoon sugar
⅛ teaspoon ground black pepper
⅛ teaspoon sea salt
¾ teaspoon celery seeds

• Combine cabbage and pickle in a large bowl; toss well. Set aside.
• Combine remaining ingredients and place in a hand food chopper or jar with tight fitting lid, blend or shake vigorously, add to cabbage mixture, tossing thoroughly to coat.

English Muffin Bread

Yield: 2 large loaves

6 cups all-purpose flour, divided
1 tablespoon sugar
2 teaspoons sea salt
¼ teaspoon baking soda
2 packages dry yeast
2 cups 1% low-fat milk
½ cup water
vegetable cooking spray
1 tablespoon yellow cornmeal, divided

• Combine 3 cups flour and next 4 ingredients in a medium bowl; stir well, and set aside.
• Heat milk and water in a large saucepan until very warm. Add to dry ingredients, stirring well. Stir in remaining 3 cups flour to form a soft dough. Divide dough in half, place each half into a lightly coated pan with cooking spray, sprinkled with ¾ teaspoon cornmeal. Sprinkle remaining cornmeal evenly over tops of dough. Cover with a clean dish towel and let rise for 45 minutes or until doubled in bulk.
• Preheat oven to 400 degrees, bake for 20 minutes or until lightly browned. Remove bread from pan, cool on wire racks.

Golden Brown Rice

Serves 6

2 cups brown rice
2 cups chicken stock or water
1 cup tomato purée
2 medium onions, chopped
2 cloves garlic, minced
1 tablespoon parsley flakes

• Toast rice lightly in a nonstick skillet stirring constantly. In a medium saucepan, bring stock and purée to a boil; add to skillet slowly. Add remaining ingredients, cover reduce heat to low. Cook for 40 minutes or until all liquid is absorbed.

Cheezy Onion-Dill Muffins

Yield: 1 dozen

2¼ cups all-purpose flour
½ cup shredded reduced-fat Cheddar cheese
2 teaspoons baking powder
1 cup skim milk
3 tablespoons vegetable oil
2 tablespoons finely chopped green onions
¼ teaspoon sea salt
¼ teaspoon dried whole dillweed
¼ teaspoon ground black pepper
3 egg whites, lightly beaten
vegetable cooking spray

• Preheat oven to 425 degrees, coat lightly with cooking spray a 12 muffin pan, set aside.
• Combine first 3 ingredients in a medium bowl, making a well in center of mixture.
• Combine milk with oil, onions, salt, and next 3 ingredients in a small bowl, add to dry ingredients, stirring just until moistened.
• Spoon batter into prepared muffin cups, bake for 18 minutes. Remove muffins from pan, cool on a wire rack.

Rice & Beans

Serves 4

3 cups cooked rice (cook as you are preparing recipe)
2 cups cooked beans, pinto, red or kidney
2 cups tomato sauce
1 large onion, chopped
1 medium green pepper, chopped
1 cup kernel corn

• Combine all ingredients except rice in a large Dutch oven; heat well. Pour vegetable mixture over cook rice.

Apple Raisin Noodle Pudding

Serves 4-6

8 ounces wide egg noodles, cooked and drained
2 apples, peeled, cored, thinly sliced
2 tablespoons fresh lemon juice
½ teaspoon ground cinnamon
1 cup low-fat (1%) cottage cheese
2 tablespoons frozen apple juice concentrate
¼ cup seedless golden raisins
1 egg white

• Combine cooked noodles with apples, lemon juice and
cinnamon in a large bowl.
• In a small bowl, combine cottage cheese, apple juice,
raisins, set aside.
• Beat egg white until soft peaks form; fold through cottage
cheese mixture. Fold cheese through noodle mixture.
Spoon into an 8 x 12 casserole dish. Bake at 350 degrees for
35 minutes or until top is lightly browned.

Scalloped Potatoes

Serves 4

6 large potatoes, pared, thinly sliced
¼ cup all-purpose flour
¼ cup finely chopped onion
1 tablespoon parsley flakes
¼ teaspoon ground black pepper
2 cups skim milk
paprika

• Combine potatoes and flour in a plastic bag, shake to coat
evenly. Alternate a layer of potatoes and onions into shallow
baking dish.
• Add milk; sprinkle with parsley flakes, pepper and paprika.
Bake for 1 hour at 350 degrees or until potatoes are fork tender.

Broccoli & Crustless Quiche
Serves 4-6

¾ pound broccoli, cut into florets
1 teaspoon olive oil
½ cup chopped onion
1 clove garlic, minced
½ cup low-fat ricotta cheese
¾ cup egg substitute
½ cup low-fat milk
½ teaspoon dried dill, crushed
⅛ teaspoon cayenne pepper
¼ teaspoon sea salt
¼ teaspoon ground black pepper
¾ cup grated low-fat Jarlsberg cheese, cut in strips
paprika

• Add broccoli florets, to boiling water and cook for 2 minutes, drain, rinse with cold water and pat dry. Chop coarsely.
• In a nonstick skillet heat olive oil on medium heat; add onion, garlic, sauté until fork tender, about 8 minutes.
• In a hand food chopper (see page 9) combine the remaining ingredients except cheese and blend.
• Preheat oven to 350 degrees, lightly spray a 9-inch quiche pan with cooking spray.
• Spread broccoli and onions in prepared quiche pan. Pour egg mixture next. Sprinkle with cheese and paprika, bake for 30 minutes. Remove from oven, let sit 5 minutes before slicing.

Poached Scallops
Yield: 4 servings

3 tablespoons dry white wine or vermouth
1 pound scallops
* garnish: fresh lemon slices

• In a nonstick skillet, heat wine or vermouth; add scallops. Cover and poach for 4-6 minutes or until scallops are fork tender.Garnish with lemon slices.

Chicken & Butternut Squash

Serves 4

2 cups butternut squash, peeled, cubed
1 pound skinless chicken breast, cut into bite-size pieces
1 cup chopped onions
½ cup golden raisins
4 cloves garlic, minced
¾ cup dry white wine
2 teaspoons curry powder
½ teaspoon red pepper flakes
½ teaspoon ground nutmeg
¼ teaspoon sea salt
¼ teaspoon sugar
2½ cups hot cooked rice
vegetable cooking spray

• Coat a large nonstick skillet with cooking spray; place over medium heat until hot.
• Add butternut squash, sauté for 9 minutes. Add chicken pieces and onion, raisins, garlic and sauté for 5 minutes. Add wine and remaining ingredients except rice, cook additional 2 minutes. Serve over rice.

Grilled Tuna or Swordfish

Yield: 4 servings

1 pound tuna or swordfish fillets
1 tablespoon olive oil
1 large clove garlic, minced
¼ teaspoon ground black pepper
* garnish: fresh lemon slices

• Place fish in a shallow casserole dish, coat fish with oil, garlic and pepper. Place cold on a smokeless grill or nonstick skillet. Cook for 3-4 minutes on each side, or just until fish flakes easily when tested with a fork.
• Garnish with lemon slices.

Baked Fish

Serves 4

juice of a small lemon
2 pounds fish fillets (grouper or red snapper)
¼ cup non-fat plain yogurt
¼ cup fat-reduced mayonnaise
¼ cup grated Parmesan cheese
1 tablespoon red wine vinegar
dash of red hot pepper sauce
6 green onions, sliced
* garnish: thinly sliced lemons, chopped fresh parsley

• Squeeze lemon over fish and let marinate for 10 minutes.
Preheat oven to 350 degrees.
• Mix yogurt, mayonnaise, cheese, vinegar, pepper sauce and ¾ of the green onions. Place fish in a 9 x 13 baking dish, pour sauce over it.
• Bake for 10-15 minutes, Canadian rule (see page 245) or until fish flakes easily. Sprinkle with remaining onions, remove to platter. Garnish with lemon and parsley.

Tuna Spread

Yield: 1 cup

1 (3oz.) can water-packed tuna, drained
3 tablespoons non-fat dry milk powder
¼ cup fat-free mayonnaise
1 clove garlic
⅛ teaspoon freshly grated lemon peel
dash of red hot pepper sauce
3 tablespoons minced fresh parsley
½ teaspoon garlic salt

• In a hand food chopper (see page 9), place tuna, milk powder, mayonnaise and garlic, chop well.
• Place tuna mixture in a small bowl, stir in garlic salt, lemon peel and parsley. Serve on a bed of mixed salad greens, assorted raw vegetables, or as a spread on crackers.

Pasta in Herbed Sauce

Serves 2

2 tablespoons olive oil
1 large onion, finely chopped
2 cloves garlic, minced
1 large red bell pepper, julienne
1 large yellow bell pepper, julienne
8 sun-dried tomatoes, halved
1 cup fresh basil leaves, loosely packed
8 ounces corkscrew or other small pasta, like shells
½ cup low-fat ricotta
½ cup low-fat plain yogurt
dash of sea salt, ground black pepper

• Cook pasta according to package directions, drain. Place cooked pasta in a large bowl, drizzle 1 tablespoon of olive oil on top, cover with a clean towel. Set aside.
• Sauté onion in remaining oil in a large non-stick skillet until the onions are translucent. Add garlic and peppers, continue cooking until the peppers are fork tender.
• Stir in tomatoes, basil and cook until peppers are soft. Meanwhile, blend the ricotta and yogurt in a hand food chopper until smooth, let sit at room temperature.
• Remove sauce from skillet pour on cooked pasta, add cheese mixture, blend, serve.

Couscous Onion

Yield: 4 servings

2 cups chicken stock
½ cup chopped onions
1 cup uncooked couscous

• In a medium saucepan bring stock to a boil; add onion and couscous. Cover and remove from heat, let stand for 5 minutes, fluff with a fork and serve.

New England Clam Chowder

Yield: 10 cups

2 teaspoons unsalted butter
1 cup chopped onion
1 (20oz.) can minced clams, undrained
4 cups water
2 teaspoon sea salt
dash of ground white pepper
2 teaspoons cornstarch
2 Irish potatoes, peeled and diced
1 (13oz.) can evaporated skim milk

• Melt butter in a Dutch oven, add onion, sauté lightly.
• Drain the liquid from the canned clams to the cooking onions, reserve the minced clams. Add water, salt, pepper, cornstarch and stir well; add potatoes, cover and cook over low heat for 10 minutes. Uncover, add milk, clam meat, simmer for 6-8 minutes stirring often, until soup is heated thoroughly.
Serve immediately.

Gazpacho

Serves 4-6

2 cups chopped peeled cucumbers
1¼ cups chopped green bell peppers
1¼ cups chopped onions
1¼ cups chopped peeled tomatoes
2 (16oz.) cans tomato juice
4 cloves garlic, minced
2 tablespoons fresh lemon juice
⅓ cup red wine vinegar
¼ teaspoon red hot sauce
½ teaspoon paprika
* garnish: chopped green onions

• Combine all ingredients well in a pitcher, chill then serve.
Garnish with chopped onions.

Baked Taco

Yield: 8-10 servings

1 pound ground beef
½ cup chopped onion
1 (1¼oz.) envelope taco seasoning mix
1 can (15oz.) tomato sauce
1 can (15¼oz.) whole kernel corn, drained
2 cups shredded Cheddar cheese
2 cups biscuit mix, (see page 407)
1 cup skim milk
2 large eggs

• Preheat oven to 350 degrees.
• In a nonstick skillet brown beef and onion, drain. Spoon mixture into ungreased 13 x 9 baking dish. Stir in seasoning mix, tomato sauce and corn; sprinkle with cheese.
• In a medium bowl blend biscuit mix, milk and eggs; pour over meat mixture. Bake for 35 minutes or until light brown. Serve with small bowls of shredded lettuce, chopped tomatoes and plain non-fat sour cream or yogurt as a topping.

Top The Hot Baked Potato

• Low-fat cottage cheese, farmer cheese, Neufchâl cheese, shredded mozzarella cheese, Parmesan cheese
• Imitation bacon bits
• Steamed fresh vegetables, carrots, broccoli, zucchini, mushrooms, tomatoes, onions, spinach, yellow squash
• Meatless chili
• Lentils, pigeon peas, black beans
• Green onions, Old Bay seasonings
• Cooked shrimp, lobster, imitation crabmeat
• Low-fat yogurt or low-fat sour cream
• Salsa, pesto, sprinkle of herbs

Pesto Dip

Yield 1½ cups

1 (8oz.) container light sour cream
⅓ cup light cream cheese, softened
½ cup fresh basil leaves, packed
2 cloves garlic, minced

• Blend sour cream and cream cheese in medium bowl.
• In hand food chopper (see page 9) combine garlic and basil until a fine paste. Stir into sour cream
• Place mixture in an air-tight container; refrigerate until ready to use.

Pancake Toppings

Combine ½ cup vanilla yogurt, ¼ cup maple syrup or ¼ cup low-fat plain yogurt, slices of banana OR ¼ cup low-fat strawberry yogurt, slices of fresh strawberries OR 2 tablespoons applesauce, sprinkle of cinnamon.

Quick Angel Cake

Serves 8-10

1 package angel food cake mix
⅓ cup cocoa powder
2 teaspoons instant coffee

• Preheat oven to 350 degrees, one tube pan (*do not oil or spray pan)*
• Prepare cake batter according to package directions, adding cocoa and coffee powder to cake mix..
•Bake for 40-50 minutes, remove from oven, invert pan over funnel, cool completely before removing from pan.

Peanut Butter Cookies

Yield: 80 cookies

⅓ cup unsalted butter
¼ cup plus 2 tablespoons sugar
3 tablespoons egg substitute or 1 egg white
1 cup low-sodium, cream-style peanut butter
½ teaspoon baking soda
¼ teaspoon ground cinnamon
1 teaspoon vanilla extract
1 cup sifted unbleached flour

• Preheat oven to 375 degrees; in a large bowl, cream together butter and sugar until well blended. Beat in remaining ingredients, except flour, until nice and smooth. Add flour and beat until well blended.
• Roll dough into balls about ¾-inch in diameter and place on ungreased baking sheets. Score in crisscross fashion with fork tines to flatten.
• Bake 10-12 minutes or until browned. Remove cookies from sheets, cool on wire racks. Store in air-tight container.

Coconut Crust Pie

Yield: Serves 8-10

4 eggs
2 cups milk
1 cup sugar
½ cup all-purpose flour
pinch sea salt
2 teaspoons vanilla
½ cup unsalted butter
1 cup coconut, flaked
⅛ teaspoon nutmeg

• Preheat oven to 325 degrees; lightly grease 9-inch pie pan.
• Place all ingredients in a large bowl in order given. Mix well.
• Pour mixture into prepared pie pan.
• Bake for 40-50 min. Remove, cool completely before slicing.

Mock Cherry Pie

Yield: Serves 6

2 unbaked 9-inch pastry shells
2 cups fresh cranberries, rinsed and pat dry
¼ cup all-purpose flour
2 cups sugar
1 cup boiling water
1 cup seedless raisins, cut into halves
1 tablespoon butter
½ teaspoon sea salt
½ teaspoon vanilla extract

• Combine flour, sugar in a large mixing bowl. Add boiling water gradually, stirring constantly. Add cranberries, raisins, butter, salt and vanilla, mix well. Pour mixture into pie pan. Top with remaining pastry shell, sealing edge and cutting several slits. Preheat oven to 400 degrees.
• Bake for 10 minutes, reduce to 350 degrees, bake for 45 min. or until crust is golden brown. Remove, cool on wire rack.

Ambrosia

Serves 6

1 cup crushed pineapple, drained
½ cup lite sour cream or non-fat yogurt
½ cup grated lite cheese
1 ripe papaya, cubed
2 ripe bananas, thinly slice

• Combine pineapple and sour cream; fold in cheese and fruit.

Sugarless Apple Pie

Yield: Serves 8

2 unbaked 9-inch pie shells
1 (6oz.) can frozen apple juice concentrate, thawed
2 tablespoons cornstarch
1 tablespoon unsalted butter
1 teaspoon cinnamon
6 apples, peeled, chopped

• Prepare pie shells, set bottom shell in pie pan, set aside.
Preheat oven to 425 degrees.
• Blend apple juice concentrate and cornstarch in medium
saucepan. Bring to a boil, stirring constantly. Stir in butter and
cinnamon, add apples, mix gently. Spoon into pastry-lined pie
pan, top with remaining pastry. Press edges of pastry making
several slits on top pastry shell.
• Bake for 25 minutes, reduce oven temperature to 350 degrees,
bake 30 minutes or until crust is golden brown. Remove, cool
on wire rack.

Apple & Pear Sauce

Yield: 2 quarts

6 large Granny Smith apples, peeled and quartered
2 large pears, peeled and quartered
¾ cup water
2 tablespoons brown sugar
1 teaspoon cinnamon

• In a Dutch oven, combine apples, pear and water. Cover and
cook over low heat, stirring often, 40-55 minutes or until apples
and pears soften and become saucy. Add sugar and cinnamon,
simmer for 15 minutes, cool and store in an airtight container in
the refrigerator.

Raisin Bars

Yield: 16 bars

1 cup raisins
½ cup unsweetened apple juice
1 cup whole wheat flour
½ teaspoon baking soda
1 teaspoon ground cinnamon
¼ teaspoon ground nutmeg
¼ teaspoon ground cloves
1 egg
2 tablespoons vegetable oil
grated orange rind
(vegetable oil for greasing pan)

• Preheat oven to 350 degrees, lightly grease 8 x 8 square pan.
• In a medium sauce pan, combine the raisins and apple juice.
Bring to a boil, remove and let cool completely.
• Combine remaining ingredients in large bowl, mix well. Add
raisin mixture, blend thoroughly. Spread into prepared pan.
Sprinkle on grated orange rind.
• Bake for 30-40 minutes, cool in pan on wire rack, then cut.

Rice Pudding

Serves 4

½ cup white rice
1½ cups skim milk
2 tablespoons dry nonfat milk
2 egg whites, slightly beaten
¼ cup golden raisins
½ teaspoon vanilla
cinnamon, nutmeg

• Bring rice and 1 cup water to a boil; cover, simmer for 15
minutes. Combine remaining ingredients except cinnamon and
nutmeg; add cooked rice, pour into a 2-quart casserole dish.
Sprinkle with cinnamon, nutmeg.
• Bake at 300 degrees uncovered for 1 hour.

Applesauce No-Sugar Cake

Serves 10

1 cup dark raisins
1 tart apple, peeled, cored, chopped
2 cups water
2 cups all-purpose flour
1 teaspoon baking soda
½ teaspoon sea salt
½ teaspoon nutmeg
1½ teaspoons cinnamon
2 eggs, beaten
1 cup unsweetened applesauce
2 tablespoons liquid sweetener
¾ cup vegetable oil
1 teaspoon vanilla
½ cup pecans, chopped

• Preheat oven to 350 degrees; lightly grease and flour 10-inch baking pan.
• Combine raisins, apple and water in medium saucepan. Cook until water evaporates and fruit is soft; set aside and cool.
• Sift flour, baking soda, salt nutmeg, cinnamon onto a piece of wax paper.
• Combine eggs, applesauce, sweetener, oil and vanilla in medium bowl, blend well. Add flour mixture gradually mixing well after each addition, pour batter into prepared pan.
• Bake for 35-40 minutes, or until toothpick inserted in the center of the cake comes out clean. Cool in pan for 5 minutes, before inverting onto serving plate.

SIT AND SIP

The calorie counts for the following cocktails are for 80 proof and do not include the garnishes.

• *Bloddy Mary:* 1oz. vodka, 5oz. tomato juice, a squeeze of fresh lemon, a dash of Worcestershire and a dash of sea salt. Shake well, pour over ice in tall glass. *(97 calories)*

• *Gimlet:* fresh juice of 1 lime, 1oz. vodka or gin and 4 drops liquid sweetener. Shake well, pour over ice in tall glass. Garnish with lime peel. *(75 calories)*

• *Whisky Sour:* fresh juice of 1 lemon, 1oz. Scotch Whisky or Bourbon and 5 drops liquid sweetener. *(73 calories)*

• *Fruit Juice:* 2 (6½oz.) bottles sparkling mineral water, 1 (12oz.) can peach nectar, ½ cup unsweetened orange juice, ¼ cup unsweetened grapefruit juice, 2 tablespoons fresh lemon juice. Combine all ingredients in a large container, mix well and pour over ice in tall glasses. *(Yield: 4 cups, 68 calories each)*

• *Chocolate Milkshake:* ½ cup diet cream soda, 5 tablespoons instant nonfat dry milk, 1½ teaspoons vanilla extract, sugar substitute to taste. Crush 5 ice cubes, stir all ingredients with crushed ice in a large pitcher, pour into tall glasses. *(90 calories)*

• *Low-Cal Egg Nog:* 2 cups skim milk, ½ cup powdered egg substitute, sugar substitute equal to 2 tablespoons sugar, 1½ teaspoons vanilla, rum or brandy flavoring, pinch of fresh grated nutmeg, Combine all ingredients in pitcher, pour over 1 ice cube in each tall glass. (*88 calories*)

Vegetable Microwave Chart

Vegetable	*Quantity*	*Preparation*
Artichokes 3½-inch diam.	1 2	Wash, cut tops off each leaf.
Asparagus spears and pieces	1 pound.	Wash, cut off hard ends.
Green beans	1 pound	Wash, cut ends off, snap or leave whole.
Beets	4 medium	Wash, leave 1-inch of beet top.
Broccoli; whole chopped	1-2½ pounds 1-2½ pounds	Remove outer leaves and split stalks.
Brussel Sprouts	1 pound.	Wash, remove outside leaves and stems.
Cabbage	½ med. head, grated 1 med. head, wedged	Remove outside leaves.
Carrots	4 sliced 6 sliced 8 sliced	Peel and cut tops off.
Cauliflower	1 med., florets 1 med., whole	Wash, cut into florets, remove core.
Celery	2½ cups 1-inch slices	Wash and slice.
Corn on Cob	1 ear 2 ears 3 ears 4 ears	Husk and cook no more than four at a time.
Eggplant	1 med., sliced 1 med., whole	Wash, peel, cut into slices. Pierce skin several times.

Time:

Microwave on high.	Amount of Water	Time Standing In Water	Hints
7-8 min.	¼ cup	2-3 min.	When done, leaves
11-12 min.	½ cup	2-3 min.	peel off easily.
2-3 min.	¼ cup	None	Stir once during cooking.
12-14 min.	¼ cup	2-3 min.	Stir once during cooking.
16-18 min.	¼ cup	None	Peel after cooking.
9-10 min.	¼ cup	3 min.	Stir during cooking.
8-9 min.	¼ cup	2-3 min.	Stir once during cooking.
5-6 min.	¼ cup	2-3 min.	Stir once during cooking.
13-15 min.	¼ cup	2-3 min.	Stir after 7 min.
7-9 min.	1 tbsp.	2-3 min.	Stir once during
9-10 min.	2 tbsp.	2-3 min.	cooking.
10-11 min.	3 tbsp.	2-3 min.	
7-8 min.	¼ cup	2-3 min.	Stir after 5 min.
8-9 min.	½ cup	3 min.	Stir once during cooking.
8-9 min.	¼ cup	2 min.	Stir once during cooking.
3-4 min.	¼ cup	2 min.	Cook in a covered 6-inch
6-7 min.	¼ cup	2 min.	dish. Rotate once
9-10 min.	¼ cup	2 min.	during cooking.
11-12 min.	¼ cup	2 min.	
5-6 min.	2 tbsp.	3 min.	Rotate once during cooking.
6-7 min.	None	None	Place on micro proof rack.

Vegetable Microwave Chart

Vegetable	*Quantity*	*Preparation*
Mushrooms	½ lb. sliced	Wash, slice, add butter.
Okra	½ pound	Wash, trim stems. Leave whole or cut.
Onions	1 lb. tiny, whole 1 lb. med. to lg.	Peel, add butter. Peel, quarter, add butter.
Parsnips	4 med., quartered	Peel and quarter.
Green Peas	1 pound	Shell and rinse.
Sweet Potatoes	1 2 4	Wash, pierce with fork. Put on paper towel in circle 1-inch apart.
White Potatoes	1 2 3 4	Wash, pierce with fork. Put on paper towel in circle 1-inch apart.
Boiled Potatoes	3	Peel, cut in quarters.
Spinach	1 pound	Wash, remove tough stems, drain.
Squash: Acorn or Butternut	1-1½ lbs. whole	Wash, pierce with fork. Put on paper towel in circle 1-inch apart.
Spaghetti Squash	2-3 lbs.	Wash, pierce with fork. Place on a paper towel.
Turnips	4 cups cubed	Peel and cube.
Zucchini	3 cups sliced	Peel and slice.

Vegetable Microwave Chart

Time Microwave on high	Amount of Water	Time Standing In Water	Hints
2-4 min.	None	2 min.	Stir once during cooking.
3-5 min.	¼ cup	2 min.	
6-7 min.	None	3 min.	Stir once during
7-9 min.	None	3 min	cooking
8-9 min.	¼ cup	2 min.	Stir once during cooking.
7-8 min.	¼ cup	2 min.	Stir once during
8-9 min.	½ cup	2-3 min.	cooking.
4-5 min.	None	3 min.	Rotate once during
6-7 min.	None	3 min.	cooking.
8-10 min.	None	3 min.	
4-6 min.	None	3 min.	Rotate once during
6-8 min.	None	3 min.	cooking.
8-12 min.	None	3 min.	
12-16 min.	None	3 min.	
12-16 min.	1 cup	None	Stir once during cooking.
6-7 min.	None	2 min.	Stir once during cooking.
10-12 min.	None	2 min.	Slice in half, remove seeds.
6 min. per lb.	None	5 min.	Serve with butter, Parmesan cheese or spaghetti sauce.
9-11 min.	¼ cup	3 min.	Stir after 5 min.
7-8 min.	¼ cup	2 min.	Stir after 4 min.

MICROWAVING

MICROWAVING means to cook, heat or defrost foods with microwave energy. Microwave cooking is moist cooking since liquids do not evaporate or thicken. Reduce liquids in recipes by one-quarter, except when cooking rice or pasta which requires established amounts of liquid for rehydration. Just like any other type of cooking it has its own characteristics. Study your microwave manual handbook

Microwave Tips:
• Always use microwave-safe utensils: plastic or glass.
• Choose the minimum cooking time. Food continues to cook after it is removed from the microwave.
• Foods that are going to be cooked for more than 5 minutes should not be covered with plastic wrap because it melts. Cover foods with a paper towel or waxed paper to allow steam to escape and to prevent popping of natural juices that soil the oven.
• Use white paper plates as lids to prevent spattering.
• When using plastic wrap, keep one corner of cover open, or make some small slits in the wrap.
• Keep your microwave clean. Built-up grease or food spatters in the microwave can slow cooking times.
• Do not use metal dishes or aluminum foil except as specifically recommended by the manufacturer of your microwave.
• If your microwave does not have a turn table, you can purchase a portable turn table in a kitchen supply store.
• Cover saucy main dishes, saucy appetizers and dips with plastic wrap. Cover other main dishes and meats with waxed paper.
• Do not cover bakery foods, griddle foods (pancakes, etc.) or beverages.
• Freshen chips and crackers by microwaving on HIGH 15-30 seconds. Let stand for 2 to 3 minutes.

• Cereal: use large enough container to avoid spill over. Start with hottest tap water to shorten cooking time. Stir half-way through cooking time. Do not cover.

• Do not cover watery vegetables which need no water added for steaming. Rinse foods and place directly in bowl.

• When doing corn on the cob, remove all but the last two layers of husks and rinse under fresh water. Place in microwave and cook, the husks become a built-in wrapper.

• Use your microwave oven to soften cream cheese and to soften or melt butter.

• Roast shelled nuts for 6-10 minutes, stirring frequently.

• Peel fruit or tomatoes by placing in 1 cup hot water. Microwave on HIGH for 30-45 seconds; skins remove easily.

• Melt chocolate right in its paper wrapper. You have nothing to clean up and there is no danger of scorching or overcooking. Make sure it is not foil wrapped.

• Cheese: soften processed cheese, cheese dips, cream cheese or cheese spreads at LOW for 1 to 2 minutes. Remove cheese from jar or wrapper, place in bowl or plate before microwaving.

• Stirring: when microwaving stir cooked portions from the outside to the center.

• Prick foods to release pressure. Steam builds up in pressure in foods which are tightly covered by a skin or membrane. Prick potatoes, eggplants, egg yolks and chicken livers to prevent bursting. Baked potato microwaves fluffy, moist and tender. Use a microwave potato holder, it's a nice tool.

• Precook barbecued ribs or chicken in the microwave until almost done, then place on the grill to sear.

• Soften brown sugar by placing it in a dish with a slice of bread or apple and microwave for 15-20 seconds, stirring once.

• Dry bread for crumbs or croutons. Place cubed or crumbled bread on paper plates. Microwave for 6 to 7 minutes, stirring occasionally.

• Drying fresh herbs: wash, dry and remove leaves from stems. May be layered between paper towels and dried in the microwave on HIGH for 1 ½ to 2 minutes or until they feel dry. Cool and store in airtight containers.
• Ripen an avocado by microwaving on LOW for 2 to 4 minutes.
• Refresh salty snacks, pretzels, popcorn and potato chips a few seconds on HIGH. Let stand a few minutes to crisp.
• Leftover casserole dishes make a perfect filler for tortillas. Spoon on top of a tortilla. Add grated or thinly sliced cheese and roll up. Roll in a paper towel and microwave on HIGH 20-30 seconds.
• Heat condensed canned soups that are diluted with water on HIGH. Use the medium setting for soups made with milk.
• Don't sprinkle salt on vegetables before microwaving. It can leave freckled-looking burn spots. Wait until vegetables are done, then season.

Basic Pastry Shell

Yield: 1, 9-inch pastry shell

1 cup unsifted all-purpose flour
1 teaspoon sea salt
6 tablespoons shortening
2 tablespoons cold water

• In a small bowl place flour and salt. Cut in shortening, until mixture resembles the size of small peas. Sprinkle water over flour-shortening mixture. Stir with fork to form ball.
• Roll out on floured pastry cloth with rolling pin to ⅛-inch thickness. Line a microwave-safe 9-inch pie plate, shaping pastry to the edge of pie plate. Prick pastry with fork. Microwave at high 6-7 minutes.

Quiche Pastry Shell

Yield: 1, 9-inch quiche pastry

1 cup unsifted all-purpose flour
½ teaspoon sea salt
3 tablespoons shortening
3 tablespoons cold butter
2½ tablespoons cold water
1 egg yolk
1 teaspoon Worcestershire sauce

• In small mixing bowl stir together flour and salt. Cut in shortening until it has the appearance of cornmeal. Cut in butter until particles form the size of peas.
• Sprinkle mixture with cold water. Blend lightly with fingers until dough holds together and can be formed into ball. Roll out to fit a microwave-safe 9-inch quiche dish. Brush pastry with mixture of egg yolk and Worcestershire sauce. Microwave on HIGH for 5-7 minutes.

Spanish Rice Plus

Serves 2

1 (16oz.) can chopped tomatoes, undrained
1 (16oz.) can zucchini, undrained
1 (4½oz.) envelope Spanish rice and sauce mix
½ pound cubed lean pork
1 small green pepper, cut into strips

• Combine tomatoes, zucchini, rice mix and pork in a 1½-quart microwave-safe casserole. Cover with lid and microwave on HIGH for 12-14 minutes or until liquid is absorbed, stirring once. Fluff with fork, garnish with pepper strips. Let stand covered about 5 minutes before serving.

➤ *Note:* You can substitute pork with cooked cubed chicken, add about 1½ cups.

Granola Chews

Yield: 24 bars

3 cups old-fashioned oats
1 cup toasted sliced almonds
1 cup wheat germ
¼ cup sesame seed
¾ cup brown sugar, packed
½ cup unsalted butter
¼ cup honey
¼ cup lukewarm water
1 teaspoon sea salt
1 cup chopped dried apricots
½ cup raisins

• Combine brown sugar, butter, honey, water and salt in a microwave-safe 3-quart glass bowl or casserole. Microwave on HIGH for 4 minutes stir, microwave 4 minutes more.
• Stir in oats, almonds, wheat germ and sesame seed; microwave on medium 3 min. Stir, microwave 9 min. more or until oats are lightly toasted, stirring after every 2 minutes.
• Stir in apricots and raisins; pour mixture into 15½ x10½x 1-inch jelly roll pan, spreading to edges of pan. Press mixture down slightly, using a spatula. Let stand 30 minutes. Cut into bars.

Nachos

Serves 2

Begin with large corn chips in a circle on a paper plate or small microwave-safe dish. Dot with jalapeño bean dip or refried bean mixture on tortilla corn chips, top with slices of hot pepper cheese. Cover with plastic wrap, leaving center space open. Microwave on HIGH for ¼ to ½ minute or until cheese is melted. Top with salsa and sour cream.

Herb-Coated Fish

Serves 4

4 (7oz.) skinless grouper fillets, about ¾ inch thick
½ cup crushed corn flakes
½ cup grated Parmesan cheese
⅓ cup minced fresh parsley
½ teaspoon garlic powder
½ teaspoon paprika
¼ teaspoon sea salt
¼ teaspoon ground black pepper
2 egg whites, lightly beaten

• Wash and pat fish dry. Combine next 7 ingredients in a
shallow dish, mixing well. Dip fillets in egg white, then in
crumb mixture, coating well. In a microwave-safe shallow
2-quart baking dish, with thickest portions to outside of dish.
• Cover with paper towels and microwave on HIGH for 8-10
minutes or until fish flakes easily when tested with a fork.

Chocolate Clusters

Yield: 2 dozen

1 package (8 squares) semi-sweet chocolate
3 tablespoons peanut butter
1½ to 2 cups cornflakes or raisin bran cereal or
1½ to 2 cups whole or coarsely chopped nuts or raisins or
2 to 2½ cups popped popcorn or
2 cups miniature marshmallows

• Melt chocolate and peanut butter in a 1½ quart microwave-
safe bowl on HIGH (100 percent) power for 2 minutes. Stir,
microwave for 30 seconds.
• Add cereal, or nuts and raisins, or popped popcorn, or
miniature marshmallows, and mix lightly until completely
coated. Drop mixture from a teaspoon onto waxed paper. Chill
until chocolate is firm.

Crunchy Italian-Style Party Mix

Yield: 10 cups

½ cup unsalted butter
1 tablespoon Worcestershire sauce
1 teaspoon dried Italian seasoning
½ teaspoon garlic powder
2½ cups small pretzels or pretzel sticks
2 cups round toasted oat cereal
2 cups bite-size wheat or bran square cereal
2 cups bite-size rice or corn square cereal or bite-size shredded wheat biscuits
1½ cups mixed nuts
¼ cup grated Parmesan cheese

• In a 2 cup glass measure, place butter, Worcestershire sauce, Italian seasoning and garlic powder. Microwave uncovered on HIGH for 1½-2 minutes or until butter melts, stirring once.
• In a 3-quart microwave-safe casserole dish, combine pretzels, cereals and nuts. Drizzle the butter mixture over the cereal mixture, tossing to coat evenly. Microwave, uncovered on HIGH for 5 min. or until hot, stirring three times. Toss with Parmesan cheese. Spread on foil, mix will become crisp while cooling.

Chili Con Queso Dip

Yield: 3 cups

1 pound block processed cheese, diced in 1½-in. pieces
1 pound can chili with beans

• In a microwave-safe 1½ quart casserole stir together diced cheese and chili. Microwave on HIGH for 8-11 minutes. Let stand a few minutes, serve with large tortilla chips.

Micro-Nachos

Serves 4-6

¾ cup Cheddar cheese or Monterey Jack cheese, shredded
tortilla chips to fill 9-inch pie plate
1 cup picante sauce or chunky salsa at room temperature
* garnish with one or more: sliced black olives, shredded crab
meat or chopped cooked shrimp

• Cover a microwave-safe 9-inch plate with tortilla chips.
Sprinkle with cheese evenly over the chips; microwave on
HIGH for 30-60 seconds or just until cheese is melted.
• Top with picante sauce or chunky salsa. Garnish with any or
all of the following; sliced black olives, shredded crabmeat or
chopped cooked shrimp, sour cream.

Swordfish with Tomato Basil

Serves 4

1 large tomato, thinly sliced
6 large fresh basil leaves
1½ pounds swordfish steaks (1-inch thick)
1 teaspoon olive oil
1 teaspoon fresh lemon juice
dash sea salt, ground black pepper

• Place sliced tomato in a microwave-safe 11 x 8½ x 2-inch
glass dish. Add basil leaves on top. Center swordfish over
tomatoes; add remaining ingredients.
• Cover tightly with microwave plastic wrap; microwave on
HIGH for 5 minutes. Remove, pierce plastic with tip of a sharp
knife, let stand, for 2 minutes covered.

Parmesan Grouper Fillets

Serves 4

4 (6oz.) skinless grouper fillets, about ¾ inch thick)
1 tablespoon lemon juice
½ cup grated Parmesan cheese
3 tablespoons chopped green onion
1 (2oz.) jar chopped pimento, drained
2 tablespoons butter, softened
1 tablespoon mayonnaise
¼ teaspoon sea salt
⅛ teaspoon hot red sauce

• Arrange fish in a microwave-safe shallow 2-quart casserole with thickest portions to outside of dish. Brush fillets with lemon juice; cover, microwave on HIGH for 4 minutes.
• Combine remaining ingredients, mix well, spread over fillets. Microwave uncovered, on HIGH for 4-6 minutes or until fish flakes easily when tested with a fork. Let stand 1 minute before serving.

Creamy Chicken Almonds

Serves 4

½ cup thinly sliced celery
¼ cup chopped onion
1 (10¾oz.) can cream of celery soup
¼ cup milk
½ cup sliced almonds
1 cup cubed cooked chicken
¼ teaspoon Worcestershire sauce
2 cups cooked rice or egg noodles

• Combine celery and onion in a microwave-safe 1½-qt. casserole. Cover, microwave for 2 minutes on HIGH.
• Add remaining ingredients; mix well, cover, microwave on HIGH 4-5 minutes stirring after 2 min. Serve over rice or noodles.

Beef Meatballs

Yield: 12 meatballs

1 pound ground beef
1 egg
½ cup fine bread crumbs
1 teaspoon sea salt
¼ teaspoon paprika
⅛ teaspoon ground black pepper

• In a medium bowl, mix all ingredients well. Shape into 12 balls, arrange in a circle in a microwave-safe 9-inch pie plate. Cover with wax paper; microwave on HIGH for 9-12 minutes or until done.

➢ *Note:* Add one of the following VARIATIONS for a great flavor combination to the above basic recipe.

• 1 tbsp. Worcestershire sauce and ¼ cup chopped onion
• 1 tbsp. steak sauce and 1 clove minced garlic or ½ tsp. garlic powder
• 1 tbsp. salsa and ¼ cup finely chopped green pepper
• 2 tbsp. red wine and 1 tsp. oregano

Curried Meat Balls

Yield: 4 dozen

½ cup crushed herb seasoned stuffing mix
⅓ cup evaporated milk
¼ teaspoon sea salt
1½ to 2 teaspoons curry powder
1 pound ground chuck beef

• In a large bowl, combine all ingredients, shape meat mixture into 48 1-inch balls. In an microwave-safe 8-inch square dish place about 24 balls, cover with wax paper.
• Microwave on HIGH for 4-5 minutes. Repeat with other half of meat balls.

Rhubarb Crisp

Yield: Serves 8

2 cups of rhubarb cut into ½-inch pieces
2 tablespoons lemon juice
½ cup sugar
½ teaspoon grated lemon peel
1 cup brown sugar
¾ cup all-purpose flour
¼ cup rolled oats
½ cup unsalted butter, softened

• Combine rhubarb, lemon juice and sugar in a 9-inch square microwave-safe dish. Spread mixture evenly in dish. Sprinkle lemon peel on top.
• In a large bowl, combine brown sugar, flour, rolled oats and butter. Sprinkle evenly over the top of the rhubarb mixture.
• Bake uncovered in the microwave oven for 15 minutes, turning the dish three times so that all sides are evenly cooked.

Sausage & Caraway Cabbage

Serves 2-4

3 cups shredded cabbage
2 cups peeled and cubed Irish Potatoes
1 medium apple, cored and chopped
2 tablespoons water
½ teaspoon sea salt
¼ teaspoon ground allspice
½ teaspoon caraway seed
1 (10oz.) package fully cooked low-fat smoked sausage links

• Combine all the ingredients except sausage in a microwave-safe 1-quart casserole; mix lightly, cover, microwave on HIGH 10-12 min. or until cabbage and potatoes are tender, stir once.
• Cut sausages in bite size pieces; add to cabbage mixture, stir once. Cover and microwave on HIGH for 2-4 minutes.

Pressure Cooking is a Pleasure

Out of the past and into the future with the versatility of the pressure cooker. Today's busy, nutrition-conscious cooks find the pressure cooker convenient, economical (they save water, fuel and time); and they make wholesome dishes.

Pressure cookers are most often used to cook food that require long, moist heat, such as stews or soups. As steam builds up in the tightly sealed pot, the pressure rises and the boiling point increases from the usual 212 degrees to about 250 degrees. This is why foods can cook in one-third of the usual time and are tender, fuller-flavored.

Your pressure cooker can also double as a steamer or spaghetti pot when you don't lock the lid and use the pressure regulator. Your cooker makes an ideal pot for carting prepared food ashore for a beach party. The locking lid keeps food from dribbling into the bottom of the dinghy or from bouncing off into deep water.

Because of the metal thickness, these pots retain heat for long periods of time. A pot of rice, for example, will stay hot in a pressure cooker for almost an hour. It can be prepared well in advance and forgotten until the whole meal is ready to go on the table. You can wrap the pressure cooker with newspaper or terry towel or place in a soft insulator bag for the meal later in the day.

A good rule of thumb to follow is to decrease the length of cooking time for a conventional recipe by two thirds. The amount of liquid used may also have to be adjusted because there is very little evaporation from the pressure cooker. Generally, decrease the amount of liquid so there is only about half a cup more than desired in the finished product. Remember, however, there must always be water or some liquid in the pressure cooker to form the necessary steam while cooking. To avoid overcooking, release pressure after the minimum recommended time.

There is often some trial and error required to become skillful. Slightly undercooked can be finished off by simmering, covered but not locked under pressure over low heat. Otherwise, re-lock and return to high pressure for another few minutes. Practice makes perfect.

I am presently using a 6-quart stainless steel FAGOR Pressure Cooker. The important features on this cooker are: Two short handles to lift pot, being able to release pressure without waiting it to come down of its own accord or using cold water to bring pressure down. You can even deep fry under pressure with this cooker. This cooker can be purchased at major boat shows or send for ordering information to: Show-Me Products 2705 61st Street #B448, Galveston, TX 77551, 409/986-5154. Taking proper care of this utensil will make it last a very long time, so your initial investment pays off.

Prescribed Pressure Pointers

• Read the manufacturers instructions for your model pressure cooker.
• After each cleaning, check valves and gaskets; make sure the vent pipe is clear before using.
• Never store your pressure cooker with the top securely on; keep rack, booklet and pressure regulator inside when storing away.
• Do not fill your cooker over two-thirds full; this allows for food expansion during cooking.
• Molds: fill molds up to two-thirds full to allow for expansion of food during cooking. *Use* 4 or 6oz. size, metal or little earthenware soufflé dishes. Molds and custard cups can be covered with aluminum foil or several layers of waxed paper securely tied with clean white string. Glass, metal and earthenware molds can be used in the pressure cooker. Place water up to rack and molds on rack cook, as directed.
• Searing meat will seal in the juices. To prevent meat from sticking, preheat pan, add a small amount of shortening or oil then sear meat.

• Another feature of the pressure cooker that makes it an important tool on a boat is its use as an oven. You can bake breads, cakes, brownies, muffins. Place small tins or pans on the rack lock lid but do not put on the pressure regulator. When doing bread directly inside pressure cooker with no pan, coat sides and bottom of pressure cooker lightly with oil, sprinkle cornmeal evenly and place dough directly in pressure cooker for second rising. The cornmeal forms an adequate heat barrier if used in conjunction with a flame tamer (usually asbestos-like material) under the pot. Remove rubber ring, place cover in place do not put on pressure regulator. Bake and check anytime for brownness on sides. Then flip out bread, return to pressure cooker and bake for 5 more minutes to brown bottom.

• If you have a pressure cooker you cannot open until pressure comes down, or by using cold water. Shorten the cooking time between 5-8 minutes. Remove from heat, allow the pressure to come down on its own accord.

• To let pressure drop of its own accord, set cooker aside to cool. This usually takes 2-4 minutes. This additional time allows cooking without any heat on. To cool cooker at once, place in sink and run cold water being careful not to get any water in vent pipe or place it in a pan of cold sea water until no steam escapes. Remove pressure regulator once pressure has completely been reduced. The Fagor pressure cooker has an extra pressure release knob that enables you to release pressure quickly. Read your manufacturer's booklet.

• When the recipe directions say: COOK 0 MINUTES, this means to cook food only until cooking pressure, (15 pounds) is reached, then remove cooker from heat and cool according to recipe.

• When quick cooking vegetables, set the timer from the moment the lid is locked into place. If the recipe states 2 minutes total cooking time, this means you should release any pressure that has built up, whether or not high pressure has been reached, after 2 minutes have elapsed. Release the pressure and remove the lid immediately.

• Under high pressure, cooking time begins from the moment that high pressure is reached.
• Don't throw away any of those vegetable peels, trimmings, corncobs, carrots, celery sticks, diced parsnips, turnips, half used onions. They still have good flavor. Wrap them in some cheesecloth and make a basic vegetable stock. (see page 427).
• To add additional flavor, divide herbs, cook half with the soup under pressure. Once pressure is down, unlock lid, stir in remainder of herbs, recover and let sit in residual steam in the pot for a few minutes.
• If a soup is too thick, thin it with water or stock. If it is too thin, purée a cup or two of the solid ingredients and stir them back in.
• Canning turkey, beef chunks, ground beef, tuna fish, conch and spaghetti sauce under pressure is possible. Read the manufacturer's instructions how to do it.

Beef Onion Beer

Serves 6-8

2½-3 pounds beef roast (bottom round, round or brisket)
1 cup ketchup
1 (12oz.) can beer or 1(12oz.) can cola or gingerale
1 envelope (1.25oz.) dried onion soup mix

• Sear beef on both sides in pressure cooker; add remaining ingredients. Secure cover, bring up to pressure, cook 20 min.
• Remove from heat, allow pressure to drop of its own accord.
• Remove meat, slice thin. Replace back into pressure cooker, simmer for 10-15 minutes or until meat is tender.

➤ *Note:* Serve on a great grain bun with a topping of horseradish, side dish of coleslaw. Make a dish of kasha and cooked bow ties, (page 272).

Vegetable Soup 1, 2, 3

Serves 8-10

1 medium onion, chopped
1 clove garlic, minced
1 cup sliced carrots
1 cup diced celery
1 cup dry mixed beans, rinse well
1 (14½oz.) can stewed tomatoes
5 cups water
1 tablespoon parsley flakes
½ teaspoon sea salt
⅛ teaspoon ground black pepper
½ teaspoon seasoning mix (see page 395)

• Place all ingredients in pressure cooker, except sea salt; secure lid and bring up to pressure. Reduce heat to maintain a slow steady rocking; cook for 20 minutes.
• Shut off heat; allow pressure to drop of its own accord.
• Open pot, stir in salt, add additional salt and pepper to taste.

➤ *Hint*: Make your own mixture of mix beans: one package each of small navy beans, black-eye peas, lima beans, red beans. Mix well, store remainder of dry bean mixture in an air-tight container.

Fish Chowder

Serves 4

1 pound fish fillet, cut into large chunks
2 (6½oz.) cans minced clams (do not drain)
2 tablespoons olive oil
2 medium onions, thinly slice
2 large Irish potatoes, cut into chunks
6 medium tomatoes, peeled, diced
4 cloves garlic, minced
½ teaspoon basil
½ teaspoon sea salt
½ teaspoon oregano
½ teaspoon ground black pepper
1½ cups water

• Place all ingredients into pressure cooker except *FISH* and *CLAMS*. Secure cover, bring up to pressure and cook for 4 minutes.
• Remove from heat; allow pressure to drop of its own accord.
• Open pressure cooker, add fish and clams and stir lightly. Place cover on but do not lock lid, simmer for 3-5 minutes.

Zucchini-Squash Mash

Serves 4-6

½ cup butter
1 cup eggplant, cut in chunks (leave on skin)
1 large zucchini, cut in chunks
½ cup sliced mushrooms
2 cloves garlic, minced
1 large tomato, peeled, diced
1 (7oz.) can pimento chopped
1 teaspoon sea salt
¼ teaspoon ground black pepper
1 cup rice
2 cups chicken broth

• Combine butter, eggplant, zucchini, mushrooms, garlic, tomato, pimento lightly, sauté lightly directly in pressure cooker. Add remaining ingredients; secure cover, cook for O minutes. (See note below and page 331.)
• Remove from heat and allow pressure to drop of its own accord.

➤ *Note:* As soon as the pressure regulator attains a rocking action, SHUT OFF HEAT IMMEDIATELY.

Cabbage Sweet & Sour

Serves 6-8

4 slices bacon, cut into small pieces
1 pound cabbage, shredded
1 medium onion, thinly sliced
¼ cup raisins
1 teaspoon sea salt
⅛ teaspoon ground black pepper
¼ teaspoon celery seeds
2 tablespoons sugar
¼ cup cider vinegar
¼ cup water

• Place bacon in pressure cooker; cook until lightly brown.
Add remaining ingredients, secure cover, cook under pressure
for 2 minutes. Remove from heat, allow pressure to drop of its
own accord. Open, stir and serve.

Beef Cabbage Soup

Yield: 4 servings

1½ pounds cabbage shredded
2 cups beef bouillon
1 cup beer
½ teaspoon ground black pepper
½ teaspoon celery flakes

• Combine ingredients in pressure cooker, secure cover, bring
up to pressure, cook for 5 minutes. Remove from heat, **cool at
once**. Sprinkle with your favorite grated cheese

Sassy Pork

Serves 4-6

2 pounds boneless pork shoulder
1 (10½oz.) can condensed onion soup
¾ cup apple juice
½ cup chopped mixed dried fruit
1 large onion, thinly sliced
3 whole cloves

• Sear meat on all sides in pressure cooker, remove excess drippings.
• Add remaining ingredients; secure cover, cook 30 minutes.
• Remove from heat, allow pressure to drop of its own accord.

Chicken à l'Orange

Serves 4

3 pounds chicken (your favorite parts cut into serving pieces)
1 tablespoon salad oil
2 cloves garlic, minced
½ teaspoon sea salt
½ cup red wine
½ cup orange marmalade
¼ teaspoon ground black pepper
¼ cup lemon juice
3 cups cooked rice (your choice)

• Brown chicken in oil, add remaining ingredients; secure cover, cook for 15 minutes. Remove from heat, allow pressure to drop of its own accord. Serve with cooked rice.

Sweet-Sour Spareribs

Serves 4

2½ pounds lean spareribs (cut 3 ribs together)
1 teaspoon sea salt
½ teaspoon dry mustard
2 tablespoons brown sugar
2 tablespoons cider vinegar
1 tablespoon ground ginger
¾ cup sherry wine
1 tablespoon soy sauce
2 cloves garlic, minced

• Place spareribs in a zip-lock bag with dry mustard, shake well to coat. Put coated ribs and remaining ingredients in pressure cooker; secure cover, bring up to pressure, cook 15 minutes .
• Remove from heat, allow pressure to drop of its own accord.

New England Corned Beef

Serves 4

2 pounds corned beef
water (see below)
4 medium Irish potatoes, peeled
4 large whole carrots, peeled
1 medium size cabbage, cut in four wedges
¼ teaspoon celery seeds

• Place corned beef on rack in pressure cooker. Add water to top of corned beef, secure cover, bring up to pressure and cook for 20 minutes.
• Remove from heat and allow pressure to drop of its own accord. Open, place on top of corned beef in this order: potatoes, carrots, celery seeds and last cabbage. Secure cover, bring up to pressure, cook for 3 minutes. Remove from heat and allow pressure to drop of its own accord.
• Place vegetables on large platter, slice corned beef.

Pressure Cooker Soda Bread

Yield: 1 bread

5 cups all-purpose flour
1½ teaspoons sea salt
2½ teaspoons baking powder
1¼ teaspoons baking soda
2 cups sour milk or buttermilk, (see pages 371,388)

• Grease the pressure cooker lightly, sprinkle the sides and bottom lightly with cornmeal.
• Combine all dry ingredients and mix well. Add milk to make a soft and sticky dough. Knead briefly on a floured board and form into a ball. Place the dough in the cooker.
• Put the lid on. DO NOT ATTACH THE PRESSURE REGULATOR VALVE. Cook over moderate heat for 20 minutes. Remove the cooker from heat and turn loaf over. Return to heat, cover and cook another 10 minutes or longer for firmness. Remove from pot and cool on wire rack.

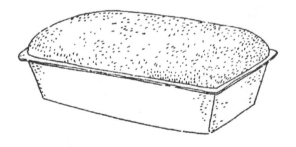

Potatoes, Pumpkin & Squashes

Serves 4

1 medium pumpkin or
1 medium to large spaghetti squash

• Cut pumpkin in half and half again if too large to fit in cooker
• or cut spaghetti squash in half (use a sharp cleaver or chef's knife).
• Scoop out seeds and pulp. Place either pumpkin or squash skin side up on rack. Place water in pot just up to rack.
• Secure cover, bring up to pressure, cook 10 minutes. Remove from heat and allow pressure to drop of its own accord.
• While cooking spaghetti squash, prepare a large bowl with pats of butter and grated Parmesan cheese. Carefully remove hot squash, place on a cutting board, have prepared bowl with butter and cheese alongside. Take a fork and scrape out squash from end to end. See how spaghetti strings come out as you do this. Place strings inside bowl, toss with cheese and butter.
• With a completely cooked pumpkin, peel, then mash with a small amount of butter and milk, serve hot. Or make a purée for use in a pumpkin pie or nut bread recipe.
• Large baking Idaho potatoes or sweet or yam potatoes: wash, make two or three slits in potatoes, place on rack. Pour in enough water to bottom of rack, secure cover, bring up to pressure, cook 5 minutes. Remove from heat, allow pressure to drop of its own accord. Top with your favorite toppings.
• Acorn squash: cut in half, scoop out seeds, put on rack skin side down, pour water up to rack. Secure cover, bring up to pressure, cook 3 minutes. Remove from heat, allow pressure to drop of its own accord, remove, top with a pat of butter and a sprinkle of brown sugar.

Dried Beans

Cooking beans in the pressure cooker are done in one quarter or less than the normal cooking time. To pressure cook soaked beans, use approximately 3 cups of water per cup of dried beans that have been soaked; use 4 cups of water for unsoaked beans. The beans must be covered with at least 1-inch of water above them; don't fill the pot more than halfway. There is very little evaporation in pressure cooking. Add only about ½-¾ cup more liquid at the start than you want at the finish. Practice at the beginning by cooking beans to a constistency to a point just before tenderness, then you can finish cooking the beans by simmering them with the cover on, but **do not** lock lid in place.

• Add 1 tablespoon of oil per cup of dried beans (helps to control foaming). Add one or more of the optional flavorings: 1 or 2 cloves garlic, chopped; 1 bay leaf; ½ teaspoon dried herbs; 1 small onion, chopped; small amount of chopped bacon, or a piece of pork or ham hock.
Do not add salt while cooking beans, it tends to harden their skins as well as prevent cooking properly. It's best to add salt after the beans are entirely cooked.

• After you have filled the pressure cooker with beans, water and seasonings secure the lid, bring up to pressure and cook for the time indicated on the cooking chart.

Pressure Cooker Bean Cooking Chart

Minutes cooking time under high pressure

Beans 1 cup Dry	Soaked 4-8 hours	Unsoaked	Yield in Cups
Black (turtle)	9-11 min.	20-25 min.	2
Black-eyed peas	Do not soak	9-11 min.	2¼
Cannellini	9-12 min.	21-25 min.	2
Chick-peas	10-12 min.	25-35 min.	2½
Great Northern	8-12 min.	25-30 min.	2¼
Lentils	Do not soak	7-10 min.	2
Limas (large) 2 tab. oil, remove loose skins before cooking.	4-7 min.	12-16 min.	2
Limas (baby)	5-7 min.	12-16 min.	2½
Peas (split, green or orange)	Do not soak	8-10 min.	2
Pigeon peas (granules)	6-9 min.	20-25 min.	3
Pinto	4-6 min.	22-25 min.	3
Navy (peas)	6-8 min.	16-25 min.	2
Red kidney	10-12 min.	17-20 min.	2

White Basmati
Yield: 3 cups

1 cup basmati white rice
½ teaspoon sea salt
1½ cups water or vegetable stock
2 cups water in cooker with rack

• Combine all ingredients in the pressure cooker. Bring heat to high and stir a few times to blend.
• Secure lid, bring up to high pressure; lower heat just enough to maintain high pressure and cook for 3 minutes.
• Remove from heat and allow pressure to drop of its own accord.
Remove cover and allow excess steam to escape. Fluff rice with fork and serve.

Spareribs with Mincemeat
Yields: 4 servings

2½ pounds spareribs (cut into serving size pieces)
1 tablespoon vegetable shortening
1 cup beef bouillon
1 cup prepared mincemeat
2 tablespoons apple cider vinegar
3 cloves garlic, minced

• Brown ribs in shortening; in a small bowl combine remaining ingredients, pour over ribs. Secure cover, cook under pressure for 15 minutes. Remove, allow pressure to drop of its own accord.

Split-Pea Soup

Serves 6

1 tablespoon safflower oil
1 large onion, chopped
2 large cloves garlic, chopped
2 large carrots, thinly sliced
½ teaspoon sea salt
¼ teaspoon ground black pepper
6 cups cold water
2 cups green split peas, picked over and rinsed
*optional: 1 soup bone or ham bone

• Heat the oil in the pressure cooker, sauté onion and garlic for
1 minute. Add remaining ingredients being careful of oil
sputtering. Secure lid, bring up to high pressure. Lower the heat
just enough to maintain the pressure at high, cook for 5
minutes.
• Remove from heat, allow pressure to drop of its own accord.
Open pot, with a potato masher mash peas and vegetables once
or twice. Season with additional salt and pepper if needed.
Simmer for an additional 5 minutes uncovered.

Baked Apples Supreme

Serves 6-8

6-8 large apples (see how many you can tightly place on bottom of cooker) cored.
¼ cup pancake syrup
⅛ cup cinnamon sugar
½ cup water
¾ cup raisins
½ cup fresh cranberries
*optional: ¼ cup brandy

• Wash, core apples, tightly place in cooker (no rack)
• Sprinkle remaining ingredients on top, except brandy. Secure cover, bring up to pressure and cook for 3 minutes.
• Remove from heat, allow pressure to drop of its own accord. Remove apples, pour brandy in juice, stir, then pour hot juice on top of apples. Serve with your favorite whip topping.

Bread Pudding

Serves 2-4

6-8 slices of dark pumpernickel bread, cubed or 14 slices of
stale Italian or French loaf bread, tear in large chunks
3 cups apple juice
1 cup chopped walnuts
½ teaspoon ground nutmeg
¼ teaspoon ground cardamom
¼ teaspoon vanilla extract
pinch sea salt
2 cups chopped mixed dried fruit
2 tablespoons strawberry or raspberry preserve

• In a large bowl combine the juice, nuts, nutmeg, cardamom,
salt and blend until smooth.
• Place a layer of bread on the bottom of a heatproof casserole
dish that will fit inside the pressure cooker. Sprinkle a small
amount of juice mixture next, then add some nuts and dried
fruit. Continue to layer, end with a bread layer.
• Press the ingredients down into the liquid so that all of the
bread is submerged in liquid. Cover with a sheet of aluminum
foil tightly. Place 2 cups of water in pot, then rack, place
casserole dish with pudding mixture on rack. Secure lid, bring
up to high pressure; lower the heat just enough to maintain high
pressure and cook for 20 minutes.
• Remove from heat, allow pressure to drop of its own accord.
Carefully remove casserole dish, remove foil and spread with
preserve. Serve warm.

Raisin-Rice Pudding

Serves 6

1 cup (4oz. raw, unsalted cashews)
3 cups water
3 tablespoons pure maple syrup
1 teaspoon ground cinnamon
¾ teaspoon ground ginger
¼ teaspoon ground cardamom
pinch sea salt
1 cup long-grain brown rice
½ cup dark raisin or dried currants

• In a hand food chopper, combine the nuts, water, maple syrup, spices, and salt. Process to a smooth texture.
• Place the rice and raisins in a 2-quart heatproof casserole that fits into the cooker; add the spice mixture and stir.
• Place rack and 2 cups of water into pressure cooker. Place casserole dish on top. Secure lid, bring pressure up to pressure, cook for 25 minutes.
• Remove from heat, allow pressure to drop of its own accord. Remove lid, stir once; if rice isn't sweet enough, stir in more maple syrup. Serve warm.

Chicken & Mango

Serve 4

1, 3-3½ pound chicken (cut in half and half again)
3 tablespoons dried herb seasoning
½ cup water
¼ teaspoon sea salt
⅛ teaspoon ground black pepper
⅛ teaspoon red pepper flakes
1 ripe medium to large mango peeled and cubed
⅓ cup soy sauce
1 large sweet onion, thinly sliced
1 large green pepper, cut in strips

• Combine mango, soy sauce, bell pepper and onion in bowl, set aside.
• Rinse chicken and pat dry with paper towel. Place chicken and remaining ingredients into pressure cooker. Secure cover, bring up to pressure, cook for 12 minutes.
• Remove from heat, allow pressure to drop of its own accord.
• Place cooked chicken on platter; add mango mixture to hot chicken juices, stir, simmer uncovered 2 minutes or until peppers are fork tender. Pour mixture on top of chicken. Serve with cooked rice. ***Substitute** 1 small can of Mandarin orange slices (drain slightly) for fresh mangoes.*

Basic Buckwheat (Kasha)

Yield: 2 cups

1 tablespoon canola oil
1 cup coarse or whole groats (kasha)
1¾ cups boiling water or vegetable stock
¼ teaspoon sea salt

• Heat oil in the pressure cooker, toast the grains over medium-high heat, stirring constantly for about 2-3 minutes. Add the boiling water slowly, watch out for spattering, and salt. Secure cover, bring up to pressure and cook for 3 minutes.
• Remove from heat, allow pressure to drop of its own accord.
• Remove cover, take a small taste of a few grains, if the grain seems too chewy, stir in a few tablespoons of boiling water or stock. Replace lid, do not turn on heat or bring up to pressure, just allow the grains to steam in the residual heat for another few minutes.

Quinoa

Yield: 4 cups

2¼ cups vegetable stock or water
1½ cups quinoa, thoroughly rinsed and drained
½ teaspoon sea salt

• Place quinoa in a very fine-mesh strainer into a bowlful of cold water. With one hand while the strainer is in water move the quinoa around. Change water and continue rinsing until water remains completely clear; drain well.
• Bring the stock or water up to the boil in the pressure cooker; stir in quinoa and salt.
• Secure cover, begin timing immediately after securing lid. Bring pressure to high heat, remove from heat after 2 minutes, even if pressure has not been reached.
• Let pressure drop of its own accord; let rest in pot for about 10 minutes. Remove cover, fluff up with fork, it should be crunchy.

Bulgur

Yield: 4 cups

1½ cups coarse bulgur
2 cups boiling water or vegetable stock
½ teaspoon sea salt
½ teaspoon thyme

• Place two cups of water in the bottom of the pressure cooker and set rack in place. Place the bulgur in a 2-quart heatproof casserole dish. Add the boiling water, stir in salt and seasonings. Place casserole dish on top of rack.
• Secure cover, bring up to pressure, cook for 5 minutes.
• Remove from heat, allow pressure to drop of its own accord. If bulgur is not tender, stir the grain, adding a few tablespoons of boiling water. Set the lid back into place, do not bring up to pressure, let it steam in the residual heat for a few more minutes. If the bulgur is tender but has not absorbed all of the water, strain.

➤ *Note:* Choose one of these optional ingredients to stir in Basic Bulgur after cooking: 1 tbsp. finely grated lemon or orange peel, ¼ cup minced green olives, ¼ cup toasted pine nuts, or ¼ cup dried currants.

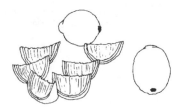

Brown Rice

Yield: 2 cups

1 cup short-or long-grain brown rice, rinsed and drained
1 tablespoon canola oil
2 cups boiling water or vegetable stock
½ teaspoon sea salt

• Place the rice in the pressure cooker, stir oil into rice. Sauté rice until lightly browned, stirring frequently for about 1 minute. Turn off the heat, carefully add the boiling water or vegetable stock and salt.
• Secure cover, bring up to pressure, cook for 20 minutes.
• Remove from heat, allow pressure to drop of its own accord.
If the rice is not tender, replace lid, do not bring up to pressure, allow it to steam in the residual heat for another few minutes.

➤ *Note: optional seasoning:* (per 1 cup of uncooked rice) before cooking, add one of the following ingredients:

• 2   cloves garlic, minced
• 1   bay leaf (remove before serving)
• ½   teaspoon dried oregano or basil
• 3   teaspoons mild curry powder
• ⅛   teaspoon ground allspice
• ¼   teaspoon ground ginger
• ⅓   cup raisins, dried currants, or chopped apricots.

After cooking , add one of the following ingredients:

• 1   tablespoon grated lemon or orange peel
• ¼ cup toasted pine nuts, or chopped walnuts
• 1-2 teaspoons poppy seeds
• ¼ cup chopped fresh herbs, basil, parsley, or dill.
• Fluff up cooked rice and serve.

Old Fashioned Chicken Soup

Serves 8-10

2½-3 pound chicken, cut up in four large pieces, use giblets (set aside liver, use for another meal or appetizer)
2 quarts cold water
1 tablespoon sea salt
1 large onion, peel, make four slits, do not cut through
3 medium carrots, scraped, cut in chunks
2 ribs celery, cut in small pieces, (use some leaves)
2 tablespoons parsley
dash of ground black pepper
2 cups cooked fine egg noodles

• Rinse, clean chicken and parts; place in pressure cooker. Add water and remaining ingredients except noodles. Secure lid, bring up to pressure and cook for 20 minutes.
• Remove from heat, let pressure come down of its own accord.
• Carefully remove chicken, discard skin and bones. Cut cooked chicken into bite-size pieces, return to soup. Add cooked noodles, simmer uncovered for 10 minutes.

➤ *Note*: If you are beginning with a fresh whole celery, rinse the top portion and cut in small pieces from the top, using the leaves as well (about 1 cup). You may want to save half of the cooked chicken for another meal like chicken salad, before returning it to the pot.

Chicken Thighs & Drumsticks

Yield: 5 servings

1 tablespoon olive oil, divided
5 chicken thighs and drumsticks cut at joints, skinned
1 cup chopped onion
3 cloves garlic, minced
¾ cup dry red wine
1 cup chicken broth
2 tablespoons tomato paste
½ teaspoon dried thyme
½ teaspoon sea salt
¼ teaspoon ground black pepper
3 cups fresh mushrooms, halved
2 cups thinly sliced carrots
2 tablespoons cornstarch
2 tablespoons water
vegetable cooking spray

• Lightly coat inside of pressure cooker with cooking spray.
Add 1½ tbsp. of oil; add thighs, cook 2 minutes on medium
high, browning on all sides. Remove cooked chicken; repeat
procedure with remaining oil and drumsticks set aside.
• Add onion and garlic to pressure cooker sauté until
translucent. Stir in wine, brandy, and broth; add tomato paste,
thyme, salt, pepper, mushrooms and carrots. Return cooked
chicken to cooker; secure lid, bring up to pressure, cook 4
minutes.
• Remove from heat, let pressure drop of its own accord. Place
chicken on large platter. Combine cornstarch and water, add to
broth mixture. Bring to a boil, cook 1 minute, stirring
constantly. Pour over chicken; serve with kasha, rice or
couscous.

Cake Baking Guide

Problem...   *Cause...*

	Butter-Type Cakes	Sponge-Type Cakes
Cake falls	Too much sugar, liquid, leavening or shortening; too little flour; temperature too low; *insufficient baking*	Too much sugar; over-beaten egg whites; egg yolks under beaten; use of greased pans; insufficient baking
Cake cracks or humps	Too much flour or too little liquid; over-mixing; batter not spread evenly in pan; temperature of oven too high	Too much flour or sugar; temperature too high
Cake has one side higher	Batter spread unevenly; un-even pan; pan too close to side of oven; oven rack or range not even; uneven oven heat	Uneven pan; oven rack or range not level
Cake has hard top crust	Temperature too high; over baking	Temperature too high; over baking
Cake has sticky top crust	Too much sugar or shortening; insufficient baking	Too much sugar; insufficient baking
Cake has soggy layer at bottom	Too much liquid; eggs under-beaten; under-mixing; insufficient baking	Too many eggs or egg yolks; under beaten egg yolks; under-mixing
Cake crumbles or falls apart	Too much sugar, leavening or shortening; batter under-mixed; improper pan treatment; improper cooling	
Cake has heavy, compact quality	Too much liquid or shortening; too many eggs; too little leavening or flour; over-mixing; oven temperature too high	Over beaten egg whites; under beaten egg yolks; over-mixing;
Cake falls out of pan before cooled		Too much sugar; use of greased pans; insufficient baking

Benne Seed Cookies

Yield: 8 dozen

½ cup butter, melted
1 cup brown sugar, packed
1 egg, beaten
¾ cup all-purpose flour
½ teaspoon salt
¼ teaspoon baking powder
1 teaspoon vanilla extract
1 cup sesame seeds, toasted

• Toss 1 cup sesame seeds in a nonstick skillet until lightly brown. Remove, cool.
• Combine all ingredients in a large mixing bowl, add seeds. Beat until smooth and creamy. Preheat oven to 350 degrees.
• Drop batter by ½ teaspoonfuls onto lightly greased cookie sheets. Bake 8-10 minutes or until edges are browned.
• Cool cookies slightly on cookie sheets, then remove to completely cool on wire racks.

No Bake Fudgey Brownies

Yield: 16 brownies

12 ounces semi-sweet chocolate
1 can (14oz.) sweetened condensed milk
2½ cups finely crushed chocolate wafers
1 cup chopped nuts

• Melt chocolate in a saucepan. Remove from heat and add milk, chocolate wafers and ½ cup of nuts. Stir in well.
• Spread mixture into a greased 8-inch square pan. Press remaining ½ cup nuts on top. Cool, cut into 2-inch squares.

Drop Brownies

Yield: 2 dozen

2 cups chocolate chips
1 (14oz.) can sweetened condensed milk
½ cup butter
1 cup all-purpose flour

• Do not grease cookie sheets.
• Melt chocolate chips, milk and butter in a medium saucepan over low heat. Stir in flour, remove from heat.
• Preheat oven to 350 degrees. Drop by teaspoonfuls onto cookie sheet. Bake 7 minutes. Do not over-bake or brownies will be soft.

➤ *Hint:* When making cookies, use 2 or 3 cookie sheets. While one batch is baking, you are preparing the next batch to go into the oven.

Peanut Butter Cookies

Yield: 2 dozen

1 cup sugar
1 cup peanut butter
1 egg
1 cup quick-cooking oats

• Combine all ingredients in a large bowl; mix well. Shape into balls; place on cookie sheet.
• Bake at 350 degrees for 10 minutes; remove from oven, cool cookies on a wire rack.

➤ *Hint:* For a pie shell which is baked before filling, always prick the bottom and side of a pie shell with the tines of a fork, which is baked before filling to prevent puffing. Brush the bottom with 1 egg white beaten with 1 tablespoon water just before the shell has finished baking to keep it from becoming soggy when filled.

Sugarless Banana Cookies

Yield: 2 dozen

3 ripe bananas, mashed
½ cup walnuts, chopped
1 cup raisins
2 cups rolled oats
1 teaspoon vanilla extract
½ teaspoon sea salt

• Do not grease cookie sheet; preheat oven to 350 degrees.
• Combine all ingredients in a large mixing bowl, mix well.
Let stand for several minutes; drop by teaspoonfuls onto cookie
sheet, press down slightly.
• Bake 15-20 minutes or until golden brown. Remove cookies
onto a wire rack to cool.

Apricot Bars

Yield: 3 dozen

1 ¼ cups all-purpose flour
¾ cup packed brown sugar
6 tablespoons butter, softened
¾ cup apricot preserves

• Preheat oven to 350 degrees.
• Mix flour, brown sugar, butter together until well blended.
• Firmly pat half of this mixture into a 8 x 8 square pan. Spread
apricot preserves on top. Sprinkle remaining half of flour
mixture on top of preserves; pat lightly.
• Bake 30 minutes or until golden brown. Cool 10 minutes
before cutting into bars.

No-Bake Oatmeal Turtle Cookies
Yield: 3 dozen

¼ cup butter
2 cups sugar
½ cup evaporated milk
5 tablespoons unsweetened cocoa
½ cup peanut butter
1 teaspoon vanilla extract
3 cups quick-cook rolled oats
wax paper

• Spread wax paper on top of wire rack.
• Bring butter, sugar, evaporated milk and cocoa to a boil in a medium saucepan. Boil 1 minute, stirring and being careful not to allow mixture to burn.
• Remove from heat, stir in peanut butter, vanilla and oats. Work quickly. Drop teaspoonsfuls of cookie mixture onto waxed paper. Cool completely before placing cookies in a airtight container.

➤ *Hint:* Make an easy fruit dessert by combining fresh fruit with a liqueur. Curaçao with oranges or pineapple slices. Grand Marnier with grapefruit or strawberries. Kirsch with sliced bananas, peaches or melon. Champagne with strawberries or peaches. Ruby port with pears or figs.

Fruit Cobbler
Serves 6

¼ cup butter
1½ cups biscuit mix, (see page 407)
¼ cup sugar
1 cup milk
1 can fruit or berry pie filling

• Preheat oven to 375 degrees.
• Melt butter in pie pan, combine biscuit mix, sugar and milk. Pour into pie pan. **Do not mix**. Pour in pie filling.
• Bake 30 minutes or until brown.

Ginger Snaps

Yield: 3 dozen

½ cup unsalted butter, softened
2 cups sugar
¼ cup dark molasses
2 eggs
1 cup sifted all-purpose flour
2 teaspoons baking soda
1 teaspoon ground ginger
½ teaspoon ground cloves
¼ teaspoon sea salt

• Preheat oven to 350 degrees; lightly grease baking sheets.
• In a large mixing bowl, cream together the butter and sugar.
Stir in the molasses, next add eggs, one at a time.
• Sift flour with soda, ginger, cloves and salt. Add flour mixture
to the batter, ⅓ cup at a time, mixing well after each addition.
Beat until the batter is smooth. Drop teaspoonfuls of batter onto
baking sheet.
• Bake 8-10 minutes, or until the cookies have browned around
the edges. Place cookies on wire rack to cool completely.

➤*Hint:* Variations: add variety to pie and tart shells by substituting
orange juice for water plus grated orange rid to add taste to your pastry.
You can substitute an equal amount of smooth or crunchy peanut butter
for the shortening in your pastry recipe. It is a taste treat and handy when
you have no shortening. Add spices such as cinnamon, nutmeg, ginger or
ground cloves to your pie dough to add interest to your fruit and custard
pies.

Key Lime Squares

Yield: 3 dozen

1 cup all-purpose flour plus 2 tablespoons
¼ cup powdered sugar
½ cup butter, melted
½ teaspoon baking powder
2 eggs, beaten
1 cup sugar
1 teaspoon grated lime rind
3 tablespoons key lime juice
powdered sugar

• Preheat oven to 350 degrees.
• Combine 1 cup flour, ¼ cup powdered sugar, butter; blend well. Pat into a 8 x 8 square pan. Bake for 15 minutes, remove from oven.
• Combine remaining flour and baking powder in one bowl. In a medium bowl combine eggs, sugar, rind and juice. Beat well. Stir dry ingredients into egg mixture, pour over crust. Return to oven, bake 25 minutes. Sprinkle with powdered sugar, cool in pan. Cut into squares.

➤ *Hint:* Make a delicious dessert sauce with 1 cup sour cream, ½ cup cup packed brown sugar and ½ teaspoon vanilla extract.

Carambolas

Serves 4

2 tablespoons unsalted butter
3 carambolas (star fruit), sliced
2 tablespoons firmly packed dark brown sugar
¼ cup dark rum

• Melt the butter in a nonstick skillet; add star fruit, sauté for a few minutes, add sugar, stir to melt. Add the rum and Flambé and cook for an additional 1-2 minutes. Serve immediately.

Pumpkin Bars

Yield: 3 dozen

½ cup canola oil
⅓ cup honey
2 eggs
1 cup plus 2 tablespoons whole wheat flour
1 teaspoon baking powder
½ teaspoon baking soda
1 cup pumpkin purée
¾ teaspoon ground cinnamon
⅓ cup pecans, chopped

• Preheat oven to 350 degrees; lightly grease 9 x 13 baking pan.
• Combine all ingredients in a large bowl, mix well. Spread into prepared pan. Bake 25-30 minutes or until a cake tester inserted in comes out clean. Cool, then cut into bars.

➤ *Hint:* To store bar cookies, place them in an airtight container with wax paper between the layers; or wrap the bars individually in plastic wrap, wax paper or aluminum foil. They will keep for up to four days in an airtight container

Easy Shortbread

Yield: 4-6 servings

1½ cups unsalted butter
¾ cups sugar
3 cups all-purpose flour
granulated sugar for topping

• Cream butter with sugar; mix in flour, pat into 9 x 13 baking pan.
• Bake at 300 degrees for 1 hour, sprinkle with sugar while hot.

No-Roll Pie Shell

Yield: one 9-inch crust

1½ cups all-purpose flour
1 tablespoon sugar
1 teaspoon sea salt
½ cup peanut oil
2 tablespoons whole milk

• Place flour, sugar, salt into a medium mixing bowl.
• Blend oil and milk well in small mixing bowl. Pour milk mixture into dry mixture and blend well.
• Place dough mixture into pie pan, press out dough gently with fingers. Follow directions for unbaked pie crust or bake at 375 degrees for 3-5 minutes or until lightly brown for baked shell.

Fruit Bake

Serves 4-6

2 (16oz.) cans peaches, sliced
⅔ cup oats, uncooked
½ cup brown sugar, packed
½ cup all-purpose flour
5 tablespoons butter, softened
2 teaspoons cinnamon
1 teaspoon nutmeg

• Preheat oven to 325 degrees; place fruit in casserole dish.
• Combine remaining ingredients in a medium mixing bowl, mix until crumbly. Sprinkle over fruit.
• Bake 45 minutes or until topping is golden brown.

➢*Note:* Variations: For above recipe try these combinations: fruit cocktail, or apricots and pears, or crushed pineapple and peaches.

Mississippi Mud

Yield: 15 servings

1 cup unsalted butter, melted
½ cup baking cocoa
4 eggs, slightly beaten
2 cups sugar
1½ cups all-purpose flour
1½ cups chopped pecans
1 teaspoon vanilla
½ teaspoon sea salt
2 cups miniature marshmallows
1 pound package confectioners' sugar
½ cup unsalted butter, melted
½ cup milk
⅓ cup baking cocoa

• Preheat oven to 350 degrees; grease a 9 x 13 baking pan.
• Mix 1 cup butter and ½ cup baking cocoa in bowl. Stir in eggs and sugar. Add flour, pecans, vanilla and salt; mix well. Pour into prepared pan. Bake for 35 minutes. Cover with marshmallows, return to oven and bake until marshmallows are melted. Remove from oven, cool slightly.
• Mix remaining ingredients in medium bowl until smooth, spread over cake.

Pistachio Pudding

Serves 4-6

1 (20oz.) can crushed pineapple, undrained
1 package pistachio instant pudding
1 envelope Dream Whip
1 cup miniature marshmallows

• Combine all ingredients in deep serving bowl.
• Chill for half an hour and serve.

➤ *Hint:* Easy quick dessert: a plate of assorted fruits and cheeses.

No-bake Quick Fruit
Serves 4-6

1 (16oz.) can peaches, drained (save ¼ cup juice)
1 (16oz.) can pears, drained (save ¼ cup juice)
1 pint fresh strawberries (sliced) or blueberries
3 tablespoons fruit liqueur
1 small container of plain non-fat yogurt

• In a deep bowl, combine all ingredients except yogurt.
• Pour yogurt on top, serve.

Chocolate Sweets
Yield: 1 dozen

4 ounces sweet dark chocolate
½ cup unsalted butter
2 eggs
1 cup all-purpose flour
1 cup sugar
dash of sea salt
1 tablespoon vanilla
½ cup chopped nuts

• Preheat oven to 325 degrees.
• Melt chocolate and butter in saucepan. Set aside to cool.
• Beat eggs, add flour, sugar and salt, mix well. Blend in chocolate mixture and vanilla. Add pecans. Pour batter into a greased 8-inch baking pan.
• Bake 20-25 minutes. Cool, then cut into 2-inch squares.

➤ *Hint:* When greasing your cookie sheets, always use vegetable shortening. Butter or oil will cause cookies to burn. Better yet, a sheet of baker's parchment on the cookie sheet yields evenly baked cookies.

Mandelbrot

Yield: 2 dozen

3 eggs, beaten
1 cup sugar
½ cup canola oil
1 teaspoon baking powder
3 cups all-purpose flour
1 cup pecans, chopped
1 teaspoon vanilla extract
cinnamon sugar mixture, (see below)

• Preheat oven to 350 degrees.
• Combine eggs, sugar, oil; blend thoroughly. Add flour blend well, add nuts, stir in lightly. Top mixture with vanilla extract, do not mix in.
• Place a sheet of aluminum foil onto cookie sheet; pour mixture making two large strips of batter onto sheet of aluminum foil. Sprinkle cinnamon-sugar mixture on top.
• Bake 30 minutes, remove, cool slightly, cut strips into ¼ inch slices, return to ungreased cookie sheet (no aluminum foil needed). Bake 5 minutes on each side or until well browned.
• Cool on wire rack. These store well in air-tight container. They are crunchy once cooled.

➤ *Hint:* Make your own cinnamon sugar mixture, store a small amount in a container for topping pancakes, french toast or when making the above recipe. Take 1 cup sugar, 3 tablespoons of ground cinnamon. Shake in container. If you need more cinnamon to make a darker mixture add ½ teaspoon at a time, shake well.

Ladyfinger Dessert

Yield: 8 servings

1 cup chocolate chips
instant coffee crystals to taste
2 cups heavy cream, whipped
2 (3oz.) packages ladyfingers

• Melt chocolate; stir in coffee, cool slightly, fold in cream.
• Layer ladyfinger; chocolate mixture ¼ at a time on a cake plate, spread chocolate mixture to frost sides.

Strawberries in Rum

Serves 4

1 pint fresh strawberries, washed and sliced
½ cup dark rum
⅓ cup sour cream
½ cup confectioners' sugar

• Combine strawberries and rum, spoon into individual glasses.
• Mix together sour cream and sugar, spoon mixture on top.

Instant Rice Pudding

Serves 2

1 package of instant vanilla pudding
1 cup cooked cold white rice
1 tablespoon sugar
dash of cinnamon

• Prepare pudding according to package directions. Add remaining ingredients, fold in gently. Chill or serve at room temperature.

Plantains in Rum Caramel
Serves 6

4 tablespoons unsalted butter
¼ cup sugar
4 ripe plantains, sliced in half
⅓ cup orange juice
1 tablespoon grated orange rind
¼ cup dark rum

• Cut off both ends of plantain, make a long slit lengthwise in the peel, remove peel. Slice plantains in half lengthwise.
• Cook butter and sugar in large nonstick skillet over low heat for 5 minutes or until sugar begins to caramelize and separates from the butter. Add orange juice and rind, rum; shake the pan to deglaze the caramel.
• Add the plantains and cook them turning once until fork tender and browned.

Chocolate Peanut Butter Pizza
Yield: 2 dozen wedges

½ cup sugar
½ cup brown sugar, packed
½ cup butter
1 egg
½ teaspoon vanilla
½ cup peanut butter
2 cups mini marshmallows
1½ cups all-purpose flour
1 cup (6oz.) semi-sweet chocolate morsels

• Combine sugar, brown sugar, butter, vanilla, egg; blend well.
• Stir in flour and press mixture evenly into a 12-inch pizza pan, forming rim along edge. Preheat oven to 375 degrees.
• Bake for 10 minutes, remove, sprinkle with marshmallows and chips. Return to oven bake for 5-8 min. or until marshmallows are puffy and lightly browned. Remove from oven, cool then cut into wedges. Can be stored in a air-tight container.

Cinnamon Tortilla Chips

Yield: 40 chips

1 small package of flour tortillas (10)
½ cup peanut oil, adding more as you fry up tortillas
cinnamon sugar (see page 367)
large brown paper bag

• Cut 5 tortillas at a time in half, and then half again, giving you 20 ¼-inch wedges.
• Heat small amount of oil in wok or deep frying pan. Place 4 wedges, one at a time, into hot oil (note how fast they puff up).
• Remove with slotted spoon put into brown paper bag with all of the cinnamon sugar. Shake, wedges and remove to platter. Continue cooking in this manner until all tortilla wedges are fried.

➤ *Note*: Unless you are serving a crowd, I suggest you make a small batch. Strain the oil into a glass container, store away and use for the next two batches. Discard oil after three batches.

Citrus Delight

Serves 2

2 grapefruits, de-seeded, cut in chunks
1 orange, de-seeded, cut in chunks
1 very ripe banana, mashed
1 cup whole cranberry sauce

• Place all ingredients in deep bowl except banana; mix well.
• Pour mashed banana on top. Let sit a 5 minutes, then serve.

➤ *Hint:* Add fresh cranberries and walnuts to your favorite apple pie.

Peach Cobbler

Serves 6-8

3 cups peaches, sliced
1 tablespoon lemon juice
2 tablespoons butter, melted
½ cup sugar
Topping:
1 cup flour
2 teaspoons sugar
3 tablespoons vegetable shortening
1 teaspoon baking powder
½ teaspoon sea salt
⅓ cup milk
cinnamon sugar (see page 367)

• Preheat oven to 350 degrees; grease 9x9 baking pan.
• Combine peaches, lemon juice, butter and ½ cup sugar into baking pan.
• Combine flour, remaining sugar, shortening, baking powder, salt; cut in shortening until fine. Add milk and stir into dough.
• Drop by tablespoonful on top of peaches. Sprinkle lightly with cinnamon sugar.
• Bake 30 minutes; cool slightly, top with ice cream or whipped topping.

➤ *Hint:* Whenever your recipe calls for liquid buttermilk or sour milk, keep on hand Saco Cultured Buttermilk Powder. It comes in a 12 oz., 340g equivalent to 3.75 quarts of liquid buttermilk. Example: when recipe calls for 1 cup buttermilk, use 4 tablespoons of buttermilk powder and 1 cup of water.

Baked Bananas

Serves 4

4 bananas, cut in half
juice of 1 lemon
3 tablespoons butter
¾ cup rum
¼ cup brown sugar, packed

• Place bananas in buttered baking dish; sprinkle with lemon juice. Mix sugar, butter and rum together, pour over bananas.
• Bake at 350 degrees for 15 minutes. Can also be done top stove in a nonstick skillet, with a cover, at low heat for 10 minutes.

➤ *Hint:* Make a delicious Dessert Sauce of 1 cup sour cream, ½ cup packed brown sugar and ½ teaspoon vanilla extract.

Mango Crisp

Serves 8-10

6 cups sliced mangoes
⅓ cup all-purpose flour
1 cup oats
½ cup brown sugar, packed
½ teaspoon sea salt
1 teaspoon cinnamon
⅓ cup melted unsalted butter

• Arrange mangoes in a layer in a lightly buttered 13 x 9 baking pan.
• Mix together remaining ingredients, except ⅓ cup melted butter; stir in butter until crumbly. Sprinkle over mangoes.
• Bake at 375 degrees for 30 minutes. Serve warm or cold.

➤ *Hint:* For a quick confectioners' sugar frosting, blend 2 tablespoons softened margarine, 2 cups confectioners' sugar and enough milk to make of spreading consistency.

No-bake Key Lime Pie
Yield: one 9-inch pie

1 (8oz.) package cream cheese
1 can (14oz.) sweetened condensed milk
3 ounces of key lime juice
1 baked graham cracker pie shell

• Blend cream cheese and condensed milk, it will have some tiny lumps of cheese.
• Add one ounce of lime juice at a time, blend well each time. Pour into pie shell, chill.
• At serving time top with one or more of the following: slices of strawberry, kiwi fruit, or other fresh fruit in season or fruit pie filling. Then top with whip cream.

Blueberry Pie
Yield: one 9-inch pie

2 unbaked pastry crusts
3 cups blueberries, rinsed and patted dry
½ cup sugar
2 tablespoons all-purpose flour
2 tablespoons fresh lemon juice
1 tablespoon butter, melted
¼ teaspoon sea salt
¼ teaspoon ground cinnamon

• Combine all ingredients in a large mixing bowl. Line bottom of 9-inch pie pan with pastry, fill with mixture. Cover with top pastry, making several slits in top crust.
• Preheat oven to 450 degrees, bake for 20 minutes. Reduce heat to 350 degrees, bake another 25 minutes. Remove, cool before slicing.

Papaya Oat Crisp

Serves 4

1 large ripe papaya, seeded, peeled and sliced
¼ cup butter
½ cup brown sugar, packed
½ cup all-purpose flour
¼ cup rolled oats
½ teaspoon ground cinnamon
½ teaspoon ground nutmeg

• Preheat oven to 375 degrees; lightly grease 13 x 9 baking pan with butter; place papaya slices in the pan.
• Combine remaining ingredients, cutting butter in with a fork until the mixture is just crumbly. Sprinkle over the papaya.
• Bake for 25-30 minutes or until top is slightly brown.

Self-Crusting Coconut Pie

Serves 6-8

2 cups milk
1 cup sugar
½ cup all-purpose flour
dash of sea salt
2 teaspoons vanilla
½ cup unsalted butter
1 to 2 cups fresh coconut, grated
nutmeg, to taste

• Grease and lightly flour a 9-inch pie pan; stir all ingredients together in a large bowl, pour mixture into prepared pan.
• Bake at 325 degrees for 40-50 minutes or until browned.

➤ *Hint:* Dust raisins and nuts with a little flour before adding them to cake batter to prevent their sinking to the bottom of the pan.

Fruity Yogurt Choices

Serves 6

#1
3 cups plain non-fat yogurt
1 cup fresh blueberries, rinsed and patted dry
1 cup fresh, seedless red grapes
honey, to taste
½ teaspoon vanilla

• Combine all ingredients very gently in a medium bowl.
• Spoon into individual dessert cups.

#2
3 cups plain non-fat yogurt
3 cups apples, peeled, cored and grated
½ cup pecans, chopped
½ cup maple syrup
dash of ground nutmeg and cinnamon
¼ cup golden raisins

• Combine all ingredients very gently in a medium bowl.
• Spoon into individual dessert cup.

#3
3 cups plain non-fat yogurt
1½ cups fresh peaches, sliced
1 cup fresh strawberries, halved
honey, to taste
1 ripe banana, mashed
½ teaspoon vanilla extract
⅓ cup sunflower seeds

• Combine all ingredients very gently in a medium bowl.
• Spoon into individual dessert cup.

Graham Cracker Crust

Yield: one 10 inch crust

2½ cups graham cracker crumbs
½ cup butter, melted
½ cup sugar

• Preheat oven to 375 degrees.
• Toss crumbs with butter and sugar in a medium mixing bowl; pour into pie pan. With fork, press mixture evenly over bottom and up side of pan.
• Bake for 5 minutes or until golden brown, cool on wire rack. Cool before filling.

➤ *Hint:* Place 4-6 whole graham crackers in a plastic bag, twist top of bag and hold. Take a crab mallet and gently bang onto bag and continue until you have fine crumbs.

Crumb Pie Shell

Yield: one 9-inch crumb pie shell

1½ cups fine crumbs (chocolate wafers, vanilla wafers or graham crackers)
2 tablespoons sugar
5 tablespoons unsalted butter, melted

• Combine crumbs and sugar, toss lightly; Add melted butter, stir well. Press crumbs firmly and evenly into pie pan with fork.
• Bake at 375 degrees for 5 minutes; remove, cool and fill.

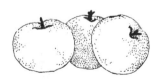

Green Tomato Pie

Serves 8

2, 9-inch unbaked pastry shells
3 cups green tomatoes, sliced unpared
½ cup brown sugar
½ cup molasses
½ cup water
2 tablespoon all-purpose flour
1 teaspoon cinnamon
¼ teaspoon ground nutmeg
boiling water to cover sliced tomatoes

• Prepare pie crusts, line pie pan with bottom crust, set aside.
Preheat oven to 425 degrees.
• Combine flour, sugar and spices on wax paper, set aside.
• Place sliced tomatoes in medium bowl; cover with boiling
water and let stand 10 minutes, drain. Place tomato slices in
unbaked pastry shells.
• Combine dry ingredients, molasses and water, blend well.
Pour mixture over tomatoes; cover with top pastry crust.
• Bake 15 minutes, reduce heat to 375 degrees and continue to
bake 30 minutes. Remove, let cool before serving.

Crustless Cheesecake

Serves 6-8

½ cup unsalted butter
¼ cup sugar
2 eggs
¾ cup milk
1 ¼ cups all-purpose flour
1 teaspoon baking powder
¼ teaspoon sea salt
Filling:
1 pound cottage or farmer cheese
2 tablespoons unsalted butter
1 egg
1 tablespoon sugar
Pinch of sea salt

• Grease well a 9-inch round shallow baking pan.
• Cream butter and sugar in a large bowl, add eggs, milk, and mix well.
• Sift together the flour, baking powder and salt. Add to the cream mixture. Pour half the batter into prepared pan.
• Blend together the filling ingredients; spoon over the batter in pan. Cover with remaining batter.
• Bake for 1 hour at 350 degrees.

➤ *Hint:* Cut a hot cake with a thread or dental floss instead of a knife.

Sweet Potato Pie

Serves 6

1 unbaked 9-inch pie shell
2 cups cooked sweet potatoes, mashed
½ cup brown sugar, packed
3 tablespoons butter, melted
3 eggs, beaten
½ cup milk
½ teaspoon nutmeg
¼ teaspoon ground cloves
¼ teaspoon cinnamon
½ teaspoon sea salt

• Prepare pie shell, set aside; preheat oven to 350 degrees.
• Combine all ingredients in a large mixing bowl, mix well.
Spoon into pie shell.
• Bake 40 minutes or until set; remove from oven, cool on wire
rack.

Gingerbread Cake

Serves 10

3 eggs, beaten
1 cup sugar
1 cup peanut oil
1 cup buttermilk
3 cups all-purpose flour
2 teaspoons ground ginger
¼ teaspoon nutmeg
½ teaspoon ground cloves
1 teaspoon sea salt, cinnamon, and baking powder
2 teaspoons baking soda

• Mix together eggs, sugar, oil, molasses and buttermilk.
• Sift dry ingredients and add to liquid mixture; blend
thoroughly but do not over-mix. Pour batter into greased and
floured 9 x 13 pan. Bake 1 hour at 325 degrees.

Apple Moist Cake

Serves 8

6 apples, peeled, quartered and thinly sliced
2 cups sugar, plus 5 tablespoons sugar
3 cups all-purpose flour
3 teaspoons baking powder
½ teaspoon sea salt
1 cup peanut oil
2 teaspoons cinnamon
4 eggs, beaten
½ cup orange juice

• Preheat oven to 350 degrees; lightly grease and flour tube pan.
• Place apples in a medium bowl, sprinkle with 5 tablespoons of sugar, 2 teaspoons cinnamon, toss well, set aside.
• Sift flour, sugar, baking powder and salt. Add eggs, oil, sugar, vanilla and orange juice and blend well. Pour ½ the batter into prepared pan, then evenly layer ½ the apples, repeat again.
• Bake 1¼-1½ hours; remove from oven and set on wire rack; cool slightly before removing from pan.

Simple Pound Cake

Serves 10

1 cup butter, softened
3 cups sugar
4 eggs
¼ teaspoon baking soda
1 teaspoon vanilla
3 cups all-purpose flour
1 cup buttermilk

• Have all ingredients at room temperature.
• Cream butter and sugar in a large mixing bowl. Add eggs one at a time, blend. Add soda and vanilla, blend. Add flour alternately with buttermilk. Preheat oven to 350 degrees, lightly grease pan.
• Pour batter into pan, bake for 1 hour. Remove, cool on wire rack before removing from pan.

➤ *Hint:* Toast pound cake; use one of the following toppings:

• Sliced fresh strawberries, non-fat strawberry yogurt .
• Mix low-fat banana yogurt with sliced bananas.
• Drizzle with coffee liqueur, whip topping.
• Kiwi fruit, slices of pear, chocolate fudge, whip topping.

Carrot Cake

Serves 16

vegetable cooking spray
2½ cups all-purpose flour
2 teaspoons baking soda
2 teaspoons ground cinnamon
1 teaspoon ground ginger
½ teaspoon sea salt
1 cup brown sugar, packed
¼ cup peanut oil
2 large eggs
½ cup plain nonfat yogurt
3 cups peeled, finely shredded carrots
Glaze:
1 cup confectioners' sugar, sifted
1 tablespoon low-fat cream cheese
½ teaspoon grated orange zest
1 tablespoon fresh orange juice

• Grease bundt pan lightly with cooking spray, set aside.
• In medium bowl, combine flour, baking soda, cinnamon, ginger and salt; mix well.
• In large bowl, mix sugar, oil, eggs and yogurt. Stir in carrots and currants and then flour mixture. Mix just until blended, spoon into prepared pan. Preheat oven to 350 degrees.
• Bake for 40 minutes or until a cake-tester comes out clean. Cool 10 minutes in pan, remove onto wire rack and cool completely before glazing. Blend glaze ingredients in a small bowl. Place cake on serving plate, drizzle glaze onto cake.

➤ *Hint:* Bittersweet and semisweet chocolate mean pretty much the same thing: slightly sweetened and without milk or cream. Domestic brands are usually called semisweet, while imported brands often use the term bittersweet.

Mango Upside-Down Cake

Serves 10-12

2 cups sliced ripe mangoes
2 tablespoons lemon juice
1 tablespoon butter
⅓ cup brown sugar, packed
¼ cup shortening
¾ cup sugar
1 egg
½ cup milk
1¼ cups all-purpose flour
2 teaspoons baking powder
¼ teaspoon sea salt

• Place mangoes in a glass bowl, pour lemon juice on top, set aside. Preheat oven to 375 degrees.
• Melt butter in an 8-inch cake pan. Add brown sugar to melted butter, spread mango slices on top.
• Cream shortening with sugar and egg in a medium bowl.
• Sift dry ingredients alternately into sugar mixture with milk.
• Pour batter over mangoes, bake 50-60 minutes. Cool slightly, turn upside down on platter. (See note below)

➢ *Note:* Let an upside-down cake cool just until you can touch the bottom of the pan, it should still be quite warm. If the cake is too hot, the sugar or custard topping will run. If too cold, it may stick to bottom of pan.

No-Egg Chocolate Cake

Serves 10

1⅔ cups all-purpose flour
1 cup light brown sugar, packed
¼ cup cocoa
1 teaspoon baking soda
¼ teaspoon sea salt
1 cup cold water
⅓ cup vegetable oil
¾ teaspoon vanilla extract

• Preheat oven to 350 degrees. Grease and flour lightly 8-inch baking pan, set aside.
• Combine all ingredients into a large mixing bowl, blend well. Pour into baking pan.
• Bake for 25 minutes or until a cake-tester comes out clean.

Easy cocoa frosting:
3 tablespoons unsalted butter
¼ cup cocoa
1⅓ cup confectioners' sugar
2-3 tablespoon milk
½ teaspoon vanilla extract

• In a medium bowl blend butter, cocoa, sugar with 1 tablespoon of milk at a time until you get a smooth spreadable consistency; spread on cooled cake.

➤ *Hint:* Prunes Purée: a unique one-to-one substitute for oil, margarine or butter. Combine 1⅓ cups pitted prunes and 6 tablespoons water in a hand food chopped. Finely chop prunes. Makes 1 cup.

Eggless Cake

Serves 10

1 cup golden raisins
2 cups water
1½ cups sugar
½ cup peanut oil
2½ teaspoons cinnamon
1 teaspoon vanilla
2½ cups all-purpose flour
1 teaspoon baking powder
1 teaspoon baking soda
¼ teaspoon sea salt

• Lightly grease and flour 9 x 13 baking pan.
• Sift flour, baking powder, baking soda and salt onto a piece of wax paper (easy cleanup).
• Combine raisins, water, sugar, oil and cinnamon in a large saucepan. Mix well, simmer for 5 minutes. Cool to room temperature. Stir in vanilla. Add sifted mixture to saucepan and blend well. Spoon into baking pan.
• Bake for 30-35 minutes or until a cake-tester or a toothpick inserted in the center of the cake comes out clean.

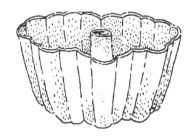

Banana Nut Bread

Yield: 2 loaves

½ cup unsalted butter
2 cups sugar
2 eggs, slightly beaten
3 medium very ripe bananas, mashed
1 tablespoon apple cider vinegar
2 cups all-purpose flour
1 teaspoon baking soda
¼ teaspoon sea salt
1 teaspoon vanilla
1 cup nuts, chopped

- Grease and flour 2 loaf pans. Preheat oven to 325 degrees.
- Cream butter with sugar in a large bowl. Add eggs and beat.
- Add bananas, vinegar to butter mixture and beat.
- Sift flour, salt, and baking soda. Stir into batter. Add vanilla then nuts. Pour batter into prepared pans.
- Bake for 1½ hours or until a toothpick inserted in the center of the cake comes out clean.

Baked Apricots

Serves 12

½ cup butter, melted
2 (28oz.) cans apricots, drained
2 cups brown sugar, packed
2 cups crushed Ritz crackers

- Preheat oven to 350 degrees.
- Place ⅓ of the melted butter in a 3 quart casserole dish.
- Layer apricots, brown sugar, crushed crackers and remaining butter, ½ at a time, in casserole dish.
- Bake, uncovered, for 1 hour. Serve hot.

Chocolate Zucchini Cake

Serves 8-10

2½ cups all-purpose flour
½ cup cocoa
2½ teaspoons baking powder
1½ teaspoons baking soda
1 teaspoon sea salt
1 teaspoon cinnamon
¾ cup unsalted butter
2 cups sugar
3 eggs
2 teaspoons vanilla
2 teaspoons freshly grated orange peel
2 cups of zucchini, grated, drained of excess juice
½ cup buttermilk
½ cup walnuts, chopped

• Grease and flour bundt pan, preheat oven to 325 degrees.
• Combine flour, cocoa, baking powder salt, soda and cinnamon in a large bowl, set aside.
• Cream butter and sugar, add eggs, one at a time, then vanilla, orange peel and zucchini.
• Add dry ingredients, stirring until well blended, then stir in nuts. Pour batter into prepared pan.
• Bake 1 hour or until a cake tester inserted in the center of the cake comes out clean.

➤ *Hint:* If you need an extra cookie sheet, grease the bottom of an inverted 9 x 13 baking pan. Cookies will brown more evenly than in a pan with sides.

INGREDIENT SUBSTITUTIONS

Ingredient	Amount	Substitution
Baking powder	1 teaspoon	¼ tsp. baking soda, ½ tsp. cream of tartar, ¼ tsp. cornstarch or ¼ tsp. baking soda plus ⅝ tsp. cream of tartar
Bread crumbs	¼ cup	¼ cup cracker crumbs, or ¼ cup rolled oats, or ¼ cup crushed corn flakes
Buttermilk	1 cup	1 cup plain yogurt or 1 tbsp. vinegar plus milk to equal 1 cup or 1 tbsp. lemon juice plus milk to equal 1 cup
Cake flour	1 cup	1 cup minus 2 tbsp. sifted all-purpose flour
Catsup	1 cup	1 cup tomato sauce plus ½ cup sugar, 2 tbsp. vinegar
Chili sauce	1 cup	1 cup tomato sauce, ¼ cup brown sugar, 2 tbsp. vinegar, ¼ tsp. cinnamon, dash of ground cloves and allspice
Chocolate, unsweetened	1 ounce (square)	3 tbsp. unsweetened cocoa plus 1 tbsp. butter or 3 tbsp. carob powder plus 2 tbsp. water
semi-sweet	1 ⅔ oz.	1 oz. unsweetened chocolate plus 2 tbsp. water
Cornstarch	1 tbsp.	2 tbsp. all-purpose flour or 1tbsp. tapioca
Corn syrup	1 cup	1 cup granulated sugar plus ¼ cup water or other liquid called for in recipe

Ingredient	Amount	Substitution
Cracker crumbs	¾ cup	1 cup bread crumbs
Cream, half & half (10-12%fat)	1 cup	1½ tbsp. butter plus ⅞ cup milk or ½ cup coffee cream plus ½ cup milk
whipping, (36-40%fat)	1 cup	⅓ cup butter plus ¾ cup milk (for baking, will not whip)
sour	1 cup	⅞ c.up buttermilk, yogurt or sour milk plus 3 tbsp. butter
Cream of tartar	½ teaspoon	1½ tsp. lemon juice or vinegar
Eggs, whole large	1 egg	3⅓ tbsp. egg yolks, thawed or 2 egg yolks (in baking)
whites	1 egg white	2 tbsp. frozen egg whites, thawed
yolks	1 egg yoke	2 tbsp. dried egg yolks plus 2 tsp. water or 3½ tsp. frozen egg yolks, thawed
Flour, sifted cake	1 cup	1 cup minus 2 tbsp. sifted all-purpose flour
pastry	1 cup	⅞ c.up all-purpose or bread flour
white, all-purpose	1 tablespoon	½ tbsp. cornstarch, potato starch, rice starch for thickening or arrowroot
white, all-purpose	1 cup	½ cup barley flour, or 1½ cup bread crumbs or 1⅛ cup cake flour (1cup plus 2 tbsp.)

Ingredient	*Amount*	*Substitution*
Garlic	1 clove	⅛ tsp. garlic powder or instant minced garlic or ½-1 tsp. garlic salt (reduce amount of salt called for in recipe)
Ginger, candied or raw	1 tbs.	⅛ tsp. powdered ginger
Herbs, fresh	1 tbs.	⅓ to ⅛ tsp. dried herbs
Honey	1 cup	1¼ cup granulated sugar plus ¼ cup water or liquid called for in recipe
Horseradish, grated fresh	1 tbs.	2 tbsp. bottled horseradish
Lemon, juice	1 teaspoon	½ tsp. distilled white vinegar
grated rind	1 teaspoon	½ tsp. lemon extract
Maple syrup	2 cups	Combine 2 cups sugar and 1 cup water; bring to clear boil; take off heat; add ½ tsp. maple flavoring
Milk, buttermilk	1 cup	1 cup sweet milk minus 1 tbsp. plus 1 tbsp. vinegar or lemon juice, let stand 5 minutes; or 1 cup sweet milk plus 1¼-1¾ tsp. cream of tarter or 1 cup yogurt
skim	1 cup	⅓ cup instant non-fat dry milk plus ⅞ cup water
sweetened, condensed	1 cup	1 cup plus tbsp. dry milk plus ½ cup warm water plus ¾ cup sugar; add dry milk to warm water mix well; add sugar; may set bowl in pan of hot water to dissolve sugar.

(milk ,cont.)

Ingredient	Amount	Substitution
whole	1 cup	½ cup evaporated milk plus ½ cup water or 1 cup reconstituted dry milk plus 2½ tsp. butter
Mint leaves, fresh chopped	¼ cup	1 tbsp. dried mint leaves
Molasses	1 cup	¾ cup granulated sugar
Mushrooms, fresh	1 pound	3 oz. dried plus 1½ cup water or 1 (8oz.) can drained slightly
Mustard, dry	1 teaspoon	1 tbsp. prepared mustard, or ½ tsp. mustard seeds
Nuts	1 cup	1 cup rolled oats, browned (use in baked products)
Onion	1 small	1⅓ tsp. onion salt or 1- 2 tbsp. instant minced onion or 1 tsp. onion powder
Orange	1 medium	6 or 8 tbsp. juice or ¾ cup diced or 2-3 tbsp. grated rind
Parsley, fresh	2 teaspoons	1 tsp. parsley flakes
Rum	¼ cup	1 tbsp. rum extract plus enough liquid to make ¼ cup
Sour cream	1 cup	3 tbsp. butter plus buttermilk or yogurt to equal 1cup or 6oz.cream cheese and 3 tbsp. milk

Ingredient	Amount	Substitution
Sugar, brown	1 cup	1 cup granulated sugar, or 1cup granulated sugar plus ¼ cup unsulphured molasses
granulated	1 cup	1 cup firmly packed brown sugar, or 1 ¾ cup confectioners' sugar (for uses other than baking)
powder	1 cup	¾ cup granulated sugar
Tomatoes, packed	1 cup	½ cup tomato sauce plus ½ cup water
canned	1 cup	1⅓ cups diced tomatoes simmered 10 minutes
Tomato juice	1 cup	½ cup tomato sauce plus ½ cup water
sauce	2 cups	¾ cup tomato paste plus 1 cup water
soup	1 (10¾ oz.) can	1 cup tomato sauce plus ¼ cup water
Yogurt	1 cup	1 cup buttermilk

Croutons

• Cut stale bread (French, Italian, whole wheat, white, corn, rye) into slices. Coat both sides of bread with butter or olive oil, sprinkle with ground black pepper. Preheat oven to 350 degrees.
• Cut the slices of bread into half-inch cubes. Spread cubes of bread on baking sheet, bake for 10-15minutes or until dried out and lightly browned. Turn over once; remove from oven, let cool thoroughly and store in an airtight container.

Variations:

• *Cheese Croutons:* follow first recipe; sprinkle grated Parmesan cheese on after spreading with butter or oil. Place on baking sheet, continue with remainder of recipe instructions.
• *Garlic Croutons:* follow first recipe; sprinkle lightly with garlic powder after spreading with butter or oil. Place on baking sheet, continue with remainder of recipe instructions.
• *Herb Croutons*: follow first recipe; sprinkle lightly with dried oregano and basil after spreading with butter or oil. Place on baking sheet, continue with remainder of recipe instructions.
• *Red and Black Pepper Croutons:* follow first recipe; sprinkle lightly with crushed red pepper flakes and ground fresh black pepper after spreading with butter or oil. Place on baking sheet, continue with remainder of recipe instructions

➤ *Note:* Croutons can be browned in a nonstick skillet over medium heat; toss crouton mixture in skillet often. Remove from heat, cool then store in airtight container.

Buy a pack of assorted paint brushes; *use* the small brush for coating croutons, the remaining sizes for basting. What a bargain buying brushes this way.

Seafood Seasoning Blend
Yield: ⅛ cup

4 teaspoons dried dillweed
2 teaspoons dried basil
2 teaspoons onion salt
2 teaspoons lemon pepper

• Mix all ingredients together in a small measuring cup; store in airtight container.

Salad Dressing Mix
Yield: ⅛ cup

3 teaspoons sea salt
1 tablespoon paprika
1 tablespoon dry mustard
½ teaspoon freshly ground black pepper

• Combine all ingredients in a small measuring cup; store in airtight container.

Salt Free Herb Mix
Yield: ⅓ cup

3 teaspoons onion powder
3 teaspoons garlic powder
3 teaspoon dried parsley flakes
1 teaspoon basil leaves
1 teaspoon thyme
1 teaspoon marjoram
1 teaspoon ground black pepper

• Mix well in a small measuring cup, store in airtight container.

Cajun Seasoning Mix

Yield: ½ cup

3 tablespoons paprika
1 tablespoon onion powder
1 tablespoon garlic powder
1 tablespoon cayenne pepper
2 teaspoons ground black pepper
1 teaspoon white pepper
2 teaspoons dried thyme
1 teaspoon sea salt
1 teaspoon oregano

• Mix well in a small measuring cup, store in airtight container.

➢ *Note*: Sprinkle on chicken, pork, beef or fish before grilling.

Spicy No-Salt Seasoning

Yield: ⅛ cup

1 teaspoon ground cloves
1 teaspoon ground black pepper
1 teaspoon coriander
2 teaspoons Hungarian paprika
1 tablespoon dried rosemary

• Mix well in a small measuring cup,
store in airtight container.

Seasoned Salt

Yield: ½ cup

1 cup sea salt
2½ teaspoons Hungarian paprika
2 teaspoons dry mustard
1½ teaspoons oregano
1 teaspoon garlic powder
1 teaspoon onion powder

• Mix well in a small bowl; store in airtight container.

Curry Powder

Yield: ½ cup

2 tablespoons ground coriander
1 tablespoon black ground pepper
2 tablespoons cumin
2 tablespoons crushed red pepper flakes
2 tablespoons turmeric
2 tablespoons ground ginger
* optional additions: a pinch of each allspice, cinnamon, ground fennel, and mace.

• Mix well in a small measuring cup; store in airtight container.

Poultry Seasoning

Yield: ⅓ cup

2 tablespoons dried marjoram
2 tablespoons dried savory
2 teaspoons dried parsley
1 tablespoon dried sage
1½ teaspoons dried thyme

• Mix well in a small measuring cup, store in airtight container.

Adobo

Yield: ¼ cup

1 tablespoon garlic powder
1 tablespoon onion powder
1 tablespoon dried oregano
½ tablespoon sea salt
½ tablespoon ground black pepper

• Mix well in a small measuring cup, store in airtight container.

➤ *Note:* Adobo is a basic seasoning in Puerto Rican cooking. It can be used for meats, poultry, pork, fish or seafood.

Mojo Criollo

Yield: ½ cup

3 tablespoons olive oil
2 tablespoons finely chopped onion
2 cloves garlic, minced
½ teaspoon oregano
¼ teaspoon cumin
⅛ teaspoon sea salt
dash ground black pepper
2 tablespoons sour orange, or
1tbsp. orange juice and 1 tbsp. lime juice
2 tablespoons water
1 tablespoon dry sherry
½ teaspoon apple cider vinegar

• Mix onions with spices in a medium bowl, toss well.
• Heat olive oil in a medium saucepan, add onion mixture and cook until onions become translucent.
• Add juice, water, wine and vinegar, simmer 5 minutes; remove, cool slightly before using.

➤ *Note:* Sprinkle on crisp fried strips of green plantains. Marinate on chicken or pork chops for grilling or a roast pork tenderloin.

Instant Dried Blends

Try one of these fantastic International flavor blends;

Yield: ¼ cup
• *Greek blend*
2 tablespoons garlic powder
1 tablespoon lemon peel
1 tablespoon oregano
½ tablespoon ground black
pepper

• Mix well in a small measuring
cup, store in airtight container.

➤ *Note:* Sprinkle ¼ tsp. over
each serving of chicken, lamb or
shrimp before baking or grilling;
sprinkle ¼ tsp. over steamed
vegetables.

Yield: ¼ cup
• *Italian blend*
2 tablespoons basil
2 tablespoons marjoram
1 tablespoon garlic powder
1 tablespoon oregano
½ tablespoon thyme
½ tablespoon crushed red pepper
flakes

• Mix well in a small measuring
cup, store in airtight container.

➤ *Note*: Sprinkle ¼ tsp. over
each serving of chicken before
baking or grilling; add ¼ tsp. to
for servings of your favorite
pasta sauce.

Yield: ¼ cup
• *Vegetable blend*
1 tablespoon marjoram
1 tablespoon basil
1 tablespoon chervil
½ tablespoon tarragon
½ tablespoon celery seed

• Mix well in a small measuring
cup, store in airtight container.

➤ *Note:* Sprinkle mixture on
steamed vegetables; use ¼ tsp.
per four servings.

Yield: ⅓ cup
• *Mexican blend*
1½ tablespoons cumin
1 tablespoon onion powder
1 tablespoon garlic powder
½ tablespoon ground ginger
½ tablespoon Hungarian paprika
½ tablespoon oregano
½ tablespoon cayenne pepper
½ tablespoon dry mustard
¼ tablespoon cayenne pepper
½ tablespoon parsley flakes

• Mix well in a small measuring
cup, store in airtight container.

➤ *Note:* Stir 1-2 tsp. into salsa
or guacamole; add ¼ tsp. to a
pot of chili (four to six servings);
or sprinkle ¼ tsp. over each
serving of meat, poultry or pork
before baking.

Sprouters & Sprouts

It's nice to have fresh vegetables every day but when you run out, don't pout: **SPROUT!** Choose a three tier plastic sprouter or glass jar with different size tops with screens, (read manufacturers instructions). Better yet, do it the ***K.I.S.S.*** way on a plain white paper plate. Spread sprouts on paper plate and cover with a paper towel. Spray clean water onto paper towel, wet well but do not soak heavily; repeat this procedure twice a day for three days and your beans will begin to sprout.

• To get a variety of seeds or beans for sprouting, go to the local health food store. It's easiy to do and this will be a pet you don't have to walk!
• Once your sprouts are ready, rinse well in cold water, drain well, pat dry with paper towel. Store the mature sprouts in a zip-lock vegetable bag or a loosely tied plastic bag. You can safely refrigerate for up to one week.
• Most beans or seeds such as alfalfa, garden cress, lentil, mustard, mung, radish, and wheat take 3-5 days for sprouting.
• Should you have a problem such as rotting sprouts, sourness, spotty germination or mold, look at the list of questions below and try again!
• Were the seeds/beans top quality and unbroken ones from a reputable natural food store? Broken seeds cause mold and rot. Old ones don't sprout well.
• Did you over soak the seeds? Did you leave too much water in the sprouting vessel? In both cases, rot and mold can again set in.
• Did you underwater and undersoak the seeds? If so, germination will be poor.
• Did you keep sprouts at too high a temperature? This causes sourness and fermentation of sprouts.

Ketchup

Yield: ¾ cup

½ cup tomato sauce
¼ cup sugar
2 tablespoons apple-cider vinegar
½ teaspoon sea salt
dash of ground cloves* optional

• Mix well in a small measuring cup; store in airtight container, refrigerate.

Chutney

Yield: 1½ cups

1 (8oz.) jar apricot or peach preserves
2 cloves garlic, minced
½ teaspoon powdered ginger or 1 tablespoon fresh grated
½ teaspoon sea salt
1 tablespoon apple cider vinegar
½ cup raisins

• Mix well in a small bowl; pour into a sterilized glass airtight container, refrigerate.

Hot Pepper & Feta Spread

Yield: 3 cups

1 red bell pepper, diced
3 tablespoons olive oil, plus extra to top the jar
½-1 teaspoon crushed red pepper flakes
2½ cups (1 pound) feta cheese, crumbled

• Warm oil in a medium saucepan; add peppers and sauté until soft, about 5-8 minutes, cool slightly. Place crumbled feta cheese, cooked peppers and pepper flakes in a hand food chopper, and blend until smooth cheese. Pour into a sterilized glass airtight container, refrigerate. Keeps 2-3 weeks.

Bouillon Sip

Yield: 2¼ cups

1 (16oz.) jar instant bouillon powder
1 (16oz.) container of grated Parmesan cheese
2 tablespoons celery seeds
3 tablespoons parsley flakes

• Mix well in a medium bowl, store in airtight container.
➤ *Note*: 2 tbsp. of mixture to 1 cup boiling water and sip slowly.

Old Sour

Yield: 2 cups

2 cups key lime juice
1 tablespoon sea salt

• Using a funnel, strain key lime juice through doubled cheesecloth into a clean sterilized bottle. Add sea salt, secure lid. Shake bottle well. Let the sauce age in a dark cool area for 4 weeks. When aged, it will have an acid-salty flavor with a bite on the tongue.
• The sauce turns brownish as it ages, but is usable as long as the flavor is tangy and salty. Splash on seafood, salads, fresh steamed vegetables.

Baking Powder

Yield: ¾ teaspoon

½ teaspoon cream of tartar plus ¼ teaspoon baking soda
OR ¼ teaspoon baking soda plus ½ cup buttermilk; reduce some other liquid from the recipe
OR
4 teaspoons quick-cooking tapioca

Russian Tea Mix

Yield: 4 cups

1 cup plain instant tea
2 cups dry instant Tang
1¼ cups granulated sugar
1 small package lemonade mix
1½ teaspoons cinnamon
¾ teaspoon ground cloves

• Mix well in a large bowl; store in airtight container.
Use 2 teaspoons of mix per cup of boiling water.

Homemade Cocoa Mix

Yield: 2½ cups

⅓ cup sugar
⅓ cup dry cocoa powder
¼ teaspoon sea salt
1½ cups nonfat dry milk powder

• Combine all ingredients in a medium bowl, store in airtight container.
Use 2 tablespoons cocoa mix into 1 cup hot boiling water.

Breading Mix

Yield: 6 cups

4 cups all-purpose flour
2½ tablespoons sea salt
1 tablespoon freshly ground black pepper
2 cups unsalted cracker crumbs
2 teaspoons dried thyme
2 teaspoons dried oregano
2½ tablespoons paprika

• Combine all ingredients in a large bowl, store in a airtight container.

Skipper's Mix

Yield: 11 cups

8 cups all-purpose flour
3 cups non-fat powdered milk
½ cup sugar
2 cups solid vegetable shortening
1 tablespoon sea salt
5 tablespoons baking powder

• Mix all ingredients in a large bowl, cut in shortening. Store in airtight container.

➢ _Note: Use_ above mix by adding water or half water and milk. It becomes a pancake mix; OR add a small amount of water to 1 cup of mix to make a pastry crust; OR add a dash of your favorite extract, 1-2 cups of mix and a small amount of water to make a soft dough, press into a nonstick skillet, and on medium heat lightly brown one side, flip over, sprinkle cinnamon sugar on top, cook additional 2-3 mins. to brown.
Remove from heat, cut in half and share a sweet cookie.

Homemade Crackers

Yield: 4 dozen (2-inch) crackers

4 cups all-purpose flour
2 tablespoons sugar
1 teaspoon sea salt
¼ cup unsalted butter
1 cup milk

• Sift together flour, sugar and salt directly into large bowl.
• Cut butter with pastry blender or two knives until mixture looks like coarse meal. Stir in enough milk to make a stiff dough. Roll about ¼ inch thick on a lightly floured board and cut with a large round cookie cutter. Prick surface of each round with fork tines and brush lightly with milk.
• Place on ungreased baking sheet. Bake at 400 degrees for 15 minutes or until golden in color.
• Remove, cool on wire rack; store in airtight container.

Soda Cracker

Yield: 4 dozen standard size

2 cups all-purpose flour
½ teaspoon sea salt
½ teaspoon baking powder
¼ cup unsalted butter, cold
½ cup milk
1 egg, beaten

• Mix together flour, salt and baking powder in a large bowl.
Cut butter into the flour mixture until the mixture is mealy in
appearance; add milk and egg.
• Preheat oven to 400 degrees; lightly grease baking sheets.
• Knead mixture on a lightly floured board until the dough has
a good spring to it. Roll the dough out very thin; cut into
rounds, place on prepared baking sheets. Prick the crackers
with fork tines, bake for 10 minutes. Remove from oven, place
crackers on wire racks to cool completely. Store in airtight
container.

Pita Bread Crackers

Yield: 3 dozen

1 package (4) whole wheat, onion, or plain pita bread

• Separate each whole pita bread. Tear into medium pieces.
• Preheat oven to 350 degrees. Place pieces on ungreased
baking sheet, bake for 12-15 minutes or until well browned.
• Remove from oven, cool completely, store in airtight
container.

Corn Chips

Yield: 2-3 cups

½ cup all-purpose flour
½ cup cornmeal
½ teaspoon sea salt
¼ cup milk, more or less
peanut oil for frying

• Mix together to form a stiff dough, adjusting milk or flour as needed.
• Divide dough mixture into golf ball sized balls. On a very well floured board, roll until very thin. Cut into half or thirds each ball of dough.
• Pour a small amount of oil in a nonstick skillet, heat and fry pieces until golden. Remove from skillet and drain on paper plate, cool completely. Store in airtight container.

Apple or Pumpkin Pie Spice

Yield: 1 tablespoon

½ teaspoon cinnamon
¼ teaspoon nutmeg
⅛ teaspoon allspice
⅛ teaspoon cardamom
¼ teaspoon ground cloves

• Mix in a small cup, enough for one 9-inch pie.

Corn Bread Mix

Yield: 5 cups

2⅔ cups cornmeal
2 cups all-purpose flour
3 tablespoons sugar
2 teaspoons sea salt
2 tablespoons baking powder

• Combine all ingredients in a large bowl, mix well.
Place in airtight container, store in a cool dry place.

Cornbread or Cornbread Muffins

Yield: 1 dozen

2½ cups corn bread mix, (see above recipe how to make mix)
2 eggs, beaten
1 cup milk
4 tablespoons unsalted butter, melted

• Preheat oven to 400 degrees; lightly grease an 8-inch square
pan or 12 muffin pan.
• Place corn bread mix in a large bowl. In a small bowl beat
eggs, milk and butter; stir into dry ingredients only until they
are moistened; do not over-mix. Spoon batter into prepared
pan or muffin cups.
• Bake bread for 25-30, muffins for 20 minutes, until golden
brown. Remove from oven and serve hot.

➢ *Note:* Variation for above recipe: ½ cup corn kernels, or 1 finely
chopped jalapeño pepper.

Basic Biscuit Mix

Yield: 8¾ cups

8¾ cups all-purpose flour
⅓ cup baking powder
¼ cup sugar
1 tablespoon sea salt
2 cups solid vegetable shortening

• Sift together the dry ingredients into a extra large bowl.
Cut in shortening 1 cup at a time. Blend until mixture looks
like coarse meal.
• Place in airtight container, store in a cool dry place.

Biscuits From Biscuit Mix

Yield: 12, two-inch biscuits

2 cups biscuit mix, (from basic biscuit mix above.)
⅔ cup milk

• Preheat oven to 475 degrees.
• In a medium bowl place mix and make a hole in the center.
Pour in milk; blend quickly, just until there is no dry mix
remaining.
• Turn the dough out onto a lightly floured board. Roll or pat
it out to form a rectangle about ½-inch thick. With a 2-inch
cookie cutter, cut out circles, place on an ungreased baking
sheet. Roll out remaining scraps of dough, cut more biscuits
until all the dough is used up.
• Turn oven down to 425 degrees, bake 12-15 minutes or until
lightly browned. Remove from heat and serve hot.

Coffee Cake

Yield: 1, 8-inch square cake

2 cups basic biscuit mix, (see page 407)
½ cup sugar
¾ cup milk
1 egg
½ teaspoon vanilla
Topping:
½ cup all-purpose flour
¼ cup brown sugar, packed
½ teaspoon ground cinnamon
2½ tablespoons unsalted butter, cut into small bits

• Preheat oven to 350 degrees; lightly grease a 8-inch square
pan.
• In a small mixing bowl, combine flour, brown sugar,
cinnamon and butter for the topping. With a pastry blender or
two knives, work the mixture together until the butter is barely
visible; set aside topping.
• In a medium bowl, whisk together biscuit mix and sugar. In
a small bowl, beat together milk, egg, vanilla, then add to
biscuit mix, stir just to moistened. Pour batter into prepared
baking pan, sprinkle with topping.
• Bake for 30-35 minutes or until a toothpick inserted in the
center comes out clean. Remove from oven and let cool
slightly in the pan. Serve warm.

Shortcake Biscuit Mix

Yield: 1 dozen

2 cups biscuit mix, (see page 407)
2 tablespoons sugar
⅓ cup heavy cream
⅓ cup milk
1 tablespoon unsalted butter, melted
slices of fresh fruit, jam and whip topping after biscuits are done

• Preheat oven to 475 degrees.
• Pour biscuit mix into a large bowl, combine with sugar. Add cream, milk, butter; blend rapidly, stirring just until there is no dry mix remaining. Turn the dough out onto a lightly floured board, pat or roll out to form a rough rectangle slightly thicker than ½-inch, cut with a biscuit cutter.
• Place biscuits on an ungreased baking sheet. Reduce oven temperature to 425 degrees, bake 12-15 minutes or until they are light brown. Remove from oven, serve warm with fruit, jam and whipped topping.

Pancakes

Yield: 4-6 pancakes

1⅓ cups milk
1 egg
2 cups basic biscuit mix, (see page 407)
½ cup blueberries or ¾ cup diced peeled apples
dash of vanilla

• In a large bowl, whisk together milk and egg. Add basic biscuit mix, ground cinnamon and vanilla, blend until smooth. Add fruit of your choice. Spoon prepared batter with a small ladle onto a hot, nonstick skillet or lightly greased griddle pan; cook until small bubbles appear, flip pancakes and brown second side.

Pancake Mix

Yield: 6 cups

6 cups all-purpose flour
1 tablespoon baking powder
1 tablespoon baking soda
1 tablespoon sea salt
6 tablespoons sugar

• Sift together all ingredients through a large strainer in a large bowl, store in airtight container.

Buttermilk Pancakes

Yield: 16 pancakes

1¼ cups pancake mix, (see above recipe pancake mix)
1 egg, beaten
1¼ cups buttermilk or use 4 tablespoons buttermilk powder mixed with 1¼ cups water
2 tablespoons peanut oil
* optional extras; 1 cup blueberries, ½ cup chopped nuts, ½ cup sliced fresh strawberries or sliced bananas.

• Place pancake mix in a large bowl. Combine remaining ingredients in a medium bowl, mixing well.
• Add liquid to pancake mix, stir until dry ingredients are just moistened. Batter will look lumpy. At this point add one of the add ins, stir once just to blend.
• Pour batter from spoon onto preheated hot griddle or nonstick skillet, cook until pancakes bubble; turn and cook until golden brown.

Pastry Mix

Yield: 6 cups

6¼ cups all-purpose flour
1 tablespoon sea salt
2⅓ cups solid vegetable shortening

• Sift flour into large bowl; mix in salt. Cut in half of shortening. Add remaining shortening, cut in until mixture looks like coarse meal. Store in airtight container.

Two Crust Pie Shell

Yield: 2, 8-inch pie crusts, unbaked

2¾ cups pastry mix, (see above recipe)
4 tablespoons cold water

• In a large bowl combine pastry mix and water. Divide dough in half; place one half of dough on piece of wax paper, place another piece of wax paper on top, top with remaining dough. Roll out dough; lift one piece of wax paper with dough crust, place on pie plate, remove wax paper gently. Repeat for top crust.
• To make one pastry shell, use 1½ cups pastry mix and 2 tablespoons ice cold water.
• To make a baked pie shell, preheat oven to 425 degrees, place unbaked pie shell in oven, reduce heat to 375 degrees, bake until golden brown. Remove from oven, cool completely before filling.

Tahini

Yield: 1 cup

4 tablespoons sesame seeds
2 or 3 garlic cloves, minced
1 teaspoon sesame oil
1 tablespoon lemon juice
½ teaspoon cayenne pepper
½ cup water, room temperature
* garnish, chopped parsley (when ready to serve)

• Place sesame seeds, garlic, oil, lemon, salt and cayenne
pepper in a hand food chopper; *use* ¼ cup water at one time,
twirl until thoroughly blended and smooth. Can be stored in a
glass jar with tight fitting lid. Refrigerate.

Ice Box Dills

Yield: 24 dills

4 large cucumber
1½ cups white vinegar
1½ cups water
scant ¼ cup sea salt
dill seed
* optional: 2-3 cloves of garlic

• Wash the cucumbers, peel if the skins are very thick or
tough. Cut into spears (1½-inch chunks). Pack them tightly
into a quart wide mouth, clean and sterilized jar. Add 1
teaspoon dill seed per quart, plus slices of garlic.
• Bring vinegar, water, salt just to the boiling point. Pour over
the cukes packed in jars and make sure you cover them
completely. Secure lid, cool to room temperature, then
refrigerate for 2 days before eating.

Skillet Dry Roast Granola

Yield: 5 cups

1 cup raw rolled oats
⅔ cup chopped pecans
⅔ cup wheat germ
⅔ cup sesame seeds
⅔ cup sunflower seeds
⅔ cup shredded coconut flakes
½ cup firmly packed brown sugar
½ teaspoon sea salt
½ cup dark raisins
½ cup dried pineapple
½ cup dried dates

• In nonstick skillet or large cast-iron skillet, place the oats
and nuts. Stir oats and nuts on medium-low heat constantly for
8 minutes or until they brown slightly.
• Add wheat germ, sesame seeds, sunflower seeds and
coconut. Continue to stir mixture constantly for additional 10-
12 more minutes.
• Sprinkle in brown sugar and salt; continue cooking for 5
minutes, lifting mixture constantly.
• Add raisins, dried pineapple and dates; remove from heat;
stir well while mixture is hot. Place in large bowl and cool
before storing in airtight container.

➢ *Note: Eat* alone as a treat. *Use* as a topping in yogurt with fresh
fruit; or *top* cooked hot cereal; *put* a dollop on low-fat cottage.

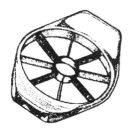

Crunchy Granola

Yield: 2½ cups

vegetable cooking spray
1 cup raw rolled oats
⅓ cup chopped walnuts
⅓ cup unblanched almonds
2 tablespoons sunflower seeds
2 tablespoons sesame seeds
2 tablespoons pecans
pinch of ground cinnamon
1 tablespoon oil
3 tablespoons honey

• Toss all ingredients together in large mixing bowl. Preheat oven to 250 degrees.
• Lightly spray baking sheet, spread mixture out very thin.
• Bake 25 minutes or until ingredients are lightly brown in color. Remove from heat, cool completely, then store in airtight container.

➤ *Note:* Variations for above recipe: add ¼ cup of one or more of the following: shredded coconut, chopped dried apricots, dates, or currants before tossing above ingredients.

Nut Puffs

Yield: 1 dozen

1 cup unsalted butter
1 ½ cups confectioners' sugar
2 cups all-purpose flour
½ cup finely chopped walnuts
⅛ teaspoon sea salt

• Beat butter and ½ cup sugar in a medium bowl until light and fluffy. Add flour, nuts, salt; mix well. Shape into 1-inch balls. Place 1-inch apart on ungreased baking sheet.
• Bake at 300 degrees for 25 minutes or until golden brown. Roll warm nut puffs in remaining sugar. Remove to wire rack to cool completely. Store in airtight container.

Cajun Cocktail Pecans

Yield: 3 cups

3 cups pecan halves
½ cup sugar
2 teaspoons ground cinnamon
½ teaspoon allspice
1 ½ tablespoons Cajun seasoning mix (see page 395)
2 tablespoons water

• Preheat oven to 350 degrees. Toast pecans in 13 x 9 baking pan; shake the pan often, for about 5-8 minutes. (They burn easily.) Remove from pan, place in a large bowl, set aside.
• Add remaining ingredients in a small saucepan over medium heat, simmer and cook until soft ball stage (234 degrees). Drizzle sugar mixture over nuts, toss quickly to coat all pecans before mixture cools off. Cool nut mixture completely before storing in airtight container.

Spiced Nuts

Yield: 4 cups

2 tablespoons unsalted butter
1 egg white
½ cup sugar
1 teaspoon cinnamon
½ teaspoon sea salt
½ teaspoon ground cloves
¼ teaspoon ground ginger
¼ teaspoon allspice
2 tablespoons water
1 cup pecan halves
1 cup almonds, whole
1 cup walnut halves
1 cup peanuts

• Melt butter on baking sheet in a 275 degree oven; remove from oven.
• Beat egg white until stiff. Combine sugar, spices and gradually beat into egg white. Stir in water and then nuts.
• Spread nut mixture in a thin layer on prepared baking sheet; bake at 275 degrees for 45 minutes. Cool completely; break into pieces, store in airtight container.

Chocolate Cake Brownie Mix

Yield: 7 cups

3 cups sugar
2 cups all-purpose flour
2 cups unsweetened baking cocoa
1½ teaspoons baking powder.

• Combine all ingredients well, store in airtight container. Place in a cool dry place.

Double Chocolate Brownies

Yield: 16 bars

2 eggs
1 teaspoon vanilla
½ cup mayonnaise
2 cups chocolate cake brownie mix (see page 416)
½ cup chopped nuts
Glaze
1 ounce sweet chocolate
1 tablespoon unsalted butter

• Preheat oven to 350 degrees; line an square 8-inch baking pan with aluminum foil; grease foil or use cooking spray.
• Combine eggs, vanilla and mayonnaise in a medium bowl. Add brownie mix blend until smooth, stir in nuts. Pour batter into pan, bake 20-25 minutes or until slight imprint remains when lightly touched with finger.
• Remove from oven, set pan on wire rack and cool 5 minutes; onto rack invert pan, remove pan and foil.
• *Glaze:* Melt the chocolate and butter in a small saucepan over very low heat, stir until smooth. Remove from heat and immediately drizzle the chocolate mixture over the top of the baked brownies, spread and let the glaze set completely before cutting into bars.

Variations:

• Peanut butter brownies: mix ½ cup quick-cooking oats, ½ cup confectioners' sugar, ¾ cup smooth peanut butter in a medium-size bowl until crumbly. Before baking, sprinkle batter with topping. Bake as directed. After cooling for 5 minutes, invert onto rack, cover with another rack and invert again to cool right side up. Do not use chocolate glaze.

• Chocolate chip brownies: add ½ cup semi-sweet chocolate chips to batter.

Chocolate Pudding Mix

Yield: 8 cups

5 cups instant dry non-fat milk powder
1½ cups sugar
1 cup cornstarch
¾ cup unsweetened cocoa
½ teaspoon sea salt

• Combine all ingredients in large bowl, mix well. Store in airtight container.

Chocolate Pudding

Yield: 6 servings

1 cup chocolate pudding mix, (see above recipe)
1 cup water
1 cup milk
1 egg
1 tablespoon unsalted butter
½ teaspoon vanilla extract

• Put mix in a medium saucepan, slowly whisk in milk and water; cook, stirring constantly over medium heat. Continue until mixture thickens and is smooth.
• Remove from heat and set aside; in a small bowl combine vanilla and egg, beat well; add ½ cup of hot pudding and blend. Return egg mixture to pot of pudding along with butter and blend again. Pour pudding into serving dishes and serve warm or cover with plastic wrap; refrigerate until ready to serve.

Chocolate Chip Cookie Mix
Yield: 9 cups

9 cups all-purpose flour
4 teaspoons baking soda
2 teaspoons sea salt
3 cups brown sugar, packed
3 cups granulated sugar
4 cups shortening

• Combine dry ingredients thoroughly; cut in shortening until crumbly, store in an airtight container in a cool dry area.

Chocolate Chip Cookies
Yield: 2 dozen

7 cups chocolate chip cookie mix, (see above recipe)
1 teaspoon vanilla
2 eggs, beaten
2 cups (12oz.) semisweet chocolate chips

• Combine mix, vanilla and eggs; mix well. Fold in chocolate chips. Preheat oven to 375 degrees.
• Drop by tablespoonful ½-inch apart onto greased baking sheet, bake for 10-12 minutes or until golden brown.
• Remove from oven, cool on wire racks.

Variations:
Add in one of the following during fold in:

• 3 (1.2oz.) Heath bars, chopped
• ½ cup smooth peanut butter
• ½ cup flaked coconut

Making Yogurt

Yield: 4 cups

4 cups milk
1 cup dry milk powder
2-4 tablespoons plain yogurt with active cultures
* *Optional:*
2 teaspoons unflavored gelatin
¼ cup cold water

• Scald milk in large saucepan; cool to temperature of 95° to 115°, checking with candy thermometer. Stir in milk powder and yogurt. Rinse thermos with very hot water; pour milk mixture in, secure lid and wrap thermos with towel and place in warm place. Incubate for 3-9 hours; check after 3 hours to see if it is set by tilting the thermos. Refrigerate immediately when set. The heat source is the most critical factor for successful yogurt making. Too low a temperature will incubate sour milk bacteria rather than yogurt bacteria; too high a temperature will kill the bacteria. Once you establish your heat source, yogurt making will be simple. *Soften gelatin in cold water; heat to dissolve and add to mixture for a firmer yogurt.

Making Yogurt Cheese (Labne)
Yield: 1 cup approximately

2 cups (16oz.) of low-fat, whole or plain yogurt
1 coffee filter or a piece of cheesecloth
1 strainer
medium bowl
plastic wrap

Yogurt cheese is a soft, spreadable cheese that is low-fat, low calorie and makes either a great spread or dip. To make yogurt cheese, drain away the liquid which leaves the cheese (curd). You can use plain or sweetened yogurt, as long as it doesn't have fruit on the bottom. Avoid brands that contain gelatin because it prevent the liquid, or whey, from draining off, and the yogurt from thickening.

Place filter or cheese cloth in a strainer, place strainer on top of bowl. Pour yogurt into filter, cover with plastic wrap. (You can also purchase yogurt strainer in a local kitchen hardware store.) Refrigerate and let drain; it should take about 4 hours but the longer it drips, the thicker it will get. Discard the remaining whey collected in the bowl.

Once the yogurt has drained add fresh herbs such as parsley, chopped basil or chopped cilantro; stir in and serve with assorted crackers or use as a dip served with assorted fresh vegetables. Select one of the dried seasonings blends (see page 398).

SOURDOUGH

Pointers about:

• *Never use* metal containers or utensils; they'll retard growth and give an off flavor. The yeast can corrode the metal, and the corrosion will affect your starter's potency.

• *Young starters* may not have as much leavening power as more mature ones. At first, use yeast plus starter, or make quick breads and pancakes which use additional rising agents such as baking soda.

• *Do not exclude* air circulation, since the yeast in your starter needs air to live. Use two or three pieces of cheesecloth held in place with a rubber band or string. Use a plastic container; sterilize first, punch holes in the lid portion for circulation.

• *Try to maintain* 1½ cups of starter. Each time a part is used, replenish with a mixture of equal amount of warm water and flour. Leave at room temperature overnight or until it is bubbly and no longer smells floury. You must feed your starter every 3 or 4 days if left at room temperature. Keeping the starter in a refrigerator, you can feed it as infrequently as every two weeks. Remember to bring starter to room temperature before using.

• *Test starter:* Sterilize a small glass bowl with hot water, wipe dry. Mix ¼ cup starter with ½ cup warm water and ½ cup all-purpose flour. Cover and let stand in a warm spot, watch it closely for bubbling. If it bubbles in 4 to 6 hours, you know the culture is alive and well. Add this test starter to the original starter batch.

Sourdough Starters

Sourdough Starter #1

1 package dry yeast
2 cups warm water or milk
2 cups all-purpose flour
1 tablespoon sugar

• Combine all ingredients in glass bowl, glass jar or plastic container; cover with cheesecloth and let stand at room temperature 24-48 hrs. Then cover loosely with plastic wrap, if using jar or plastic container, punch a few holes in lid and store in refrigerator. Allow starter to come to room temperature before using.

Sourdough Starter # 2

3 tablespoons instant potato flakes
⅓ cup sugar
1 cup warm water

• Sterilize a large plastic container before making your starter. Punch holes in the top lid so starter can breath. Combine all ingredients in container, let sit at room temperature 2-3 days. As soon as bubbles appear, it's ready for use. Then keep remainder of starter in refrigerator. Allow starter to come to room temperature before using.

Sourdough Starter # 3

1 cup skim or low-fat warm milk
1 cup all-purpose flour
3 tablespoons plain yogurt

• Sterilize glass bowl with hot water and dry it. Stir in yogurt and one cup milk, cover with a piece of cheesecloth secured by rubber band or string, keep in a warm place overnight. This mixture should look like a curd consistency of yogurt, with a layer of liquid on top. If the liquid is pink at this point, discard the starter and try again; all equipment must be sterilized. Once you receive your yogurt culture, stir in one cup flour. Cover with a cheesecloth and let stand at room temperature three to five days. When your starter is ready, it should be full of bubbles and have a good sour smell. Take a peak at your starter each day and if it is separating, simply stir the separating fluid with a sterilized spoon.

Gingham Sourdough Bread

Yield: 2 loaves

1 package dry yeast
1¼ cups warm water
¼ cup firmly packed brown sugar
2 teaspoons sea salt
⅓ cup unsalted butter
4 to 4½ cups sifted all-purpose flour
1½ cups sourdough starter #1 (see page 423)
3½ cups raw oats

• Lightly grease and flour 2 loaf pans, set aside.
• Combine yeast in ¼ cup of the warm water, set aside.
• Pour remaining water over sugar and butter in large bowl, stir well. Add two cups of flour, sourdough starter, oats and yeast mixture. Stir in enough additional flour to make a stiff dough.
Knead on floured board until smooth, about 10 minutes. Round dough into ball, place in a greased large bowl. Lightly grease surface of dough; cover and let rise in warm place until nearly double in size, about 1 hour.
• Punch dough down, cut in half. Shape and place in loaf pans; cover, let rise in warm place until nearly double in size again, about 40 minutes. After second rise, with a sharp knife cut a shallow slash down center or a few small ones on a angle on each loaf. This will prevent cracking while baking.
• Preheat oven to 350 degrees, bake 35-40 minutes. Remove from oven and set pans on wire rack; cool first before removing bread from pans.

Gray Ghost Sourdough Bread

Yield: 2 loaves

1 cup sourdough starter #2 (see page 423)
1 teaspoon sea salt
⅓ cup oil
1 tablespoon sugar
1⅓ cups warm water
6 cups bread flour

• Mix all ingredients well in large bowl. Turn onto flour board and knead 10 minutes. Place dough in large lightly greased bowl, cover and let sit overnight in warm place.
• Next morning, punch down dough and divide into 2 loaves. Lightly grease and flour pans, place dough in pans, cover and let rise about 1 hour.
• After second rise, preheat oven to 350 degrees. Cut a shallow slash down center or a few small ones on a angle on each loaf with a sharp knife. This will prevent cracking while baking.
• Bake 35-40 minutes; remove breads from oven, cool in pan 5-10 minutes, remove breads to cool completely on wire rack.

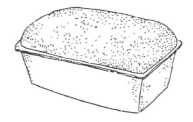

Lorca Sourdough Bread

Yield: 1 loaf

1 tablespoon dry yeast
¼ cup warm water
1 cup warm milk
½ cup sourdough starter #3 (see page 423)
dash of sea salt
2 tablespoons sugar
4 cups all-purpose flour
2 tablespoons cornmeal

• Lightly grease baking sheet, set aside.
• Dissolve yeast in warm water in a large bowl. Stir in all
remaining ingredients to make a stiff dough. Turn dough onto
a floured board and knead 10 minutes. Place in a large greased
bowl, cover and let rise 1 hour or until double in size.
• Sprinkle half of the cookie sheet with cornmeal, place
dough on cookie sheet, sprinkle with remaining cornmeal.
Cover, let rise for about 40 minutes.
 • Preheat oven to 350 degrees, bake for 20-25 minutes or until
lightly brown in color.

➤*Hint*: No oven? Use your pressure cooker! Coat lightly with oil the
inside of the pressure cooker, sprinkle cornmeal on sides and bottom.
Place dough on second rise in pressure cooker. After it has risen second
time secure with top, DO NOT place pressure valve on. On medium
flame bake 15-20 minutes; open to check if sides are slightly brown.
Flip out bread, replace bread unbaked side down back in pressure
cooker, secure cover, DO NOT place pressure valve on, bake additional
5 minutes, so bottom will brown.

Make Your Own Stocks

Below are a few basic homemade stocks to make. Whenever you cook grains or vegetables, use stock for additional flavor. Please note **no salt** is added to any of the stocks, salt as desired can be added in individual recipes later on. Salted stock used in a bean soup, for example will toughen the bean skins and lengthen cooking time. If at all possible, freeze your stock in small containers or ice cube trays. Once frozen in the ice cube trays they can be popped out and stored in a plastic bag. This way it's easy to use one or two cubes needed for broth when cooking grains, fish, rice, etc.

Vegetable Stock #I

Yield: 2 quarts

2 large unpeeled Irish potatoes, washed and quartered
2 large carrots, peeled and thickly sliced
1 large onion, peeled and quartered
1 celery rib, chopped
1 apple or pear, cored, cut in chunks
1 bay leaf
12 peppercorns, crushed
10 cups cold water (2½ quarts)

• Place all ingredients into a large stock pot and bring to a boil; reduce heat, cover and simmer for 45 minutes to an hour. Remove from heat, cool, then strain.

➤ *Note:* Use your pressure cooker for the above recipe. Lock and secure lid, bring up to pressure and cook for 15 minutes, remove from heat and let pressure drop of its own accord. Strain.

Vegetable Stock #II

Yield: 2½ quarts

10 cups cold water (2½ quarts)
6 asparagus ends
2 broccoli stalks
2 bay leafs
celery tops with leaves
2 cloves garlic, unpeeled and crushed
1 large onion, peeled and quartered
2 Irish potatoes, wash unpeeled and quartered
2 sweet potatoes, peeled and quartered
1 turnip, peeled and quartered

• Place all ingredients into a stock pot, bring up to a boil,
reduce heat, cover, simmer for 45 minutes to 1 hour. Remove
from heat, cool slightly, strain.
➤ *Note:* Use your pressure cooker. Lock and secure lid, bring up to
pressure, cook for 15 minutes. Remove from heat, let pressure drop of
its own accord. Cool slightly, strain.

Chicken Stock #1

Yield: 1½ quarts

2½ pounds of necks, wings, backs
1½ quarts cold water
1 large onion, peeled and quartered
1 rib of celery with leaves, cut in chunks
1 bay leaf
½ teaspoon dried thyme
2 parsley sprigs
5 whole peppercorns, crushed

• Place all ingredients into a stock pot bring up to a boil,
reduce heat, cover, simmer 45 minutes to 1 hour. Cool
slightly, strain.
➤ *Note:* Use your pressure cooker: lock and secure lid, bring up to
pressure, cook for 15 minutes. Remove from heat, let pressure drop of
its own accord. Cool slightly, strain.

Chicken Stock #II
Yield: 2 quarts

2 ½ pounds of necks, wings, backs
2 quarts of cold water
1 large onion, peeled and quartered
1 leek, white part only, cleaned and sliced
2 whole cloves
1 bay leaf
2 medium-sized carrots, scraped and quartered
¾ teaspoon dried thyme
6 peppercorns, crushed

• Place all ingredients into a stock pot, bring to a boil, reduce heat and simmer covered for 45 minutes to 1 hour. Cool slightly, strain.

➢ *Note:* Use your pressure cooker: lock and secure lid, bring up to pressure, cook for 15 minutes, remove from heat, let pressure drop of its own accord. Cool slightly, strain.

Simple Beef Stock
Yield: 2 quarts

1½ pounds beef bones
1 pound chunk of lean beef, leave whole
2 onions, peeled and quartered
2 medium-sized carrots, scraped and cut into chunks
3 celery ribs with leaves, cut in chunks
2 quarts of cold water

• Place all ingredients into your pressure cooker. Lock and secure lid, bring up to pressure and cook for 20 minutes. Shut off, and let pressure drop of its own accord. Remove the fat that rises to the top. Strain stock through a cheesecloth, place in jars and refrigerate. Will keep for 5 days. OR cook in stockpot for 45 minutes to 1 hour, cool slightly then strain.

➢ *Note:* Make a chili that day, add cooked beef cut into chunks after above stock recipe has been made.

Fish Stock #I

Yield: 2 quarts

2 pounds white-flesh fish with trimmings: head, tail, skin and bones.
2 quarts cold water
1 medium-sized carrot, scraped and chopped
1 bay leaf
2 cloves garlic, crushed
4 parsley sprigs
½ teaspoon dried thyme
10 peppercorns, crushed
* optional: 1 cup dry white wine

• Put all ingredients into a stockpot, bring slowly to a boil and skim. Reduce heat, simmer, uncovered 30 minutes if fish is used, 20 minutes if only trimmings are used. Remove from heat, strain. Store stock, covered in refrigerator up to three days or pour into containers and freeze.

➤ *Note:* Use your pressure cooker. Lock and secure lid, bring up to pressure, cook for 15 minutes, shut off, let pressure drop of its own accord. Cool slightly, strain.

Fish Stock #II

Yield: 2 quarts

2 pounds of fish bones, heads and tails
8 cups of cold water
1 tablespoon fennel seeds
2 leeks, white part only, cleaned and chopped
*optional: ½ cup white wine

•Place all ingredients into a stock pot. Bring slowly to a boil and skim. Reduce heat, simmer, uncovered for 20 minutes. Remove from heat and strain. Store stock, covered in refrigerator up to three days or pour into containers and freeze.

➤ *Note:* Use your pressure cooker. Lock and secure lid, bring up to pressure, cook for 15 minutes, shut off, allow pressure to drop of its own accord. Cool slightly, strain.

Cruising Contributors

Toby Ackerman
Marilyn Aiches
Mary Ann Albright
Loree Alderisio
Becky Aldrich
Mary Ann Albright
Alice Allchin
Linda Amos
Patricia Anderson
Kimi Atwell
Caroline Auer
Pat Bartell
Karen Beal
Frannie Beckley
Karen Bhirdo
Linda Blaise
Kaye Boland
Ruth Bowman
Frankie Boyd
Nancy Burroughs
Betty Brock
Bill Butler
Phyllis Cady
Helen Caesar
Johanna L. Clester
Rebecca Conkling
Niki Coxwell
Marcia Davis
Mary Ann Degraw
Doris DeGroodt
Carol Dingley
Ronnie Doughty
Kate Drew
Debby Dye
Becky Elston
Fritz Feldman
Jeanne Fijux
Eleanor Fisher
Heather FItzgerald
Rae Flanders
Gail Vera Fyhrie
Jeanne Gaudia
Gabriela German
Gail Gisel
Pat Godfrey
Sandy Goodman
Georgia Gordon
Louise Gray
Danny Greene
Joan Casanova Hawksworth
Elaine Heine

Linda Henly
Katrin Henzi
Mary Herrick
Linda Hixon
Joanne Hoffman
Skippy Hoffman
Thelma Holt
Kathy Johnson
Heidi Jones
Sally Jones
Ruth Kates
Carol Kaeser
Maxine Karlovsky
Brenda Kennerly
Leslie Kettlewell
Susan Kiser
Lyn Klarmin
Phyllis Knight
Jim Kontur
Marge Lamb
Arlene Landry
Thelma Langley
Sara Lewis
Beth Liggett
Mary Kay Lindquist
Nancy Lobdell
Erica Lowery
Sara Marsh
Mary Mauck
Michele Michael
Fiona McCall
Marilyn McCrory
Barbara Muller
Glenyse Mitchell
Patty Moffat
Ann Marie
Morgenstern
Joan Morse
Martha Mullis
Margo Murray
Elsie K. Nelson
Ann Nesbitt
Mary Ochse
Kay O'Mara
Nora Papy
Laura Parisi
Delores Parker
Nancy Payson
Cindy Plante
Suzanne Pogell
Dee Dee Plummer

Nancy Primrose
Liz Raedeke
Jeannie Rainek
Sandy Rawe
Pat Ready
Janet Reckord
Karen Rettie
Toni Robertson
Loretta Rosenberg
Carmen Rubei
Joan Russell
Dorothy Salvagin
Ruth Sarrett
Pat Sasser
Judy Saxton
Shirley Schindler
Whitey Schmidt
Jude Schooner
Marianne Schuler
Beverly Shields
Shug Skarda
Joan Smith
Maggie Smith
Suzanne Stein
Joan Stewart
Sally Stewart
Sandy Stone
Lucille Strubell
Ken Swantz
Mary Thomson
Nancy Turner
Susan Uhlman
Harriet Ungeloff
Orletha Van Etten
Susan Lee Voss
Louise Weiss
Angela Wellman
Diane Wheeler
Howard Whitney
Mary Ellen
Williams
Dottie Williamson
Bea Willis
Faith Winkler
Elizabeth Worden
Priscilla Wormell
Karen Zambrzicky
Pat Zimmerman
U.S. Department
of Agriculture

EQUIVALENT CHARTS

Butter and Shortenings

1 ounce butter	2 tablespoons
½ stick butter	¼ cup
1 stick butter	½ cup
1 pound butter	2 cups
1 pound shortening	2 cups

Baking

1 square chocolate	1 ounce = 4 tbsp. grated
6oz. semisweet chocolate chips	1 cup
1 pound cocoa powder	4 cups
1 ounce of baking powder	2½ tablespoons
1 package dry yeast	¼ oz. or 1 tbsp. or 1 cake

Breads & Cereals

1 pound loaf	14 regular or 20 thin slices
1 slice fresh bread	½ cup soft crumbs or cubes
2 slices bread	1 cup soft bread crumbs or cubes
4 slices bread	1 cup fine dry crumbs
1 slice dry bread	¼ cup dry crumbs
1 ounce dry bread crumbs	¼ cup
28 saltines	1 cup fine crumbs
15 graham crackers	1 cup fine crumbs
22 wafers	1 cup fine crumbs
15 gingersnaps	1 cup fine crumbs
19 chocolate wafers	1 cup fine crumbs
3 cups uncrushed cornflakes	1 cup crushed cornflakes
3.4 ounces rolled oats	1 cup
1lb. uncooked rolled oats	5 cups cooked oats
1 cup uncooked rolled oats	1¾ cups cooked oats

Cornmeal

1 pound cornmeal	3 cups uncooked cornmeal
1 cup cornmeal	4 cups cooked cornmeal

Cheese & Milk

4 ounces cheese (Cheddar, Swiss)	1 cup shredded
1 pound cheese	4 cups shredded
1 cup freshly grated cheese	¼ pound
8 ounces cottage cheese	1 cup
¼ pound crumbled blue cheese	1 cup
¼lb. hard cheese (Parmesan, Romano)	1¼ cups grated
4oz. soft cheese (American, Monterey Jack)	1¼ cups shredded
3 ounces cream cheese	6 tablespoons
8 ounces of sour cream	1 cup
½ cup heavy cream	1 cup whipped cream
1 (5oz.) can evaporated milk	⅔ cup evaporated milk
1 (12oz.) can evaporated milk	1⅔ cup evaporated milk
1 (14oz.) can sweetened condensed	1¼ cup milk

Eggs

2 egg yolks	1 whole egg (for custards and sauces
2 egg yolks + 1 tbsp. water	1 whole egg (for baking purposes
1 egg yolk	1½ tbsp.
1 egg white	2 tbsp.
1 medium egg	3 tbsp.
5 large eggs	3 tbsp.
6 large egg whites	1 cup
12 large egg yolks	1 cup

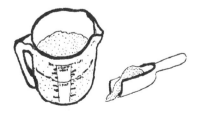

Fruits

1 pound apples	3 medium or 3 cups sliced
4 medium apples	4 cups sliced or chopped
1 pound dried apricots	3¼ cups chopped
3 medium or 1 pound bananas	1⅓ cups mashed
2 cups pitted cherries	4 cups unpitted
8oz. pitted dates or candied fruit	1 cup
8 ounces coconut	2½ cups shredded
1 pound cranberries	4 cups
1 medium lemon	3 tablespoons juice
1 medium lemon	1 tbsp. grated rind
1 medium orange	⅓ cup juice
1 medium orange	2 tbsp. grated rind
8 medium peaches	4 cups sliced
12oz. pitted prunes	2 cups
1 pound raisins	2¾ cups
1 pint berries	1¾ cups

Meats

1 (5 pound chicken)	4 cups chopped cooked
1 pound cooked meat	3 cups diced cooked
1 pound cooked ground meat	2 cups cooked ground

Nuts

4 ounces shelled	1 cup chopped
1 pound nuts in shell	2 cups shelled

Pasta

1 cup uncooked medium noodles	1 heaping cup cooked
1 pound noodles	6 cups uncooked or 7 cups cooked
8oz. or 2½ to 3 cups uncooked	3½ cups cooked
1 cup uncooked macaroni	2 cups cooked
8oz. or 2½ cups uncooked macroni	4 cups cooked
1 pound spaghetti	4 cups uncooked or 8-10 cups cooked

Rice

1 cup uncooked quick-cooking	2 cups cooked
14 ounces quick-cooking rice	4 cups uncooked or 8 cups cooked
1 cup uncooked converted rice	3 to 4 cups cooked
14 ounces converted rice	2 cups uncooked or 8 cups cooked
1 cup long grain rice	3½ cups cooked
1 pound long grain rice	2¼ cups uncooked or 6¾ cups cooked
1 cup uncooked wild rice	3 to 4 cups cooked
1 pound wild rice	3 cups uncooked or 11-12 cups cooked
12 ounces brown rice	2 cups uncooked or 8 cups cooked

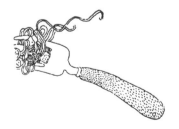

Vegetables

1 pound dried beans	2½ cups dry or 6 cooked
1 cup dried beans	2½ cups cooked
½lb. fresh or 1 (6oz.) can green	2 cups cooked beans
1 pound beets or 16oz. can	2 cups cooked and diced
1 medium bell pepper	1 cup chopped
1 pound cabbage	4 cups shredded
1 large carrot	1 cup grated
1 pound celery	4 cups diced
1 pound fresh mushrooms	6 cups sliced
1 large onion	1 cup chopped
1 (16oz.) can tomatoes	2 cups
1 pound fresh peas unshelled	1 cup shelled
4 medium potatoes	4 cups sliced or diced
1 pound potatoes	3 cups chopped

Miscellaneous

1 cube bouillon	1 tsp. instant or 1 envelope
1 pound coffee	3⅓ cups ground
1 ounce cornstarch	3 tablespoons
1 envelope unflavored gelatin	¼ oz. or 1 tablespoon
1 small package flavored gelatin	3 ounces
1 large package flavored gelatin	6 ounces
¼ pound marshmallow	16 regular-size or 1 cup packed
1 ounce salt	1 tablespoon
1 gill	½ cup
1 jigger	1½ ounces
1 wine glass	¼ cup
1 pony	1 ounce
dash	8 drops
pinch	⅓ of ¼ teaspoon
4 pecks	1 bushel

INDEX

563 recipes, cross-reference index by main ingredient

BEEF CUT CHART

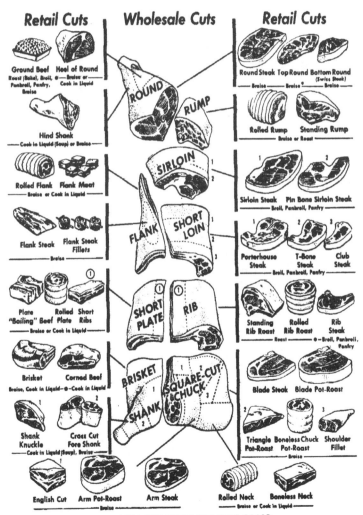

Retail Cuts   Wholesale Cuts   Retail Cuts

Prime and choice grades may be **NATIONAL LIVE STOCK AND MEAT BOARD**
broiled, panbroiled or panfried

PORK CUT CHART

Retail Cuts ### Wholesale Cuts ### Retail Cuts

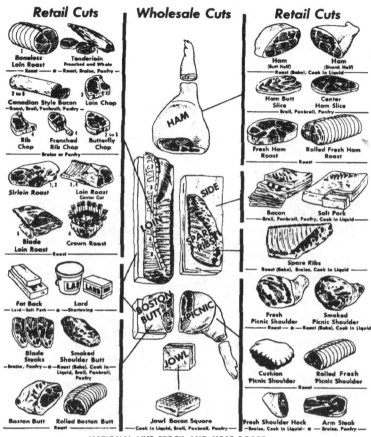

NATIONAL LIVE STOCK AND MEAT BOARD

LAMB

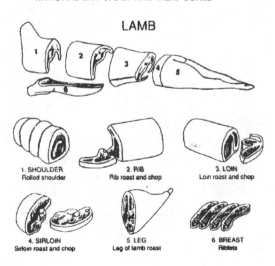

1. SHOULDER
Rolled shoulder

2. RIB
Rib roast and chop

3. LOIN
Loin roast and chop

4. SIRLOIN
Sirloin roast and chop

5. LEG
Leg of lamb roast

6 BREAST
Riblets

Epilogue

Mother and Father go sailing, you know
Every autumn they pack up and go
Far from the winds and the cold and the
snow,
South to the sun and the sea.
I love to think of them sailing there,
The blue of the water, the gold of the air.
Skimming the whitecaps without a care;
imagine a life so free.
I build up a picture of sea and sky;
of lazy harbors and bays drifting by.
I build up this image of pie-in-the-sky;
till their first letter reaches me.

Oh! The propeller shaft is knocking
and the fuel injector's clogged.
There is dry rot in the transom
and the hull is waterlogged.
The heat exchanger's bugged up
and it won't exchange its heat.
When the spinnaker blew out last night;
we lost another cleat.
But, in spite of these small incidents,
when all is said and done;
it's great to spend our holidays sailing in
the sun.

Mother and Father are sailing, you know,
Down in the south where the fair winds
blow,
Basking all day in the warm sun's glow
while sea brids circle and dive.
I think of them strolling the silver shore,
Small dinghy bobbing, the flash of an oar;
Sleek hull shadowing ocean's floor.
Then a second letter arrives.

Oh! We lost both anchors overboard
And now the gasket's blown.
A connecting rod has broken
And the piston rings have gone.
Some moron ran aground last night
And blocked the harbor's mouth.
But we couldn't leave here anyway;
The wind's not from the south.
But, in spite of these small incidents,
When all is said and done,
It's great to spend our holidays sailing in
the sun.

Yes, Mother and Father are sailing
today;
crisp bow throwing a fine salt spray.
Sails stretched taut as they cleave
their way,
through the crystal waters clear.
I like to think of them browned by the
sun,
enjoying the speed of a long clear run,
to a small still bay when day is done.
But a third letter is here.

Oh! The captain gets quite anxious,
when the oil pressure drops.
The main bearing seizes solid
and the halyard ties in knots.
We hit a small reef yesterday,
so now the bilge is full.
And he says the blasted bilge pump,
is clogged with knitting wool!
But in spite of these small incidents,
when all is said and done.
It's great to spend our holidays sailing
in the sun.

P.S. I am indebted to my husband for
technical assistance. I wouldn't have
known if bearings seized and propeller
shafts knocked, or the other way
around.

P.P.S. He says it could be the other
way around!

A COOKBOOK! A PERSONAL TREASURE

A LOVING GIFT FOR FRIEND OR RELATIVE

Ordered by:

Name:_____

Address:_____

City:_____ State:_____ Zip:_____

Quantity	Title / Description		Price	Amount
	The Cruising K.I.S.S. COOKBOOK	@	24.95	
	The Galley K.I.S.S. Cookbook	@	13.95	
	SAILOR'S MULTIHULL GUIDE	@	24.95	
	Sub total			
	Florida residents add 6.5% sales tax			
	Shipping and handling @ 3.75 per book			
	Total Books	Grand Total	.	

Autograph to:
_____

Mail to:
(if different than ordered by)_____
Address:
_____

City:_____ State:_____ Zip:_____

Autograph to:
_____

Mail to:
(if different than ordered by)
_____

Address:
_____

City:_____ State:_____ Zip:_____

Please make all checks payable to: *SAILco Press*
P.O. Box 2099
Key Largo, FL 33037
Tel. & Fax: (305) 743-0626
e-mail: kisscook@aol.com

Credit cards accepted: ☐VISA   ☐MASTERCARD   (check one)

_____

Card number:_____ Exp. Date:_____

_____

Print name on Card

_____

Signature:

Metric Conversion Tables

Formulas Using Conversion Factors
When approximate conversions are not accurate enough, use these
formulas to convert measures from one system to another.

Measurements	*Formulas*
ounces to grams	# ounces x 28.3 = # grams
grams to ounces	# grams x 0.035 = # ounces
pounds to grams	# pounds x 453.6 = # grams
pounds to kilograms	# pounds x 0.45 = # kilograms
ounces to milliliter	# ounces x 30.00 = # milliliters
cups to liters	# cups x 0.24 = # liters
inches to centimeters	# inches x 2.54 = # centimeters
centimeters to inches	# centimeters x 0.39 = # inches

Ounces to Grams

Ounces	*Convenient Equivalent*	*Actual Weight*
1 oz	30 g	28.35 g
2 oz	60 g	56.70 g
3 oz	85g	85.05 g
4 oz	115 g	113.4 g
5 oz	140 g	141.8 g
6 oz	180 g	170.1 g
8 oz	225 g	226.8 g
9 oz	250 g	255.2 g
10 oz	285 g	283.5 g
12 oz	340 g	340.2 g
14 oz	400 g	396.9 g
16 oz	450 g	453.6 g